Islamic Politics, Muslim States, and Counterterrorism Tensions

The US Global War on Terror and earlier US counterterrorism efforts prompted a variety of responses from Muslim states despite widespread Islamic opposition. Some cooperated extensively, some balked at US policy priorities, and others vacillated between these extremes. This book explains how differing religion–state relationships, regimes' political calculations, and Islamic politics combined to produce patterns of tensions and cooperation between the United States and Muslim states over counterterrorism, using rigorous quantitative analysis and case studies of Pakistan, the United Arab Emirates, and Turkey. The book combines recent advances in the study of political institutions with work on religion and politics to advance a novel theory of religion and international relations that will be of value to anyone studying religion, terrorism, or Islamic politics. It also provides numerous insights into current events in the Middle East by extending its analysis to the Arab Spring and rise of the Islamic State.

Peter S. Henne has more than ten years of experience in international relations, Middle Eastern and South Asian politics, religion, and counterterrorism. He teaches Middle Eastern politics at the University of Vermont, and has previously worked on international religious politics and counterterrorism as a consultant with the US government and analyst at various think tanks. Dr. Henne has published articles in numerous scholarly journals and has discussed international religious issues in print media and radio. He holds a doctorate from Georgetown University and a bachelor's degree from Vassar College, and was a fellow at the University of Virginia's Miller Center.

Islamic Politics, Muslim States, and Counterterrorism Tensions

PETER HENNE

University of Vermont

CAMBRIDGE UNIVERSITY PRESS

CAMBRIDGE
UNIVERSITY PRESS

University Printing House, Cambridge CB2 8BS, United Kingdom

One Liberty Plaza, 20th Floor, New York, NY 10006, USA

477 Williamstown Road, Port Melbourne, VIC 3207, Australia

314-321, 3rd Floor, Plot 3, Splendor Forum, Jasola District Centre, New Delhi - 110025, India

79 Anson Road, #06-04/06, Singapore 079906

Cambridge University Press is part of the University of Cambridge.

It furthers the University's mission by disseminating knowledge in the pursuit of education, learning and research at the highest international levels of excellence.

www.cambridge.org
Information on this title: www.cambridge.org/9781316507667

© Peter Henne 2016

First published 2016
First paperback edition 2018

A catalogue record for this publication is available from the British Library

ISBN 978-1-107-14322-7 Hardback
ISBN 978-1-316-50766-7 Paperback

Cambridge University Press has no responsibility for the persistence or accuracy of URLs for external or third-party internet websites referred to in this publication, and does not guarantee that any content on such websites is, or will remain, accurate or appropriate.

Contents

Introduction

Understanding US–Muslim Counterterrorism Cooperation

In 2002, under pressure from the United States, Pervez Musharraf – the president of Pakistan – implemented several policies intended to combat the influence of extremist groups in the country's educational system.[1] Musharraf had reason to believe that the United States took its efforts seriously: US Deputy Secretary of State Richard Armitage had reportedly threatened to bomb Pakistan "back to the stone age" if Pakistan did not take action against al-Qaeda elements in the country.[2] Domestic backlash to these policies was significant and almost immediate. One Islamic figure claimed these reforms were aimed at "removing Quranic . . . verses on Jihad and fundamentals of Islam," and that US "talk of curbing extremism" was a "garb for invading Muslim countries."[3] A newspaper editorial attacked Musharraf for trying to remove "jihad" from the curriculum, arguing that jihad is not only a "basic concept of Islam," but also "part of the motto of the Pakistani Army since independence."[4] In response to this opposition, Musharraf backed down on his reforms, resulting in little substantive change to the country's educational system.

This is just one example of the complex exchanges involving Muslim states, US counterterrorism pressure, and domestic Islamic politics

---

[1] "Pakistan: Government to Amend Law Regarding Registration of Islamic Seminaries," September 28, 2005. Accessed through World News Connection.

[2] "US 'Threatened to Bomb' Pakistan," *BBC News Online*, September 22, 2006.

[3] Pakistani Leader: USA 'Biggest Terrorist' on Earth, Musharraf Acting as Servant, December 10, 2005. Accessed through World News Connection.

[4] "Pakistan: Editorial Disapproves US Demand of 'Excluding Jihad' From Curriculum," August 22, 2005. Accessed through World News Connection.

that took place during the United States' "global war on terrorism."
On September 20, 2001, US President George W. Bush gave a speech
to a joint session of Congress, in which he laid out the US response
to the deadly 9/11 terrorist attacks. This was followed by a worldwide
effort to disrupt the al-Qaeda network – the group that perpetrated the
attacks – and reform political systems in the "Muslim world" to prevent
similar violent movements from arising. The effort included two invasions, numerous negotiations in international forums, and covert actions
around the world. US counterterrorism efforts also built on more than
a decade's worth of US policies designed to understand and counter the
growing threat from international and transnational terrorism.

US counterterrorism efforts quickly became a religious issue among
Muslims, however. As the United States increased its activities against
Islamic groups in the 1990s, many saw these as directed against Muslims or Islam in general. After 9/11, when US policymakers discussed
the need to reform Muslim societies and promote a "moderate Islam,"
these concerns grew stronger. Many Islamic groups came to oppose US
counterterrorism efforts on religious grounds, and saw Muslim states'
cooperation with the United States as un-Islamic or detrimental to Muslims. Even Muslims who were not part of organized Islamic groups or
were generally secular perceived US efforts as an attack on the worldwide
Muslim community. US counterterrorism efforts – and Muslim states'
participation in those efforts – were thus met with widespread opposition, much of it religious in nature.

The previous example on Pakistan came to constitute a pattern: US
pressure on Muslim allies to step up their counterterrorism efforts, followed by backlash and backtracking. This was emblematic of interactions
between the United States and Muslim states over counterterrorism before
and after the 9/11 attacks.

In the 1990s, Saudi Arabia, a long-time and crucial US ally in the Middle East, dragged its heels on counterterrorism as the United States pressed
the Saudis to combat support for Osama bin Ladin and his al-Qaeda network in that country. As Steve Coll put it, "Saudi Arabia competed with
Pakistan for the status of America's most frustrating counterterrorism
ally," due to the significant financing going to al-Qaeda from the country and its government's hesitance to do anything about it.[5] After the
9/11 attacks, anger at the fact that many of the hijackers came from

---

[5] Steve Coll, *Ghost Wars: The Secret History of the CIA, Afghanistan and Bin Ladin, from the Soviet Invasion to September 10, 2011* (New York: Penguin Press, 2004): 516–517.

Saudi Arabia nearly derailed US-Saudi relations. Rachel Bronson relays the "palpable anger" in the United States "at the lack of outward Saudi contrition" in her study of US-Saudi relations; as she discusses, one high-level meeting after the 9/11 attacks even discussed options for targeting Saudi Arabia.[6]

Other countries frustrated US counterterrorism initiatives in different ways. Turkey had been a US ally and member of the North Atlantic Treaty Organization (NATO) since the 1940s. It participated in US military operations in Iraq in the early 1990s and worked closely with the United States on many issues. When the United States began gathering allies for its planned invasion of Iraq in 2003, it turned to Turkey to support the operation. To the shock of US officials, however, Turkey decided to not participate in American military actions, significantly complicating US plans. A different sort of uncooperative behavior emerged in some countries in sub-Saharan Africa. Starting in 2009, Nigeria dealt with a significant terrorist threat from Boko Haram, an Islamic group that emerged in the country's north. The Nigerian state struggled to significantly disrupt this group, and Boko Haram continued to wage a brutal war against the state and its citizens.

To some, it appeared that Muslim countries – many of whom had been tied to the United States – were slipping away from US influence as it launched its Global War on Terrorism after the 9/11 attacks. Widespread popular opposition – much of it tied to or spearheaded by Islamic groups – appeared throughout Muslim countries, limiting their leaders' ability to work closely with the United States on counterterrorism. At times this expanded into violent insurgencies that threatened the state itself. And occasionally, it seemed that Muslim leaders who had previously been allies of the United States were sympathizing with al-Qaeda and affiliated groups by dragging their feet on counterterrorism initiatives.

But this does not tell the entire story. For every example of a Muslim state being uncooperative on counterterrorism in the face of Islamic opposition, there is a counterexample of a different state walking in lockstep with the United States despite very real domestic political costs.

Many states posed no problems for the United States as it launched the Global War on Terror. Egypt, which had previously repressed Islamic groups, continued this repression and expanded its efforts to focus on US priorities like extremist messaging and support for al-Qaeda. Central

---

[6] Rachel Bronson, *Thicker Than Oil: America's Uneasy Partnership with Saudi Arabia* (New York: Oxford University Press, 2006): 235–236.

Asian states like Uzbekistan kept a firm hold on Islamic activism in their society, frequently clashing with Islamic groups that became too active. Not all examples of cooperation were so repressive: in relatively democratic Bosnia, the government at times struggled to adequately control its borders, but it for the most part implemented US counterterrorism priorities.[7]

In fact, many of the states that stood out as particularly uncooperative examples actually worked closely with the United States at other points. Turkey may have refused to help invade Iraq, but this was nearly its only example of uncooperative counterterrorism behavior in the years after 9/11. The state launched mass arrests of suspected al-Qaeda members, reformed its financial restrictions, and was an active supporter of US counterterrorism efforts in international forums. Saudi Arabia continued to drag its heels on counterterrorism after the 9/11 attacks, but it moved quickly to crack down on al-Qaeda supporters after a string of terrorist attacks there in 2003.

The story is further complicated by the nature of states' uncooperative behavior. In most of these cases, the uncooperative behavior was not the result of regimes joining with Islamic groups to support a rejection of US hegemony. Instead, leaders responded to complicated political situations by attempting to avoid domestic backlash for not supporting supposed Islamic causes. This can be seen in Pakistan, where the late Prime Minister Benazir Bhutto – speaking about Pakistan's support for the Taliban in Afghanistan – argued that Pakistani regimes were often "slowly sucked into" policies like supporting Islamic militants by pressure from powerful political groups.[8] None of this uncooperative behavior was the result of a society-wide desire to join al-Qaeda in its struggle. Some militants, of course, did – as in Somalia – but many Islamic groups were more critical of their states' cooperation with the United States than they were sympathetic to al-Qaeda. In addition, these Islamic groups did not represent all, or even a majority, of Muslim societies. For example, as Cohen notes in his history of Pakistan, few Islamist movements in the country had a broad following; until 2002, no Islamist party received greater than 5 percent of the vote in elections.[9]

---

[7] "Country Reports on Terrorism 2003," ed. US Department of State (2004).

[8] Quoted in Coll, *Ghost Wars: The Secret History of the CIA, Afghanistan and bin Ladin, from the Soviet Invasion to September 10, 2011*, 293.

[9] Stephen Philip Cohen, *The Idea of Pakistan* (Washington, DC: Brookings Institution Press, 2004).

MAKING SENSE OF THIS PUZZLE, AND WHAT IT MEANS
FOR INTERNATIONAL RELATIONS

The scholar, policymaker, or general observer of international relations thus encounters a puzzle when trying to make sense of the dynamics of religion and US–Muslim counterterrorism cooperation. Namely, why was there such variation among states – and even within states across time – in the extent to which they cooperated in the US Global War on Terror? If relations were marked by widespread Islamic opposition, why did so many states cooperate? On the other hand, if one tries to argue that Islam was really irrelevant to these decisions, then how do we explain cases of states refusing to cooperate in contentious areas despite significant US pressure? We can readily develop plausible, detailed explanations of particular states' cooperation – or lack thereof – but would struggle to generalize from this specific observation to explain these overall patterns of cooperation.

Understanding this puzzle is crucial to anyone interested in religion and international relations, US influence over the world, or contemporary events in Muslim countries. My primary motivation for launching this investigation was to better understand the complicated relationship between religion and international relations. Since the 9/11 attacks, scholars, policymakers, and the general public have been grappling with the question of what role religion plays in world events, and what role it will play in the future.[10] As an example of a highly contentious issue with widespread religious opposition, the case of US–Muslim counterterrorism cooperation is a crucial one for those studying the importance of religion. At the same time, it is also an area that has direct

---

[10] For examples, see Thomas Banchoff, ed. *Religious Pluralism, Globalization and World Politics* (New York: Oxford University Press, 2008); Eva Bellin, "Faith in Politics: New Trends in the Study of Religion and Politics," *World Politics* 60, no. 2 (2008); Erik Gartzke and Kristian Skrede Gleditsch, "Identity and Conflict: Ties That Bind and Differences That Divide," *European Journal of International Relations* 12, no. 1 (2006); Peter S. Henne, "The Two Swords: Religion-State Connections and Interstate Conflict," *Journal of Peace Research* 49, no. 6 (2012); Michael Horowitz, "Long Time Going: Religion and the Duration of Crusading," *International Security* 34, no. 2 (2009); Daniel Philpott, "Has the Study of Global Politics Found Religion?," *Annual Review of Political Science* 12 (2009); Monica Duffy Toft, Daniel Philpott, and Timothy Samuel Shah, *God's Century: Resurgent Religion and Global Politics* (New York: W. W. Norton and Company, 2011); Daniel H. Nexon, *The Struggle for Power in Early Modern Europe: Religious Conflict, Dynastic Empires and International Change* (Princeton: Princeton University Press, 2009); Ron E. Hassner, "To Halve and to Hold: Conflicts over Sacred Space and the Problem of Indivisibility," *Security Studies* 12, no. 4 (2003).

effects on states' security and even their survival. If religion affects counterterrorism cooperation, this indicates how important it is in international relations, as it can influence behavior even in life or death situations.

Another area where understanding of this question is crucial is the
United States' ability to influence weaker states' foreign and domestic
policies, and the broader nature of hierarchy in the international system.[11]
Since the end of the Cold War, scholars have debated whether or not the
United States is in decline, and how this purported decline relates to the
influence that the US is able to wield over other states. The Global War on
Terrorism was a case of a powerful state – the United States – organizing
international efforts by exerting pressure on weaker states to comply
with its policy priorities. Yet, domestic and transnational opposition (in
this case, religious contention in Muslim countries) at times complicated
and undermined these efforts. The nature of US influence over Muslim
states' counterterrorism cooperation in the face of domestic opposition
indicates the varying power of the United States over others' domestic
and foreign security policies. Moreover, if religious politics complicated
US counterterrorism efforts, this also suggests that contentious politics in
weak states can undermine hierarchical relationships.

Finally, an examination of the religion and international relations
question can provide insight into other situations in which the United
States or other states are attempting to direct Muslim states' behavior on
contentious issues. The US Global War on Terrorism will undoubtedly
not be the last time the United States becomes involved in the Middle
East or South Asia on religiously salient issues. The current turmoil in
the Middle East – beginning with the Arab Spring protests and continuing with the rise of the brutal Islamic State movement in Iraq and
Syria – is arguably a similar case of Muslim states reacting to a religious
issue with distinct security implications. Understanding how this religious

---

[11] For discussions on these points, see Stephen G. Brooks and William C. Wohlforth,
World Out of Balance: International Relations and the Challenge of American Primacy
(Princeton: Princeton University Press, 2008); Robert J. Lieber, *The American Era:
Power and Strategy for the 21st Century* (New York: Cambridge University Press,
2007); Charles A. Kupchan, *The End of the American Era: US Foreign Policy and
the Geopolitics of the Twentieth Century* (New York: Random House, 2002); Daniel
H. Nexon and Wright, "What's at Stake in the American Empire Debate?," *American
Political Science Review* 101, no. 2 (2007); Alexander Cooley, *Logics of Hierarchy:
The Organization of Empires, States and Military Occupations* (Ithaca, NY: Cornell
University Press, 2005); David A. Lake, "Escape from the State of Nature: Authority
and Hierarchy in World Politics," *International Security* 32, no. 1 (2007).

contention interacts with regional states' security concerns will be crucial to policymakers and observers.

I will answer these questions and provide insight into these areas of international relations through a new theory on institutional religion–state relationships, a quantitative analysis, and case studies of Pakistan, the United Arab Emirates (UAE), and Turkey. In this introduction, I first discuss existing explanations for US–Muslim counterterrorism cooperation and why they are insufficient. I will then present my explanation before previewing the book's chapters.

Existing Explanations

There have been numerous attempts to explain the response of Muslim states to US counterterrorism efforts. Some focus on Islam or Muslim culture, others on security and material interests, and still others on anti-Americanism not directly related to religion. All of these various explanations have been useful in illuminating particular aspects of US–Muslim counterterrorism relations. None, however, have been able to provide a comprehensive explanation for all aspects of these interactions or the role of religion in them.

One prominent set of explanations for US–Muslim counterterrorism cooperation focuses on Islam, or Muslim culture. The specifics vary, but these explanations generally argue that trends within Muslim societies explain their hostility toward the United States and US efforts, such as counterterrorism. In an extreme form, the argument runs that Muslims reject modernity and support a group like al-Qaeda as the vanguard for their ideal society. Following this argument, Muslim states either agree with this sentiment or are compelled to follow along to appease Muslim constituents. Most scholars do not go this far, however. Instead, they may argue that Muslim societies are currently facing turmoil due to the effects of globalization or the political weakness of Muslim states, and that this turmoil makes Muslim societies and states look unfavorably on US efforts such as counterterrorism cooperation. In this explanation, al-Qaeda is a symptom of this turmoil. Refusal to work with the United States, then, is a by-product of the struggles within Muslim states. For example, Mousseau points to the tension between Muslim societies and market forces.[12] And Lieber argues "tensions over individual and national

---

[12] Michael Mousseau, "Market Civilization and Its Clash with Terror," ibid. 27, no. 3 (2002).

identity" in Muslim countries has given rise to tensions that come to focus on the United States.[13] Likewise, Lewis discusses a long-running struggle within Muslim societies to make sense of why Muslims have declined in importance in the past two centuries.[14] Alternately, some argue that Muslims identify more with each other than they do with their respective states, so uncooperative behavior on counterterrorism is the result of this universal Muslim alignment and its opposition to US power. The most famous model for this argument is Huntington's "clash of civilizations" thesis, in which he argues that civilizations – rather than states – will be the dominant mode of political organization, and a major fault line will lie between the Muslim and Western civilizations.[15]

This category of explanations is too broad to explain the dynamics of US–Muslim counterterrorism cooperation. A "civilization"-wide motivation or tensions among all Muslims would not be able to explain why some Muslim countries cooperated with US counterterrorism efforts and others did not. Moreover, as I discussed earlier, it would be confounded by the strategic nature of Muslim states' uncooperative behavior. Additionally, some of these explanations operate on a different level than this book. It may be that scholars like Lieber are right that tensions within Muslim countries explain much of the anger at the United States. But this is separate question from understanding why religious opposition to counterterrorism resulted in different effects in different Muslim countries.

Others would argue that US–Muslim counterterrorism cooperation has nothing to do with religion, and everything to do with conventional matters of statecraft. To these scholars, Muslim states cooperated on counterterrorism for the same reasons they cooperate on anything; it was in their best interest. Likewise, Muslim states did not cooperate when they had no reason to or were unable to cooperate. For example, Lieber and Alexander argue that examples like Turkey refusing to invade Iraq stem from regional security dynamics and domestic politics, not a broader rejection of the United States.[16] Byman also argues that many

---

[13] Lieber, *The American Era: Power and Strategy for the 21st Century*, 183.

[14] Bernard Lewis, *The Crisis of Islam* (New York: Random House Trade Paperbacks, 2003).

[15] Samuel P. Huntington, *The Clash of Civilizations and the Remaking of World Order* (New York: Simon & Schuster, 1996).

[16] Kier A. Lieber and Gerard Alexander, "Waiting for Balancing: Why the World Is Not Pushing Back," *International Security* 30 no. 1 (2005).

of the issues the United States faced in getting its allies to cooperate on counterterrorism had to do with the weakness of these states and their limited capacity.[17] Likewise, some recent studies point out the differing effects of foreign aid on terrorism. One study indicates increased foreign aid can improve a country's counterterrorism efforts, while another study suggested greater dependence on the United States can promote the rise of terrorist groups.[18]

These explanations are not necessarily wrong, but they are incomplete. Much counterterrorism cooperation can be partially explained by non-religious factors. However, it is difficult to make sense of these dynamics without taking Islamic politics into account. As I will discuss in the chapter on Pakistan, both the weakness of the Pakistani state and its security concerns about India were closely tied to religious politics within the country. Likewise, domestic politics did help drive the counterterrorism policies of states, but it was a specific type of domestic politics arising from religious contention. Moreover, the security concerns that led, for example, Turkey to not participate in the Iraq invasion relate to its reasons for cooperating in other areas of counterterrorism. Turkey's uncooperative behavior on Iraq, and its cooperation in other areas of counterterrorism, was partly related to its concerns over Kurdish separatism in Turkey. Despite these security concerns, Turkey did face intense Islamic opposition to its US ties before and after 9/11. Any explanation of Turkish counterterrorism must be able to explain how Turkey was able to ignore this opposition. Finally, sometimes states were not acting according to their interests by being uncooperative on counterterrorism. Dragging their heels on counterterrorism was a potentially dangerous prospect when it involved angering the most powerful state in the international system that had recently invaded two countries.

Still others would argue that while uncooperative counterterrorism behavior is related to domestic backlash against US efforts, this backlash itself has little to do with religion. Instead, it is related to anger at US actions or broader North-South political divisions. That is, both Muslim and non-Muslim societies were upset with the United States because

---

[17] Daniel Byman, "Friends Like These: Counterinsurgency and the War on Terrorism," ibid. 31, no. 2 (2006).

[18] Thomas Griesa, Daniel Meierrieksb, and Margarete Redlinc, "Oppressive Governments, Dependence on the USA, and Anti-American Terrorism," *Oxford Economic Papers* 67, no.1 (2015): 83–103; Subhayu Bandyopadhyay, Todd Sandler, and Javed Younas, "Foreign Aid as Counterterrorism Policy," ibid. 63, no. 3 (2011).

its counterterrorism efforts involved controversial policies or because the United States is the dominant power in a system that disadvantaged many of them. Driven by this sentiment, Muslim states refused to cooperate. For example, Finnemore argues that US counterterrorism efforts lack legitimacy.[19] Keohane and Kaztenstein's edited volume on anti-Americanism also highlights the numerous causes of US opposition within Muslim states that had little to do with Islam.[20] Moreover, while he does not focus on counterterrorism, Voeten analyzed states' votes in the United Nations and found that there were a distinct divide between developed and developing states on many international issues.[21] It would be easy to expand this to point toward such a "North-South" divide on counterterrorism.

This explanation is not actually in direct conflict with a religion-focused explanation. Much of the anti-Americanism in Muslim countries does relate to religion, especially the sense that US counterterrorism policy or its broader foreign policies – such as its support for Israel – are targeting Muslims or Islam itself. It is difficult to explain anti-American attitudes and anger at US actions without reference to religious beliefs or identity. At the same time, much of the opposition of Islamic groups to US counterterrorism efforts, and their critiques of Muslim governments more generally, are related to religion. As I will discuss in this book's case studies, numerous Islamic groups contend with their governments and point to Islam or religious causes to justify their anger.

Finally, many eschew broad explanations and focus instead on the dynamics of particular states. For example, Hussein Haqqani provides an in-depth discussion of how the Pakistani military developed ties to extremist Islamic groups and how this affected the state's foreign policies, including its counterterrorism relationship with the United States.[22] Hakan Yavuz also discusses how the rise of the Justice and Development Party (*Adelet ve Kalkinma Partisi*, AKP) – the conservative religious party that has ruled Turkey since 2002 and shaped its current politics – relates to socioeconomic changes in the 1980s and 1990s and why the party

---

[19] Martha Finnemore, "Legitimacy, Hypocrisy, and the Social Structure of Unipolarity: Why Being a Unipole Isn't All It's Cracked up to Be," *World Politics* 61, no. 1 (2009).

[20] Robert O. Keohane and Peter J. Katzenstein, *Anti-Americanisms in World Politics* (Ithaca, NY: Cornell University Press, 2007).

[21] Erik Voeten, "Resisting the Lonely Superpower: Responses of States in the United Nations to US Dominance," *The Journal of Politics* 66, no. 3 (2004).

[22] Husain Haqqani, *Pakistan: Between Mosque and Military* (Washington, DC: Carnegie Endowment for International Peace, 2005).

implemented the policies it did, including the refusal to cooperate with the US invasion of Iraq.[23]

These studies are incredibly useful, but do not allow us to produce a generalizable explanation for US–Muslim counterterrorism cooperation. Moving beyond single case studies to a cross-national study and generalizable explanation can put the details of a single case into context, helping analysts uncover the most crucial aspects of the case and compare them to similar and differing outcomes in other countries. For example, as I will discuss in the case studies, my comparative analysis allows us to reject some explanations for a state's counterterrorism cooperation by pointing to other states with similar situations but different outcomes. At the same time, these detailed single case studies can provide insights into broader dynamics. Particularly, Hussein's discussion of the historical processes through which early decisions by Pakistan's elites had significant later ramifications on the country's later counterterrorism policies offers potential insights for historical explanations in other countries.

Thus, existing explanations for US–Muslim counterterrorism cooperation are useful but incomplete. They leave those attempting to make sense of this crucial episode in US foreign policy at a loss or resorting to ideographic explanations that focus on one or a few countries at a time. More importantly, for the purposes of this book, they do little to expand our understanding of how religion influences international security issues. Explanations focused solely on Islam struggle, as Islam does not seem to have a direct influence on counterterrorism policies. Non-religious explanations, while not complete, have pointed successfully to other factors that seem to influence counterterrorism cooperation.

So, do the limits of many religion-based explanations mean religion has little influence on high-stakes security issues? Or, more dramatically, does it call into question all works emphasizing religion's importance?

An Institutional Approach to Religion and International Relations

I argue that all of the examples I raised previously of US–Muslim interactions over counterterrorism are due to religion, specifically Islamic contention in Muslim countries. But the answers to these questions lie not with Islam itself, or the specific rhetoric or actions of Islamic groups. Instead, they lie with the numerous institutions and policies that have

---

[23] M. Hakan Yavuz, ed. *The Emergence of a New Turkey: Democracy and the Ak Parti* (Salt Lake City: University of Utah Press, 2006).

developed in Muslim states in response to and because of this Islamic contention. These institutional religion–state relationships structure the nature of Islamic politics in Muslim countries and determine the influence of Islamic groups. States with close religion–state ties are amenable to Islamic groups' policy demands and gain politically from advancing religious causes. Over time, the close relationship to religion becomes taken for granted, driving policies on religious issues and making it difficult for leaders to change course. In contrast, states with more distant relations between religion and state provide limited opportunities for Islamic groups to influence regime behavior, and at times actively repress them. These states gradually develop durable policy tools to insulate the state from religious pressure, and a professional cadre dedicated to upholding this distant religion–state arrangement.

The effects of these differing religion–state relationships are obvious in certain ways. In officially Islamic Saudi Arabia, the government in the 1960s built a television station, which was met with strident – and ultimately violent – opposition from groups in society. The country's close ties to religion had empowered conservative Islamic sentiment and opened the regime to charges of hypocrisy for countering it. By contrast, officially Islamic Turkey has restricted the ability of women to wear Islamic head coverings in civil service, education, and other areas. After the conservative Islamic AKP was elected to power in 2002, debates wracked the country over the party's attempts to loosen these restrictions. Turkey's political institutions had developed in the opposite direction of Saudi Arabia; secular limits on religiosity were instantiated and powerful forces in society opposed any attempts to change this.

The importance of these religion–state relationships and their differing effects on numerous spheres of society has been extensively studied in several high-quality works.[24] But my argument in this book is that these religion–state ties do not only affect legal systems or cultural policies. Instead, the religion–state relationship is *inextricably connected to security policies* on *contentious religious issues*, particularly Muslim states' *responses to US counterterrorism efforts*. In those states with a close religion–state relationship, the political institutions operate in a situation

---

[24] Ahmet T. Kuru, *Secularism and State Policies Towards Religion: The United States, France and Turkey* (New York: Cambridge University Press, 2009); Brian J. Grim and Roger Finke, *The Price of Freedom Denied: Religious Persecution and Conflict in the Twenty-First Century* (New York: Cambridge University Press, 2010); Toft, Philpott, and Shah, *God's Century: Resurgent Religion and Global Politics*.

in which Islamic groups are influential enough – and some elites are sympathetic enough to religious sentiment – that the state's behavior will often be driven by a desire to leverage or deflect Islamic contention. As the United States began pressuring Muslim states on counterterrorism, those regimes with close ties to religion found it difficult to cooperate extensively.

Scholars of religion and politics have made significant advances in understanding religion. We have moved past essentialist explanations that posit a direct link from fixed religious doctrine to political behavior, and now analyze religion as a set of symbols and actions that religious actors deploy to advance political goals. Religion still can have dramatic effects on political struggles, though. It increases the pressure that leaders face to be responsive to society, colors political debates through the infusion of religious beliefs, and promotes religious connections across national boundaries. Yet, I hold with a few studies that argue religion alone does not result in changes in state behavior; instead, it is the political context in which religious discourse arises that matters.

Specifically, I draw from a variety of studies that focus on institutions to understand political struggles.[25] Numerous influential works have pointed to the important role that institutions play in politics. They influence the "winners and losers" of debates by strengthening some groups and weakening others. They also affect the nature of debates themselves by constraining the options available to political actors. And they are "sticky," developing slowly over time and proving resistant to change, so political outcomes may be determined by actions taken far in the past. In the context of religion, a few studies highlight how institutions can channel religious contention, giving groups influence over the regime or insulating the regime from religious pressure.

I synthesize and expand these studies to present a soft rationalist theory on religion and international relations that focuses on institutional

---

[25] I will discuss this in further detail in the next chapter. For general examples see Bruce Bueno de Mesquita *et al.*, *The Logic of Political Survival* (Cambridge, MA: The MIT Press, 2003); James Mahoney, "Path Dependence in Historical Sociology," *Theory and Society* 29, no. 4 (2000); Daron Acemoglu and James A. Robinson, *Why Nations Fail: The Origins of Power, Prosperity and Poverty* (New York: Crown Business, 2012). The studies focusing specifically on religion are Daniel Philpott, "Explaining the Political Ambivalence of Religion," *American Political Science Review* 101, no. 3 (2007); "The Religious Roots of Modern International Relations," *World Politics* 52, no. 2 (2000); Anthony Gill, *The Political Origins of Religious Liberty* (New York: Cambridge University Press, 2008); Grim and Finke, *The Price of Freedom Denied: Religious Persecution and Conflict in the Twenty-First Century*.

religion–state relationships. I argue that religion is a transformative force in politics. At the same time, I also argue that a regime's primary motivation is to survive. As a result, religion will only influence a regime's behavior if it affects regime elites' survival calculations. This is most likely to happen when a state's political institutions tie religion and state closely together. Close religion–state relationships make religious issues more salient in a country's politics, strengthen religious groups' positions, and make it likely that regime elites will be sympathetic to religious groups or even be part of them. As a result, religious groups can threaten a regime's survival by withdrawing their support and even defecting from the regime, thereby destabilizing it. When an international religious issue arises, those states with close religion–state relationships will adopt policies in line with religious sentiment, while those with more distant relationships will be insulated from religious pressure and effectively ignore it.

This theoretical approach to religion and international relations can explain the general trends of US–Muslim counterterrorism cooperation. Islamic contention over counterterrorism is intense and generally opposed to close ties to the United States; as a result, Muslim states will be under pressure to not cooperate extensively on counterterrorism. Those states with close religion–state relationships will generally be less cooperative due to the enhanced political power of religious issues and groups in those states. In contrast, states with more distant religion–state relationships will have greater freedom of action from religious groups, and will tend to be more cooperative.

My theory can also explain the specific dynamics of US–Muslim counterterrorism cooperation. Muslim states' uncooperative behavior is not due to regimes' embrace of Islamic groups: it is because of regime's survival calculations in the face of powerful Islamic pressure. As a result, when states do not cooperate they will often attempt to still work with the United States in some areas that are less contentious or more able to be hidden from domestic audiences. Likewise, states may be uncooperative at first due to concerns over upsetting domestic Islamic groups, but will increase their cooperation if they come under increased US pressure and are able to minimize the threat that Islamic groups pose.

Finally, the dynamics of US–Muslim counterterrorism cooperation are not due only to short-term political calculations. Instead, these dynamics are the result of the manner in which the religion–state relationship developed over time. The institutional configurations and state policies that tied religion and state together – or kept them separate – in Muslim states were incredibly durable arrangements, persisting well past the initial political struggles that formed them and structuring countries' politics for decades. These religion–state relationships strengthened some political actors at the expense of others, made it difficult for opposition groups or even regime elites to change course and helped give state policies regarding religion a "taken for granted" nature. Thus, what appears to be regimes responding to immediate political pressure and limiting their cooperation with the United States is actually the result of long-term, gradually developing environments structured by the states' institutions.

I use this theory to explain US–Muslim counterterrorism cooperation through a multi-methods research design.[26] Quantitative methods are useful in highlighting patterns in a large number of observations and identifying the relative effects of different variables. As a result, a quantitative analysis can help us understand the relationship between religion–state relationships and other factors and counterterrorism cooperation among all Muslim countries. At the same time, it is less useful for understanding the reasons why a certain factor leads to an outcome and what processes connect variables to each other. Qualitative methods are therefore needed to ascertain whether the specific claims I made regarding religion–state relationships' effects are actually what explain the differences in counterterrorism cooperation among Muslim states.

My investigation thus draws on a combination of quantitative and qualitative methods in this book to analyze US–Muslim counterterrorism cooperation. I developed original quantitative measures of religion–state relationships and counterterrorism cooperation and use these in a statistical analysis of all Muslim states between 1996 and 2009. I then conduct case study analysis of Pakistan, Turkey, and the United Arab Emirates using both cross- and within-case methods. The quantitative analysis finds states with closer religion–state relationships tend to be less cooperative on counterterrorism, and that this is particularly the case for domestic aspects of counterterrorism. The case studies demonstrate that this is due to the different attitudes toward Islamic groups in Muslim states and the differing pressure regimes face from Islamic opposition to counterterrorism. They also demonstrate that this political environment is shaped

---

[26] For a discussion of multi-methods research designs, see Evan S. Lieberman, "Nested Analysis as a Mixed-Method Strategy for Comparative Research," *American Political Science Review* 99, no. 3 (2005); Alexander George and Andrew Bennett, *Case Studies and Theory Development in the Social Sciences* (Cambridge, MA: MIT Press, 2005); James Mahoney and Gary Goertz, "A Tale of Two Cultures: Contrasting Quantitative and Qualitative Research," *Political Analysis* 14, no. 3 (2006).

by the institutional religion–state relationship, which structured Islamic politics over several decades.

There are a few caveats I must raise to my explanation. The first is that I focus specifically on religion–state relationships in Muslim states. Religion–state relationships in other states or in the context of different issues may involve different dynamics, and I do not address them in this book. Second, as I will make clear in the theory chapter, my focus is on states' responses to religious contention over counterterrorism cooperation. I thus do not focus on why Muslims or Islamic groups adopted the specific stances they took or how counterterrorism became religiously contentious. Finally, I focus on whether or not Muslim states complied with the United States on counterterrorism, but this does not imply that Muslim states *should* or *should not* have complied with the United States. That is, I am making no normative claims about US power or counterterrorism. The fact of the matter is that the United States is the dominant state in the international system, and is often able to set the terms of the debate for issues like counterterrorism.

Definitions

Before proceeding with the theoretical discussion and empirical analysis, it is helpful to clarify the definitions I use in this book. I use Christian Smith's definition of religion as a "system of beliefs and practices oriented towards the sacred or supernatural."[27] However, I approach religion not as a direct influence on behavior but rather along the lines of international relations scholar Daniel Nexon, who argues that "religious beliefs, experiences, and frameworks draw boundaries...around what constitutes acceptable arguments and warrants."[28] Similarly, as Jack Snyder – paraphrasing Nexon – puts it, "religion works as a discursive field in which political claims play out in a process that involved religious conviction and strategic calculations."[29] As a result, much of my discussion does not deal with religion per se, but rather religious contention, religious policies,

---

[27] Christian Smith, "Correcting a Curious Neglect, or Bringing Religion Back In," in *Disruptive Religion: The Force of Faith in Social-Movement Activism*, ed. Christian Smith (New York: Routledge, 1996): 6.

[28] Daniel H. Nexon, "Religion and International Relations: No Leap of Faith Required," in *Religion and International Relations Theory*, ed. Jack Snyder (New York: Columbia University Press, 2011): 158.

[29] Jack Snyder, "Introduction," ibid.: 16.

and religious groups. McAdam, Tarrow, and Tilly defined contention as social groups' sustained engagement with the state.[30] I thus define "religious contention" as sustained engagement by social groups with the state based at least in part on religious sentiment. This is different from religious beliefs or sentiment; these attitudes need to be mobilized as part of contention in order to produce observable political effects. "Religious policies," in turn, are state actions influenced by religious contention, and "religious groups" are groups engaging in religious contention. I also use the term "religious politics" to generally discuss political struggles involving religious groups, or contention.

As this book is focused on Muslim countries, I use versions of these terms that are specific to Islam. I should note that in theoretical or general discussions I rely on the term "Islamic group" as an Islamic example of a religious group, rather than the more commonly used term "Islamist." This is due to disagreements and controversy surrounding this term, although I do use the term Islamist in specific instances, especially when it appears in my source material. Finally, I discuss "Muslim states" in this book, which refers to states with majority-Muslim populations. This does not refer to the official ideology of states, which I discuss in terms of religion–state relationships. I present an expanded discussion of each of these points in the next chapter.

I follow Bruce Hoffman's definition of terrorism: "The deliberate creation and exploitation of fear through violence or the threat of violence in pursuit of political change."[31] There is admittedly controversy over this term, as well as whether groups should be called "terrorist groups" and whether all behaviors the United States refers to as terrorism actually falls within this definition. As the focus of this book is on counterterrorism efforts, not terrorism itself, I do not engage deeply with these debates. In order to avoid ambiguities, however, I often discuss groups that engage in terrorist violence as militant groups.[32] Accordingly, I describe "militant" or "terrorist" groups that draw on Islam to justify their actions and mobilize followers "Islamic militant groups." Again, I recognize controversy over these terms, but use them for the sake of clarity. Finally, as I will discuss in subsequent chapters, I use the term *counterterrorism* to

---

[30] Douglas McAdam, Sidney Tarrow, and Charles Tilly, *Dynamics of Contention* (New York: Cambridge University Press, 2001).

[31] Bruce Hoffman, *Inside Terrorism* (New York: Columbia University Press, 2006): 40.

[32] For a similar approach, see Charles Tilly, "Terror, Terrorism, Terrorists," *Sociological Theory* 22, no. 1 (2004).

refer to state policies that are in line with US counterterrorism efforts. There is understandable debate over this approach, but as my focus is on compliance with US counterterrorism pressure, it is desirable.

Finally, regarding non-English terminology, I use popular terminology, specifically for political groups. This can be either the non-English version of an acronym or the English version of a group's name. I do this to avoid confusion over differing interpretations, although I include the English-language version of names when I draw on non-English acronyms.

Book Overview

I will present this theory and apply it to the case of US–Muslim counterterrorism cooperation over the next six chapters. I include technical details for the quantitative and qualitative analysis in a methodological appendix at the end of the book.

In the first chapter, I present my theory of religion and international relations. I discuss existing theories on institutions, politics, and religion and how I synthesize and expand on them. I then lay out my institutional approach to religion and international relations, specifying how religion–state relationships influence international relations.

Chapter 2 applies this to US–Muslim counterterrorism cooperation. I first touch on the background of the topic, including the development of US counterterrorism operations since the 1980s and the history of terrorism, the rise of Islamic militant groups as the primary focus of US efforts, and the diverging reactions of Muslim groups to US counterterrorism pressure. I also provide background on religious politics in Muslim countries and the development of various religion–state relationships in Muslim states. I then explain how the different religion–state relationships lead to various effects from religious politics on counterterrorism cooperation, presenting specific hypotheses for each type of religion–state relationship.

Chapter 3 demonstrates how religion–state relationships influence counterterrorism cooperation among all Muslim states through a quantitative analysis. It includes a brief discussion of the original variables on counterterrorism cooperation and religion–state relationships, the other variables included in the analysis, and the methods used, to provide a context for the quantitative findings. I then present different aspects of these findings, the variation in Muslim states' counterterrorism cooperation, and how individual states' levels of counterterrorism cooperation changed between the 1990s, the immediate post-9/11 era, and later in the 2000s.

Following this, I present the results of the quantitative analysis. I first show the consistent negative effect of close religion–state relationships on counterterrorism cooperation, even when numerous other explanations are controlled for. I then present the findings dealing with the specific types of counterterrorism cooperation, highlighting the manner in which religion–state relationships have a stronger impact on domestic aspects of counterterrorism cooperation than on international initiatives.

Chapter 4 discusses Pakistan, highlighting how the close religion–state relationship channels the widespread religious opposition in the country into intermittent cooperation with the United States on counterterrorism. Pakistan is a case of extensive ties to religion and a relatively open political system.[33] In Pakistan, religion and state gradually grew closer since the country's founding, so that by the 1990s religious groups were very influential in politics, numerous religious laws were in place, and the state had ties to several religious groups. When the United States began pressing Pakistan on counterterrorism, there was widespread religious contention, much of it involving attacks on Pakistani regimes for working with the United States. The intensified salience of religious issues in Pakistani politics and ties between the state and religious groups – including the military's sponsoring of violent and nonviolent Islamic groups in the region – made regimes hesitant to work too closely with the United States on counterterrorism. Yet, under pressure from the United States, Pakistan attempted to cooperate in some areas. The end result was a mixture of cooperation and non-cooperation, with Pakistan hesitating on many domestic policies – such as cracking down on militant groups and reforming the educational system – but working with the United States, often covertly, on areas such as US drone strikes. I also highlight the inadequacy of alternative explanations – including the weakness of the state and tensions with India – to explain the US-Pakistan counterterrorism relationship.

Chapter 5 presents a discussion on the United Arab Emirates (UAE). The UAE is a conservative Islamic state and society, but, unlike Pakistan, the regime maintains strict control over society, including the political activity of religious groups. The state is officially Islamic, with some provisions for Islamic law and restrictions on religious activity; the government is composed of conservative princedoms, however, with little

---

[33] There may be some debate over this characterization. See Chapter 4 on Pakistan, as well as the discussion on my coding for the religion–state variable in Chapter 3 and the methodological appendix for more information.

role for societal religious groups to influence state behavior. As a result of the conservative Islamic nature of the state and society, the Emirati regime allowed suspected financing of terrorist movements – including al-Qaeda – throughout the 1990s. After the 9/11 attacks, though, the United States pressed the UAE to crack down on financing in the country. Although this was controversial, the regime's control over society and distance from religious groups in society allowed it to enact policies in line with US counterterrorism initiatives. The chapter also rejects alternative explanations, such as the claim that Islamic activism is absent in the UAE or that the outcome was entirely the result of the state's strength.

Chapter 6 discusses Turkey. Turkey also has an open political system – like Pakistan – but, unlike Pakistan, has minimal religion–state ties. In Turkey, religion and state have been separate since modern Turkey emerged in the early twentieth century. The state is officially secular, with limitations on Islamic political activity and a role for the military to enforce this secularism. This has persisted into the twenty-first century, even though a religiously influenced political party came to power in 2002. There has been widespread religious contention in Turkey, however, similar to that in Pakistan; some groups have pressed the state to increase the role of religion, and called for foreign policies in line with religious sentiment, including opposing US counterterrorism efforts. The distant religion–state relationship has persisted in Turkey, however, with secular groups pushing back against religious contention and the military threatening to take action against Islamic activism. This has given the government the freedom of action needed to cooperate with the United States on counterterrorism, as the state is more insulated from religious contention. Even though tensions emerged in some areas of international politics between the United States and Turkey, counterterrorism cooperation remains close. The chapter also rejects alternative explanations, such as the apparent strength of the Turkish state and Turkish interest in counterterrorism actions, as they are insufficiently specified or inaccurate.

I conclude the book with a summary of the findings and brief discussion of other countries that I included in the quantitative discussion but not the case studies: Egypt, Saudi Arabia, and Azerbaijan. I then consider what the book tells us about religion and international relations, US international influence, and tensions in Muslim countries. The rest of the chapter expands the book's findings. I provide tentative analysis on the prospects for institutional change in religion–state relationships and what this means for international relations, discussing specifically the case of

Turkey. Finally, I discuss how my findings could apply to understanding Middle Eastern states' responses to the Arab Spring and the Islamic State, as well as broader implications for understanding US foreign policy. The book also includes a methodological appendix, which provides in-depth information on the quantitative measures and methods I used, as well as the qualitative analyses.

I

Religion–State Relationships and Religious Politics

Beginning in the 1990s, numerous scholars and pundits claimed that religion is becoming a dominant and transformative force in the international system. The earliest, most influential such argument was Samuel Huntington's "clash of civilizations" theory, arguing that civilizations – many of which fall along religious lines – will become the primary geopolitical pressure points.[1] Numerous other books proclaimed similar grand changes as a result of increasing religious beliefs, some positing a positive future as a result – such as Beyer's argument that religion will produce a global civil society – and others a messy one, like Juergensmeyer's books on the rise of violent religious extremism.[2] And this intensified after 9/11, focusing primarily on Islam, as many claimed politics in Muslim countries were defined by Islam and driven by a rejection of modernity and Western values.[3] This followed earlier interest in religion and American politics, as the rise of evangelical Christians as an influential voting bloc suggested a major shift in the importance of religion.[4]

While overgeneralizations about Muslim politics are both inaccurate and ethically problematic, I do agree with many of these studies that the increasingly public role that religion has been playing in Muslim

---

[1] Huntington, *The Clash of Civilizations and the Remaking of World Order*.
[2] Peter Beyer, *Religions in Global Society* (New York: Routledge, 2006); Mark Juergensmeyer, *The New Cold War?: Religious Nationalism Confronts the Secular State* (Berkeley: University of California Press, 1993).
[3] Bernard Lewis, "The Roots of Muslim Rage," *The Atlantic Monthly* (1990).
[4] Kenneth D. Wald and Clyde Wilcox, "Getting Religion: Has Political Science Rediscovered the 'Faith Factor,'" *American Political Science Review* 100, no. 4 (2006).

states – and non-Muslim states – for the past several decades has broad ramifications for international relations. Unfortunately, although evidence of religiosity is apparent, evidence for religion transforming the manner in which states operate on a large scale is difficult to find or complicated. As a result, some have questioned whether religion does matter on a large scale in international relations.[5]

These complications in understanding whether religion matters in international relations arise from a few puzzles in religious politics. The first is the indeterminacy of religious identity and beliefs. For example, even if we discard Huntington's admittedly problematic definition of civilizations, many studies of religion and conflict – including my own – do not find, for example, that Muslim states are more likely to fight with Christian states.[6,7] The second is the strategic use of religion. For example, in the 1990s, then-Iraqi leader Saddam Hussein used Islam to try and gain the support of Muslims in his ongoing tensions with the United States.[8] But this behavior was primarily instrumental, as Hussein had previously been a leftist nationalist who repressed Islamic groups in Iraq. The third is the persistence of statecraft – and indeed states themselves – belying grand claims of religion undermining the established international system. Even among states with religious populaces and leaders, religious issues only affect states' interactions at certain times. For example, the United States and Saudi Arabia have been close allies since the 1940s, and economic and military concerns drove the alliance's dynamics as much as religious issues did.

These puzzling aspects of religion and politics complicate our attempts to understand them. Studies claiming religion drives state behavior would struggle to explain with the variation in which it does. Likewise, the many instances of states' strategic use of religion seem to undermine religion's importance. And the fact that religion has not dramatically transformed international relations, with religious influences apparent only in certain circumstances, further complicates analysis. Do these numerous

[5] For one example, see Brenda Shaffer, "Introduction: The Limits of Culture," in *The Limits of Culture: Islam and Foreign Policy*, ed. Brenda Shaffer (Cambridge, MA: MIT Press, 2006).

[6] Henne, "The Two Swords: Religion-State Connections and Interstate Conflict"; Gartzke and Gleditsch, "Identity and Conflict: Ties That Bind and Differences That Divide."

[7] Shaffer, "Introduction: The Limits of Culture."

[8] James P. Piscatori, "Religion and Realpolitik: Islamic Responses to the Gulf War," in *Islamic Fundamentalisms and the Gulf Crisis*, ed. James P. Piscatori (Chicago: University of Chicago Press, 1991).

complications suggest religion is an irrelevant, or at best, minimal force in contemporary world politics?

I argue that the answer to this question is no. Religion is incredibly important. Yet, it influences international relations not directly, but rather through varying types of state institutions. I combine a soft rationalist approach to religion and politics with selectorate theory to demonstrate how varying religion–state relationships lead to differing effects of religion on state behavior. Because regimes' primary motivation is survival, religion only affects regimes' behavior when it affects their survival. This is most likely to occur when there is a close institutional relationship between religion and state, which amplifies the political salience of religious issues and the power of religious groups. When an issue arises that religious groups press the state to take action on, these religion–state ties give regimes an incentive to act in line with religious sentiment in order to expand their support among religious groups and avoid provoking a backlash. These religious policies do not arise from states sharing religious sentiment, however; they are the by-product of institutional configurations set up often decades earlier that structure a state's politics and influence the nature of religious contention it faces. US counterterrorism efforts – and religious opposition to close counterterrorism cooperation – are one example of this dynamic.

In this chapter, I present the theoretical argument I will use to assess the effects of religion on US–Muslim counterterrorism cooperation in the rest of this book. This chapter involves a rather broader survey of theoretical literature, which is necessary both to set the stage for my theory on religion and international relations – and my specific focus on US–Muslim counterterrorism cooperation – and to do justice to the high-quality work in this area in a manner that allows for knowledge accumulation in these research programs. I first present its theoretical background, particularly studies of institutions and religion and politics. I then discuss my general theory, specifying how religion influences politics and the effects of differing religion–state relationships.

THEORETICAL BACKGROUND

I base my explanation for US–Muslim counterterrorism cooperation on several existing research programs. The first research program is work on institutions and politics, studies that highlight the significant role that institutions play in structuring political outcomes and how variations in institutions lead to different types of outcomes. The other research program is recent advances in the study of religion and politics, which highlight the dramatic effects of religion on politics and the interaction between political institutions and religious groups. I focus specifically on one aspect of religious politics these studies highlight – *religion–state connections* – which existing studies have shown to have significant effects on political contention. I discuss each of these in turn.

Institutions

I situate my theory among a growing set of works that emphasize the manner in which institutions structure politics. In their influential 2012 book *Why Nations Fail*, economists Acemoglu and Robinson highlight how variations in political institutions significantly affected the economic trajectories of states, leading some to experience significant growth and others stagnation and crisis.[9] Similarly, Bueno de Mesquita *et al.*'s selectorate theory focuses on differences in political institutions – particularly the segment of society a state represents (the selectorate) and the group able to choose a state's leaders (the winning coalition) – to explain a variety of political outcomes, ranging from economic growth to international conflict. Since they introduced this theory with 2005's *Logic of Political Survival*, numerous other studies have expanded selectorate theory and applied it to international relations and domestic political topics.[10] And several scholars have emphasized the historical processes leading to institutional development and change, and how these institutional processes affect later political conditions. This includes the field of comparative historical analysis, such as the works of Mahoney and Thelen.[11]

[9] Acemoglu and Robinson, *Why Nations Fail: The Origins of Power, Prosperity and Poverty.*

[10] Bruce Bueno de Mesquita and Alastair Smith, "Leader Survival, Revolutions, and the Nature of Government Finance," *American Journal of Political Science* 54, no. 4 (2010); Bueno de Mesquita *et al.*, *The Logic of Political Survival*; James D. Morrow *et al.*, "Retesting Selectorate Theory: Separating the Effects of W from Other Elements of Democracy," *American Political Science Review* 102, no. 3 (2008); Alastair Smith and Bruce Bueno de Mesquita, "Contingent Prize Allocation and Pivotal Voting," *British Journal of Middle Eastern Studies* 42, no. 2 (2011); Fiona McGillivray and Alastair Smith, *Punishing the Prince: A Theory of Interstate Relations, Political Institutions and Regime Change* (Princeton, NJ: Princeton University Press, 2008).

[11] James Mahoney, "Strategies of Causal Assessment in Comparative Historical Analysis," in *Comparative Historical Analysis in the Social Sciences*, ed. James Mahoney and Dietrich Rueschemeyer (New York: Cambridge University Press, 2003); "Path Dependence in Historical Sociology"; James Mahoney and Kathleen Thelen, eds., *Explaining Institutional Change: Ambiguity, Agency and Power* (New York: Cambridge University Press,

One key argument of these studies is that institutions are not only the product of political struggles or the arena in which they occur: they structure these struggles. As Acemoglu and Robinson argue, political institutions are:

the rules that govern incentives in politics. They determine how the government is chosen and which part of the government has the right to do what. Political institutions determine who has power in society and to what ends the power can be used.[12]

Likewise, selectorate theory argues that the size of the winning coalition and selectorate affects the incentives of leaders to adopt certain policies, as leaders will adopt policies or provide goods that benefit those in society who can remove them from power. Because the type of institution – which influences the winning coalition and selectorate sizes – determines the groups in society that have political power, these institutions hold considerable sway over the actions a regime takes.[13]

Another argument is that different types of institutions produce different types of political outcomes. For example, Acemoglu and Robinson focus on the difference between extractive and inclusive institutions to understand economic growth.[14] And selectorate theory focuses on variation in two aspects of institutions: selectorate and winning coalition.[15] When these are small – limiting the segments of society that participate in politics or are able to select the regime – regimes have an incentive to provide *private goods*, goods or policies that benefit the limited number of elite regime members, often to the detriment of society in general. When they are large, however, the regime has an incentive to provide goods or implement policies that benefit everyone in society, as the general public has the power to remove a regime from power. Moreover, later advances in selectorate theory have highlighted not just the effects of small winning coalitions but the makeup of the winning coalition; regimes will

2010); Sven Steinmo, Kathleen Thelen, and Frank Longstreth, eds., *Structuring Politics: Historical Institutionalism in Comparative Politics* (1992); Wolfgang Streeck and Kathleen Thelen, "Introduction: Institutional Change in Advanced Political Economies," in *Beyond Continuity: Institutional Change in Advanced Political Economies*, eds. Wolfgang Streeck and Kathleen Thelen (New York: Oxford University Press, 2005).

[12] Acemoglu and Robinson, *Why Nations Fail: The Origins of Power, Prosperity and Poverty*: 79–80.

[13] Bueno de Mesquita *et al.*, *The Logic of Political Survival*.

[14] Acemoglu and Robinson, *Why Nations Fail: The Origins of Power, Prosperity and Poverty*.

[15] Bueno de Mesquita *et al.*, *The Logic of Political Survival*.

implement specific types of policies to reward groups for their support, so these institutions can affect not just the type of policies – private or public goods – but also the content of the policies.[16]

Finally, many argue that these institutions are "sticky"; once created, they become path dependent, affecting politics well after their founding and in a manner possibly unintended by their founding, and proving incredibly difficult to change. This relates to what Pierson refers to as "thinking more explicitly about the role of time in politics"; that is, not just analyzing institutional arrangements to understand their effects, but looking into how they developed.[17] One implication of this is that a complete understanding of many political outcomes requires analyzing the historical process through which they came to be.[18] It also means that institutions not only structure politics, they are also extremely durable arrangements that prove resistant to change and often maintain themselves independently of any political actor's efforts. Mahoney, for example, argues that institutions are often characterized by "mechanisms of reproduction" that can "'lock-in' a given institutional pattern, making it extremely difficult to abolish."[19] Likewise, the effects of institutions and the manner in which they are perpetuated may not be related to or have been the intended effects of their causes; in Thelen's words, "the forces behind the creation of a particular institution may be quite different from the forces that sustain it over time."[20]

My focus on institutions, then, and the claims I will make regarding their effects on religious politics, come from this broad set of works on political institutions. I draw primarily from rationalist studies of institutions, although I expand them to take into account the importance of religious beliefs. I argue that political actors are primarily self-interested, and will direct their activities toward advancing their interests. As a result, a regime's primary goal is to maintain its power, or survive. The policies

---

[16] Alastair Smith, "Political Groups, Leader Change, and the Pattern of International Cooperation," *Journal of Conflict Resolution* 53, no. 6 (2009); Smith and Bueno de Mesquita, "Contingent Prize Allocation and Pivotal Voting"; Alastair Smith, Bruce Bueno de Mesquita, and Tom LaGatta, "Group Incentives and Rational Voting," *Journal of Theoretical Politics* (forthcoming).

[17] Paul Pierson, *Politics in Time: History, Institutions and Social Analysis* (Princeton, NJ: Princeton University Press, 2004), 8.

[18] Ibid. Chapter 3.

[19] Mahoney, "Path Dependence in Historical Sociology": 515.

[20] Kathleen Thelen, "How Institutions Evolve: Insights from Comparative Historical Analysis," in *Comparative Historical Analysis in the Social Sciences*, eds. James Mahoney and Dietrich Rueschemeyer (New York: Cambridge University Press, 2003): 218.

that regimes enact will be their best efforts at ensuring that goal. Institutions affect politics by changing the power of different groups in societies and the optimal strategies that regimes will follow in order to survive. I differ with some strict rationalist studies, however, by arguing that some groups in society are motivated by beliefs, in this case religion. Religious groups or segments of society will not be motivated by narrow self-interest – such as economic acquisition – but rather by their desire to ensure that society follows their religious standards.[21]

I thus distinguish between the motivations of leaders and the motivations of religious groups in society. I believe that individuals in society have principled, sincere beliefs, and they will at times act on them. In the case of religious politics, this means religious groups are truly attempting to advance their religious causes through their contention with leaders and other groups in society. Regimes, in contrast, act based on their self-interest. Individual members of a regime may hold sincere religious beliefs, but the importance of maintaining power – and the often-severe penalties for failing to do so – limits the extent to which leaders will act in a manner that does not focus on their survival. It is this dual nature of political behavior – survival-seeking leaders and principled ideological religious groups – and the tension between religious groups' beliefs and leaders' self-interest that motivates my theory on religion–state relationships and can help to explain the more puzzling aspects of US–Muslim counterterrorism cooperation. Moreover, as I will discuss next, I draw on several influential studies of religion and politics that take a similar approach to this topic.

Religion and Politics

The previously mentioned works highlight how institutions can structure politics. Work on religious politics, in turn, can tell us something about the nature of the political struggles these institutions structure. As I discussed in the introduction, I follow recent advances in the study of religion and politics and approach religious politics not as a fixed application

---

[21] Although this is a different approach from many rationalist studies, there is room in the rationalist approach for the role of beliefs and ideas. For example, Fearon discussed the importance of norms or beliefs in determining the interests of individuals in society. And Bueno de Mesquita *et al.* have highlighted the potential importance of *affinity*, or belief-based ties between a regime and society, in affecting regime's survival calculations. James D. Fearon, "Domestic Political Audiences and the Escalation of International Disputes," *American Political Science Review* 88, no. 3 (1994); Bueno de Mesquita *et al.*, *The Logic of Political Survival*.

of religion to political behavior but rather a discourse that infuses and alters political contention. This can have dramatic effects on political struggles. Several studies emphasize not just religious politics, however, but the important role leaders' self-interest and political institutions can have in influencing the nature of religious politics. This broad "religious economies" approach to religious politics provides room for synthesis with the previously mentioned studies that will produce my institutional theory on religion and international relations.

Drawing on existing studies, we can identify three effects that religious contention has on politics. First, it induces a normative debate in society, increasing the application of religious standards in politics.[22] Before the increasing public expression of religion, debates focused on economic issues, security concerns, nationalism, or anti-imperialism. Once religious contention increases, however, pressure groups will increasingly draw on religious symbols and beliefs when advancing their causes, even if the causes themselves are not inherently religious. This can also catalyze a debate in society between religion and secular groups over the proper role of religion in politics.[23] We can see this in Muslim countries, as Islamic groups have gradually gained influence over leftist or nationalist movements, and political debates increasingly revolve around the proper application of Islam. And in some Muslim countries intense religious-secular clashes have broken out.

Moreover, religious contention makes it harder for leaders to act without regard to their citizens.[24] Because of the intensity of religious

---

[22] Jose Casanova, *Public Religions in the Modern World* (Chicago: University of Chicago Press, 1994); Kwame Anthony Appiah, "Causes of Quarrel: What's Special About Religious Disputes?" in *Religious Pluralism, Globalization, and World Politics*, ed. Thomas Banchoff (New York: Oxford University Press, 2008); John D. Carlson and Erik C. Owens, "Introduction: Reconsidering Westphalia's Legacy for Religion and International Politics," in *The Sacred and the Sovereign: Religion and International Politics*, eds. John D. Carlson and Erik C. Owens (Washington, DC: Georgetown University Press, 2003); Scott Thomas, "Religion and International Conflict," in *Religion and International Relations*, ed. K. R. Dark (New York: St. Martin's Press, 2000).

[23] See Gilles Kepel, *Jihad: The Trail of Political Islam* (Cambridge, MA: The Belknap Press of Harvard University, 2002); Kuru, *Secularism and State Policies Towards Religion: The United States, France and Turkey*; John M. IV Owen, *The Clash of Ideas in World Politics: Transnational Networks, States, and Regime Change, 1510–2010* (Princeton: Princeton University Press, 2010); Olivier Roy, *Globalized Islam: The Search for a New Umma* (New York: Columbia University Press, 2004).

[24] See K. R. Dark, "Large-Scale Religious Change and World Politics," in *Religion in International Relations*, ed. K. R. Dark (New York: St. Martin's Press, 2000); Jonathan Fox and Shmuel Sandler, *Bringing Religion into International Relations* (New York: Palgrave MacMillan, 2004); Pratap Bhanu Mehta, "On the Possibility of Religious Pluralism," in *Religious Pluralism, Globalization, and World Politics*, ed. Thomas Banchoff

sentiment, leaders will face greater backlash from taking actions that upset religious groups than they would from policies upsetting economic interests. And the organizational strength of religious groups – based on existing structures such as places of worship – enables coordinated action against the state. This is also apparent in Muslim countries. Studies of Egypt have highlighted how successive regimes have tread warily in dealing with Islamic groups, granting them some privileges over secular groups even as they repress more politically active Islamic elements.[25] The state policies were in part a response to the superior organizing power of Islamic groups as they could draw on religious networks to advance their agendas.

Finally, religion intensifies transnational influences in the domestic sphere. Increasing societal religiosity tends to correspond to greater identification with coreligionists abroad and global religiously salient issues.[26] Religion also creates tangible transnational connections through networks of activists, scholars, and religious institutions.[27] This leads

(New York: Oxford University Press, 2008); Susanna Hoeber Rudolph, "Introduction: Religion, States and Transnational Civil Society," in *Transnational Religions and Fading States*, eds. Susanna Hoeber and James Piscatori Rudoplh (Boulder, CO: Westview Press, 1997); Smith, "Correcting a Curious Neglect, or Bringing Religion Back In"; Scott Thomas, *The Global Resurgence of Religion and the Transformation of International Relations: The Struggle for the Soul of the Twenty-First Century* (New York: Palgrave Macmillan, 2005); Nukhet Sandal, "Religious Actors as Epistemic Communities in Conflict Transformation: The Cases of South Africa and Northern Ireland," *Review of International Studies* 37, no. 3 (2011).

[25] Daniel Brumberg, "Survival Strategies versus Democratic Bargaining: The Politics of Economic Reform in Contemporary Egypt," in *The Politics of Economic Reform in the Middle East*, ed. Henri Barkey (New York: Palgrave MacMillan, 1992); "Authoritarian Legacies and Reform Strategies in the Muslim World," in *Political Liberalization and Democratization in the Arab World*, eds. Rex Brynen, Bahgat Korany, and Paul Noble (Boulder, CO: Lynne Reiner Publishers, 1995); Carrie Rosefsky Wickham, *Mobilizing Islam: Religion, Activism, and Political Change in Egypt* (New York: Columbia University Press, 2002); "Interests, Ideas and Islamist Outreach in Egypt," in *Islamic Activism: A Social Movement Approach*, ed. Quintan Wiktorowicz (Bloomington, IN: Indiana University Press, 2004).

[26] Casanova, *Public Religions in the Modern World*; "Globalizing Catholicism and the Return to a 'Universal' Church," in *Transnational Religion and Fading States*, eds. Susanna Hoeber and James Piscatori Rudoplh (Boulder, CO: Westview Press, 1996); Thomas, *The Global Resurgence of Religion*; Fox and Sandler, *Bringing Religion into International Relations*; Dark, "Large-Scale Religious Change and World Politics"; Rudolph, "Introduction: Religion, States and Transnational Civil Society"; Carlson and Owens, "Introduction: Reconsidering Westphalia's Legacy for Religion and International Politics."

[27] Thomas Banchoff, "Introduction: Religious Pluralism in World Affairs," in *Religious Pluralism, Globalization, and World Politics*, ed. Thomas Banchoff (New York: Oxford University Press, 2008).

domestic politics to fuse with global concerns, as religious groups see international religious issues as directly relevant to their lives, pressuring leaders to act on them accordingly.

A few studies have taken the significance of religious politics as a starting point, and analyzed how religious politics and state institutions interact, which is where I situate this book. Some of these studies approach religion as a type of marketplace, in which religious groups attempt to broaden their "share" of society and states attempt to regulate this "market" in order to maintain control over society and advance their goals.[28] For example, Gill argues that self-interested leaders will implement restrictions on religious practice in order to gain the support of religious groups and extend their hold over society.[29] And Grim and Finke argue that governments regulate religious practice in order to maintain control of society.[30] Just as an economic monopoly distorts business practices, however, a religious monopoly increases the incentives of both the state and religious groups to persecute others. Finally, Philpott works from what he calls "the two roles of ideas" to argue that religion can both drive social contention and be an instrumental source of power for leaders.[31] He also emphasizes the effects of political institutions on religious belief, arguing that close religion–state ties can provoke disruptive religious contention.[32]

The Effects of Religion–State Connections

Existing works on religion highlight the dramatic effects that religious contention can have on politics. Likewise, works that highlight the interaction between religion and institutions can provide a few key insights. First, while religious contention is driven by sincere religious beliefs, state policies toward religion often arise from leaders' political calculations, particularly their attempts to gain the support of powerful religious groups. Second, these state attempts to gain religious support often create durable institutional configurations that strengthen the favored groups in society and give leaders an incentive to adopt policies these groups support. These *religion–state connections* provide the most favorable

---

[28] Lawrence Iannaccone, Roger Finke, and Rodney Stark, "Deregulating Religion: The Economics of Church and State," *Economic Inquiry* 35, no. 2 (1997).

[29] Gill, *The Political Origins of Religious Liberty*.

[30] Grim and Finke, *The Price of Freedom Denied: Religious Persecution and Conflict in the Twenty-First Century*.

[31] Philpott, "The Religious Roots of Modern International Relations."

[32] "Explaining the Political Ambivalence of Religion."

intersection point between works on political institutions and religious politics. Existing works provide a few indications of their effects.

Some studies highlight how religion–state relationships affect the nature of religion in a country, with close religion–state connections producing more intense or extreme religious contention. For example, Gill – among others – has noted that "deregulation" of religious practice promotes increased religious diversity and practice.[33] And Toft, Philpott, and Shah discussed how restrictions on religious practice or the promotion of a certain religious tradition can marginalize disapproved groups, exacerbating tensions among groups and with the state and possible leading religious groups to take up violent tactics.[34] Likewise, the previously mentioned work – as well as others, including Grim and Finke – found that favoring a certain religious tradition can strengthen more extreme elements in that tradition, leading to greater religious contention in society; this can also enable these extreme elements to use violent tactics to advance their goals.[35]

Several scholars have noted the political nature of religion–state relationships. That is, religion–state relationships represent dynamics of religious belief, but political struggles are often as important in their emergence. Gill found that the extent to which regimes depend on religious groups for support – or are threatened by secular groups – can determine the extent to which religion and state are separated.[36] Similarly, Kuru found that ideological struggles between political opposition and an entrenched regime tied to religious authorities can produce strict religion–state separation-check.[37] And in an influential recent study, Sarkissian found that the combination of low political competition and intense religious differences can lead to widespread religious repression.[38]

Most importantly for this book, however, religion–state relationships structure the extent to which religious contention in society affects a state's policies. Political institutions in general influence a regime's decisions and the outcomes of political struggles by allocating resources to

[33] See Anthony Gill, *Rendering Unto Caesar: The Catholic Church and the State in Latin America* (Chicago: University of Chicago Press, 1998).
[34] Toft, Philpott, and Shah, *God's Century: Resurgent Religion and Global Politics.*
[35] Ibid.
[36] Gill, *The Political Origins of Religious Liberty.*
[37] Kuru, *Secularism and State Policies Towards Religion: The United States, France and Turkey.*
[38] Ani Sarkissian, *The Varieties of Religious Repression: Why Governments Restrict Religion* (New York: Oxford University Press, 2015).

different groups in society, changing the sorts of policies that are viable choices for actors and determining the sources of a regime's support. religion–state relationships function in a similar manner, altering the chances of a state adopting policies in line with religious contention by changing the power of religious groups and issues. This occurs through three specific effects of the religion–state relationships.

First, religion–state relationships increase the political power of religious groups. Political ties between religious groups and the state give religious groups an avenue through which they can petition the regime to adopt policies these groups support. And the ties between religion and state give these groups some power over the regime. This can involve threats to withhold votes from a ruling party in a parliamentary setting, or authoritarian regimes' dependence on religious groups to administer the state or provide cover for unpopular state actions. Moreover, the active funding that often makes up religion–state relationships further strengthens religious groups. As they are supported by the state, these groups have an advantage in political debates over secular groups – including groups advocating for a lessened role for religion in politics or groups focusing on non-religious issues, like economic concerns or political liberalization. Religious groups thus become prominent in a country partly through these religion–state ties, further enhancing their political power. This is most apparent in Gill's work on religious freedom, which found that ties between religious groups and the state gave religious groups an avenue to discourage state support for new religious groups or broader secularism that could undermine the groups' position. Several other studies have found a similar dynamic in a variety of cases.[39] Even cases where the religion–state ties were accompanied by repression – as in countries like Egypt – these ties did give religious groups some prominence in society.[40]

Second, religion–state relationships intensify the salience of religious issues in a country's political debates. In officially religious states, elites use religion to legitimate their rule and justify their actions. This makes

---

[39] Grim and Finke, *The Price of Freedom Denied: Religious Persecution and Conflict in the Twenty-First Century*; Shirin Tahir-Khelli, "In Search of an Identity: Islam and Pakistan's Foreign Policy," in *Islam in Foreign Policy*, ed. Adeed Dawisha (New York: Cambridge University Press, 1985); S. V. R. Nasr, *Islamic Leviathan: Islam and the Making of State Power* (New York: Oxford University Press, 2001).

[40] Brumberg, "Survival Strategies Versus Democratic Bargaining: The Politics of Economic Reform in Contemporary Egypt"; "Authoritarian Legacies and Reform Strategies in the Muslim World."

it more likely that debates will be framed in religious terms; if a leader is trying to explain why his policy is the right one through appeal to God, it is likely his supporters and opponents will draw on similar appeals when debating the policy. As a result, religious symbols and rhetoric will suffuse a country to a greater extent when there are close religion–state ties. In addition to a change in the debate, however, close religion–state relationships make it more likely regimes will be threatened by religiously grounded opposition. By justifying their rule through religion, regimes will be open to charges of hypocrisy by religious groups if their actions do not follow religious standards. Thus, regimes ignoring religious issues or not taking a stance in line with religious sentiment will face significant opposition. Several studies of religion and politics have noted this dynamic as well.[41]

Finally, religion–state relationships increase the likelihood of regime elites being members of or sympathizing with religious groups. That is, in states with close religion–state ties, the regime may not only face greater pressure from religious groups and over religious issues, but they may be more inclined to agree with this religious sentiment. This is partly because, over time, the close ties between religion and state – and the prominent religious groups they produce – make it likely members of the regime will be religious and possibly be associated with religious groups.[42] This has also been noted in studies on rhetoric and norms that do not deal explicitly with religion.[43]

Thus, religion–state relationships increase the political power of religious groups and issues and the affinity between regimes and religious groups. Regimes with close religion–state relationships face greater political pressure from religious groups than those in states with more distant relationships. Leaders will thus fear losing power from crossing religious

---

[41] Douglas W. Blum, "Beyond Blood and Belief: Culture and Foreign Policy Conduct," in *The Limits of Culture: Islam and Foreign Policy*, ed. Brenda Shaffer (Cambridge, MA: MIT Press, 2006); John Esposito, *The Islamic Threat: Myth or Reality?* (New York: Oxford University Press, 1992); Adeed Dawisha, "Islam in Foreign Policy: Some Methodological Issues," in *Islam in Foreign Policy*, ed. Adeed Dawisha (New York: Cambridge University Press, 1985); James P. Piscatori, "Islamic Values and National Interest: The Foreign Policy of Saudi Arabia," ibid. (1983); Nasr, *Islamic Leviathan: Islam and the Making of State Power*.

[42] For a similar argument, see Nexon, *The Struggle for Power in Early Modern Europe: Religious Conflict, Dynastic Empires, and International Change*.

[43] Ronald R. Krebs and Patrick Thaddeus Jackson, "Twisting Tongues and Twisting Arms: The Power of Political Rhetoric," *European Journal of International Relations* 13, no. 1 (2007).

groups. Additionally, the affinity between the regime and religious groups makes it more likely religious individuals will be part of the regime or the regime will be sympathetic to their arguments. Regimes with close ties to religion may also have a greater preference for the policies that religious groups support than those with distant religion–state relationships. Finally, they increase the likelihood that policies perceived to be contrary to religious beliefs will be viewed as unacceptable. The intensity of religious issues in countries with close religion–state relationships mean these regimes will be perceived as hypocritical for proposing policies out of line with religious sentiment. This is in line with several studies that have highlighted how ties between religion and state can affect a variety of issues in international relations.[44]

AN INSTITUTIONAL APPROACH TO RELIGION AND INTERNATIONAL RELATIONS

As we saw earlier, many existing studies on religion and politics highlight the nature of religious contention and the specific political effects of religion–state connections. Close ties between religion and state can relate to a regime's attempts to maintain control over society and have significant effects on politics, increasing the salience and intensity of religion in political debates. Some studies even suggest how these religion–state ties could influence international relations. In this section, I extend these studies to present a generalizable theory on how and when domestic religious contention affects international relations by focusing on the political effects of religion–state connections. I do this by synthesizing the insight from the broad "religious economies" approach I discussed earlier – relating to the effects of religion–state connections – with selectorate theory's insights into the dynamics of political institutions.

When an international religious issue arises, religious groups will pressure the regime to act on the issue; these religion–state ties give leaders an incentive to follow the religious pressure and enact religious policies. Drawing on selectorate theory, I argue religion–state relationships

44 Jonathan Fox and Nukhet Sandal, "State Religious Exclusivity and International Crises between 1990 and 2002," in *Religion, Identity, and Global Governance: Theory, Evidence, and Practice*, ed. Patrick James (Toronto: University of Toronto Press, 2010); Philpott, "The Religious Roots of Modern International Relations"; Ron E. Hassner, "Blasphemy and Violence," *International Studies Quarterly* 55, no. 1 (2011); Henne, "The Two Swords: Religion-State Connections and Interstate Conflict"; "The Domestic Politics of International Religious Defamation," *Politics and Religion* 6, no. 3 (2013).

vary according to the extent of religion–state ties and the size of the winning coalition, with the strongest religious effects on international relations occurring in states with large winning coalitions and extensive religion–state ties. This institutional theory of religion and international relations provides insight into numerous aspects of religious politics, and can readily explain religion and US–Muslim counterterrorism cooperation. In this section, I first discuss how I conceptualize differing religion–state relationships. I then discuss how religion–state connections would affect international relations.

Conceptualizing Religion–State Relationships

Existing studies of religious politics – specifically the works of Gill, Grim and Finke, and Philpott – highlight that one of the key elements in understanding how religion influences politics is the institutional relationship between religion and the state. For Grim and Finke, this was the extent to which the state regulated religious belief and practice. For Gill, it was the political connections between religious groups and the regime. And for Philpott, it was the leverage religious groups were able to wield over leaders. Many other studies have pointed to the importance of various types of religion–state ties as well; for example, Jonathan Fox – an influential scholar of religion and politics – has highlighted religious institutions as a means to understand religious conflict and state attitudes toward religion in several of his studies.[45]

By religion–state relationships, I refer to the institutional configurations, state policies, legal frameworks, and official rhetoric that define the relationship between religion and state. Institutional religion–state connections include: provisions for an official religion; active support for religious causes; a role for religious groups in the government; and policies restricting the activities of a certain religious community, either disapproved minorities or elements of the approved religious community that do not follow the official state approach to the religion.[46] And

---

[45] Jonathan Fox, "Ethnoreligious Conflict in the Third World: The Role of Religion as a Cause of Conflict," *Nationalism and Ethnic Politics* 9, no. 1 (2003); *A World Survey of Religion and the State* (New York: Cambridge University Press, 2008); Fox and Sandal, "State Religious Exclusivity and International Crises between 1990 and 2002"; Fox and Sandler, *Bringing Religion into International Relations*; "Global Restrictions on Religion," (Washington, DC: Pew Research Center, 2009).

[46] Fox, *A World Survey of Religion and the State*; Grim and Finke, *The Price of Freedom Denied: Religious Persecution and Conflict in the Twenty-First Century*.

institutional separation between religion and state involves: the establishment of a state as secular; the lack of an official religion; restriction on the public expression of religion; and insulation of the government from religious groups, through either the power of secularist forces in society or active discrimination of religious groups' involvement in politics.[47]

Scholars have taken varied approaches to conceptualizing religion–state connections. Some look at numerous discrete examples of religion–state ties, combining them into a numeric index.[48] Others look at a few broad types of religion–state connections to establish categories of religion–state connectivity.[49] I follow the latter approach, emphasizing three aspects of religion–state connections. The first is ideological ties to religion and the use of religion to justify the state; these include constitutional provisions for an official religion, the rhetorical use of this religion to legitimate the state's existence, and favoritism toward the official religion in terms of subsidies for religious activities. The second is political connections between the regime and religious groups. This includes: powerful religious political parties in democracies; the inclusion of religious groups in governing coalitions in closed political systems; or official roles for religious groups, like advising the regime on legal matters. And the third is restrictions on religious practice, such as limitations on what groups can preach in public, proselytizing and conversion efforts, or religious broadcasting. The more of these factors that are present, the greater the connections between religion and state.

How Religion–State Connections Affect International Relations

By combining insights into the nature of religion–state relationships with selectorate theory, we can see both *how* and *when* political institutions lead to religious influences on international relations. These religion–state connections are a specific example of the general institutional configurations I discussed earlier that structure states' politics. As a result, the insights of institutional studies – while not addressing religion, for the

---

47 Gill, *The Political Origins of Religious Liberty*; Kuru, *Secularism and State Policies Towards Religion: The United States, France, and Turkey*; Philpott, "Explaining the Political Ambivalence of Religion."
48 Fox, *A World Survey of Religion and the State*; Grim and Finke, *The Price of Freedom Denied: Religious Persecution and Conflict in the Twenty-First Century*; "Global Restrictions on Religion."
49 Kuru, *Secularism and State Policies Towards Religion: The United States, France, and Turkey*; Philpott, "Explaining the Political Ambivalence of Religion."

most part – can synthesize the various arguments of studies on religion and politics and provide expectations for how these institutions channel religious politics. As selectorate theory would argue, regimes' policies toward religious groups are driven by political survival calculations, not belief systems or ideologies. And both the stability of a regime and the manner in which religious groups are tied to the regime influence the extent to which a regime will adopt policies that religious groups support.

First, religion is an incredibly important aspect of contemporary world politics, and has significant effects on states and societies. Religion will not always dominate a country's politics, and religious individuals and groups may often focus their attention or activities on non-religious goals. But when a religious issue arises, religious groups will focus on religious causes and political debates will increasingly be driven by religious appeals. Members of society will call on the state to follow what they see as religious standards, such as taking actions in support of the religious cause or refusing to implement policies deemed contrary to their religious belief. In cases of religious issues that transcend a particular state's boundaries, religious people in a society will also identify more greatly with co-religionists abroad. And if this religious issue is international in nature, the pressure on states will involve calls for them to adopt certain foreign policies, which would affect international relations.

Widespread religious contention, however, is not sufficient for religious influences on state behavior. Except for a few rare instances, religious sentiment is not shared by everyone in society – or there is disagreement among religious individuals in society over an issue – so religious groups pressing for a policy response to a religious issue will have to compete with other actors. Moreover, a regime's primary goal is to survive, not advance an ideological cause or remain true to the faith. Even if leaders or important regime members are personally pious, their religious views will be constrained by the need to maintain their rule. Thus, religious fervor can be sweeping a country and religious groups can uniformly demand a certain policy be enacted, but unless this contention threatens a leader's hold over the government or it is otherwise in the leader's interest to act in line with the pressure, it will not change a state's behavior.

Instead, the institutional effects of religion–state relationships influence how states respond to religious issues. When religious issues emerge, their effects on international relations do not arise from the beliefs of religious groups in society themselves. Likewise, the manner in which they shape state policies depends not on the specific debates about the issue, or the intensity of social beliefs about them. Instead, the effects of religion on states' behavior come from institutions, particularly the religion–state relationship present. In states with close religion–state relationships, religious groups' contention over an issue will be more salient and gain greater support among the public and some members of the regime. This is due to the political influence of religion in such states stemming from official provisions for the religion and state support for religious groups. Moreover, the political power of religious groups, arising from their historical ties to the state, will allow them to threaten leaders' survival, incentivizing the regime to act in line with their pressure. And the official ties between religion and state mean leaders' legitimacy will be threatened if they do not act in a manner deemed religiously appropriate.

Approaching religious politics in this manner – by focusing on the institutional effects of religion rather than religious beliefs themselves – can tell us numerous things about religious politics we would not be able to understand otherwise. The first is the varying conditions under which religious politics lead to changes in state behavior. One of the key aspects of political institutions is whether they are open or closed. Open systems – like democracies – will allow society direct access to regimes' decision-making. In the case of religious issue, this will mean that social groups advocating for a certain policy in response to the issue will be able to pressure a leader through voting or similar mechanisms. Closed systems, in contrast, insulate regimes from society. But what institutional studies point to as even more significant are the specific manner in which the regime is connected to or relates to society. Even in closed political systems, social groups that are well-connected to the regime – through either affinity between regime members and the group or actual group presence in the regime – will have some influence over the regime. The regime will craft policies to ensure the group's continued support, and the ties between the social group and regime will limit regime members' ability to take stances the group opposes. The religion–state ties I discussed previously are a specific example of this, as they tie the regime to a specific religious group, granting this group outsize influence over the policy process.

The effects of religion on a state's international relations will vary by the combinations of these institutional types. The strongest effects will be in states with open political systems and close ties to religion. In these states, society is able to directly pressure leaders to act – giving religious groups a channel through which to influence policymakers – and religious groups are strengthened by the close ties between religion and state. When an international religious issue arises, these groups will be able to place great pressure on regimes to act in line with their religious views due to

TABLE 1.1 *Religious Influence over State Foreign Policy*

	Open Political System	Closed Political System
High religion–state connections	Significant religious influence	Moderate religious influence
Low religion–state connections	Low religious influence	Minimal religious influence

this heightened influence. Noticeable, but less significant, influence will be present in states with closed political systems and close ties to religion. These states have the intensified salience and leverage of religion as in the first category, but the closed political system provides the regime some freedom of action. Thus, when faced with religious pressure to act the state will follow along in many areas but could still resist when desired. Religion will have less of an influence in states with minimal religion–state ties. In such states with open political systems, religious groups may still be able to pressure the state occasionally through electoral means but the lack of close ties between religion and state will diffuse these groups' influence. Closed political systems without religion–state ties, in turn, will easily be able to ignore – or actively repress – religious groups attempting to pressure the state (see Table 1.1.).

In addition to understanding how religious effects will vary across state, we can also understand variation in religion's effects on a state within the same state. No state, not even the most explicitly religious regime, will always follow religious sentiment. As I noted, leaders are driven first and foremost by a concern for survival. While they will implement religious policies in order to increase their changes or survival – by either avoiding domestic backlash or gaining supporters – they will not do so to the extent of threatening their survival. That is, we see few "Samson" states, as one study critical of religion's importance called states whose religious policies lead to self-destruction.[50] Because leaders following religious policies are acting in their self-interest, they will stop following such policies when it ceases to benefit them. Moreover, because of their ultimately self-interested nature, leaders will avoid implementing religious policies they do not desire to follow if they can. This is most likely to happen in policy areas that leaders are easily able to hide from the public.

---

[50] See Brenda Shaffer, ed. *The Limits of Culture: Islam and Foreign Policy* (Cambridge, MA: MIT Press, 2006).

This approach can also inform us about some of the more puzzling aspects of religious politics I discussed earlier. Religious policies will rarely seem to be coherent applications of religious standards onto politics. This is not due to religion's lack of importance, but rather the balance leaders strike between religious pressure and self-interest as well as the root of leaders' actions in their down desire for survival, not piety. And leaders will often appear to be paying "lip-service" to religious groups, by adopting policies they champion while trying to hedge their way around them or privately discounting the importance of the religious issue for similar reasons. Likewise, leaders will often display a mixture of religious and secular justifications precisely because they are *not* acting according to *religious beliefs*; they are acting based on the *political power* of groups in society *with religious beliefs*. Religious policies, moreover, will almost never be clear extensions of religious identity. That is, we will rarely see the behavior some critics of religion's importance claim will be the effects of religion, namely states only allying with those of the same religion and fighting states of different religions. Declaring war and forming alliances are some of the more important policies that a state can undertake, as they may – quite literally – determine whether or not a state survives. As a result, even if there is significant religious pressure on a state to ally or fight based on religious identity, states will usually follow their self-interest although this religious pressure can affect other aspects of war-fighting.

Finally, taking an institutional approach to religion and international relations indicates the longer-term impact of religious struggles. As institutional studies indicate, institutions – once created – are "sticky," and difficult to change. Moreover, they structure the possible decisions leaders can make and even their incentives to undertake certain actions well after their initial founders are gone. And they are self-perpetuating; institutions create a positive feedback loop in which they make later decisions that uphold and strengthen them more likely, further increasing the hold of the institutions into the future. Thus, religion–state relationships and policies that states enact in response to religious pressure will have significant consequences for a states' policies long after the initial struggle ended.

CONCLUSION AND TAKEAWAYS

Thus, religion has a dramatic effect on countries' politics by infusing religious appeals into political debates and increasing pressure on leaders to follow society's preferences. But religion alone does not affect international relations, as regimes' primary motivation remains survival even in the face of widespread religious contention in society. Instead, the institutional religion–state relationships produce religious effects on international relations by channeling and intensifying religious contention to incentivize regimes to act on religious issues. When these relationships are close – in countries with extensive religion–state ties and large winning coalitions – regimes will enact policies in line with religious pressure in order to gain religious groups' support and avoid provoking a domestic backlash.

So what, specifically, does this mean? What does a focus on religion–state relationships to understand religious politics – rather than religious beliefs or discourses – tell us? The first is that the primary influence on whether or not a state adopts a religious policy – defined as a policy advocated for by religious groups or seen as religiously appropriate – is the extent of institutional ties between the state and religion. The nature of the debate, the intensity of religious activism, and the personal beliefs of the leader matter because they determine the content of the pressure leaders face. But these ideational factors on their own do not determine states' responses. Moreover, these religion–state ties are not simply a proxy for religiosity in society or the influence of religious groups. Often religious groups will have disproportionate power over a state due to the religion–state relationship. The second is that this influence has nothing to do with piety, religious ideologies, or sentiment. Again, while this matters for social groups' actions and what they pressure regimes over, regimes' ultimate decisions – and the details of the policies they enact – are not related to religious beliefs. Instead, regimes adopt policies that are mostly likely to avoid backlash from religious groups without unduly undermining the leaders or regimes' agendas. As a result, any religious influence on a state will emerge from a balancing act between state interests and religious pressure, with the outcome often unrecognizable to both.

I should note what this theory focuses on, however, and what it does not. I focus primarily on the effects of religious contention on international relations once religious groups in society began advocating over a religious issue. That is, I do not attempt to explain why religious individuals believe what they do or how they decide which policies to advance. Likewise, I do not attempt to understand what issues become contentious among religious groups and lead to international activism. These are all worthy pursuits, but are outside the scope of this book; moreover, as I focus on one particular religious issue – counterterrorism among Muslim countries – with a clear direction of religious pressure against cooperation with the United States, these aspects of religious politics are not essential to my analysis.

What does this say about religion itself? Or, in other words, is this really a theory about religion? In one sense, this is not a book about religion. As I noted, the scope conditions for this theory limit its investigation of how religious issues arise and become politicized. Moreover, as I also noted, I believe that these political institutions play more of a role in religious politics than religion itself. As a result, this theory – and the empirical chapters of the book – does not deal with religion, but rather the political effects of religion as filtered through institutional religion–state ties. At the same time, this is very much a book about religion, and one of my key intended takeaways is that we cannot understand the dynamics of Muslim cooperation with US counterterrorism efforts without understanding religious contention in Muslim countries. It is not just political institutions that matter; it is the specifically *religious nature* of these institutions that interact with intense religious contention to alter states' behavior. Just as we would be missing out on important variations by looking just at religious contention, we would also be missing out on important context for political struggles by ignoring religion to focus just on institutions and political calculations.

This discussion has, by necessity, been rather general. The specifics of religious issues will vary greatly across time and space, so it would be impossible or overly simplified to provide specific expectations for their nature and timing. Likewise, the type of pressure religious groups place on a regime – the policies they call on regimes to enact or oppose – will also vary according to the specific religious issue at play. Finally, the details of various religion–state ties will depend on the religious makeup of the state and other contingent factors. The previous discussion, however, provides the theoretical justification for my focus on religion–state relationships and the general logic of the argument. In the next chapter, I will address the specific topic of this book – US–Muslim counterterrorism cooperation – and provide the nature of the general aspects of this theory.

2

Muslim States and Counterterrorism

The institutional theory of religion and international relations I presented in Chapter 1 can comprehensively explain the dynamics of religion and US–Muslim counterterrorism cooperation. Over the past few decades, Muslim states have experienced widespread religious contention as Islamic groups came to prominence in society and Islamic causes suffused political debates. This contention took place in greatly varying institutional contexts, though, ranging from explicitly Islamic states to secular authoritarian ones that repressed any Islamic activity. As US counterterrorism efforts began in earnest in the 1990s, they took on a religious tone in Muslim countries, due to their focus on Islamic groups and Muslim societies. As a result, Islamic groups opposed Muslim states' cooperation with US counterterrorism, and broader Islamic sentiment saw such cooperation as distasteful. In states with closer religion–state relationships, this Islamic opposition translated into states' hesitating cooperation with the United States. States with more distant religion–state ties, in contrast, were able to ignore religious opposition and work closely with the United States.

In this chapter, I apply the general theory of religion and politics from the previous chapter to the specific topic of this book. I first discuss the background of this topic, going through the various religion–state relationships that have developed in Muslim states and how these relationships affect their politics. I then discuss the history of US counterterrorism operations and relations with Muslim countries related to counterterrorism. Following this, I use the institutional theory of religion and international relations to present expectations for how the differing religion–state relationships in Muslim states affect their counterterrorism cooperation with the United States. I also present the multi-methods research design I use in this book.

ISLAMIC CONTENTION AND RELIGION–STATE TIES AMONG MUSLIM STATES

The Muslim states I focus on in this book experienced intense Islamic contention that resulted in recurring clashes between societies and states. The nature of Islamic contention varied greatly according to the specific country context, but they generally increased the prominence of Islam in political debates, sparked religious-secular struggles, and promoted a transnational identification among some Muslim groups. These clashes produced a variety of differing religion–state relationships that have influenced Muslim states' behavior in many areas, including cultural policies and debates in international forums.

Islamic Contention and Muslim States

Muslim societies since the second half of the twentieth century have been characterized by widespread and intensifying religious contention. Examples range from the officially Salafist state of Saudi Arabia to the Pakistani homeland for South Asian Muslims. Moreover, as pan-Arabism declined in influence after the 1967 Arab-Israeli War, political Islam came to be the dominant ideology and motivating principle in Middle Eastern politics. And political Islam became prominent beyond this region, taking root from Turkey to Indonesia.

Islamic politics in Muslim states varied greatly in nature, however. Some Islamic groups participated in electoral politics, as seen in Algeria in the 1980s and early 1990s when an Islamist party rose to prominence in elections before the military intervened. Other Islamic groups focused primarily on social issues, such as the Muslim Brotherhood, at times. Moreover, though many Islamic groups attempted to create Islamic states, some attempted only to expand the role of religion in a country's politics. A prominent example is Turkey's Justice and Development Party (*Adelet ve Kalkinma Partisi*, AKP), which arguably pursued this course for much of its time in power. Beyond this, some Islamic groups were violent, ranging from the transnational al-Qaeda network to ethnoreligious insurgencies in the Philippines.

At the same time, there were some similar effects of Islamic politics on Muslim societies. Political debates have come to be dominated by Islamic symbols and rhetoric. The Muslim Brotherhood remains popular in Egypt in the face of persistent state repression, and the formerly leftist Palestinian groups have given way to the Islamic Hamas. Likewise, debates over what counts as Islamic and what role Islam should play in societies have had wide-ranging effects. This includes the ongoing secular-Islamic conflict in Turkey I will discuss in that chapter and official attempts to limit Islamic activity in Bangladesh.

This intensifying Islamic politics has altered the nature of Muslim states around the world. States that had only loose associations with Islam, like Pakistan and Malaysia, adopted stronger ties to Islam after facing Islamic pressure.[1] And nationalist or leftist regimes like that in Egypt established connections to Islam in order to head off domestic opposition. Even Saudi Arabia felt compelled to strengthen its ties to Islam, with the Saudi king taking the title of "Defender of the Two Holy Places" in the 1980s.

Moreover, Islamic contention has had a transnational element, as connections and campaigns spread across state boundaries. Islamic groups often frame their struggles as part of worldwide Islamic causes, or claim to be serving the *ummah* or global Muslim community. This can be seen in the discussion on Pakistan in this book, in which some groups tie the conflict in Kashmir to conflicts involving Muslims in other countries. Additionally, many Muslim groups focus not just on domestic issues but often identify with the suffering of Muslims in other countries, such as transnational mobilization to aid Muslims in Afghanistan, Bosnia, Burma, Iraq, and Russia.

Diverse Religion–State Relationships

While religious contention has been widespread throughout Muslim states, the relationship between religion and state among Muslims has varied greatly. This diversity is apparent when looking at different Muslim states. In this book, I present in-depth analyses of three Muslim states with vastly differing religion–state relationships. Pakistan was formed initially as a homeland for Muslims. It increasingly became officially Islamic, with laws being required to be based on or in line with Islam and active state support for domestic and international Islamic groups. The United Arab Emirates (UAE), in contrast, was formed as a confederation of conservative Islamic city-states based on traditional authorities. The UAE

---

[1] Nasr, *Islamic Leviathan: Islam and the Making of State Power.*

contains laws based on Islam but limits the political power of Islamic groups to a greater extent than does Pakistan. And Turkey has been officially and aggressively secular since its founding, due to the Westernizing reforms of its first post-Ottoman leader Mustafa Kemal. Other states I do not cover in chapters further indicate the range of religion–state relationships. For example, states like Egypt were historically secular authoritarian states that adopted some trappings of Islam to co-opt opposition, while authoritarian Central Asian states like Uzbekistan actively distance themselves from any religious politics.

The differing religion–state relationships come in part from the great diversity among Muslims themselves, as well as historical ideological struggles and political struggles. The "Muslim world," which analysts and pundits sometimes refer to when discussing Islamic politics, stretches from sub-Saharan Africa to Southeast Asia. Some Muslim states – like Nigeria and Burkina Faso – are made up of numerous African ethnicities, and Muslims live alongside Christians and animists. Many others are ethnically Arab, although some have significant non-Arab minorities; this includes most of the states in the Middle East, from Algeria to Iraq. In contrast, the two most populous Muslim states – Pakistan and Indonesia – are not Arab, and both are made up of numerous ethnicities. Nigeria in West Africa formed out of European colonial projects. Southeast Asian states like Indonesia, in contrast, formed out of colonial efforts and revolutionary postcolonial struggles. Turkey and Iran had never been colonized, but formed out of precolonial political structures and pressure from colonial projects. And Central Asian states like Uzbekistan and Kazakhstan formed from the breakup of the Soviet Union.

Thus, religion–state relationships in Muslim states differ greatly. These differences may have arisen from aspects of the previously mentioned diversity of Muslim states, with differing cultures, ethnicities, and colonial legacies producing distinct religion–state arrangements. Once formed, however, these religion–state relationships have an independent effect on Muslim states' behavior, structuring religious politics in line with my general theoretical argument stated earlier. Those states with closer religion–state ties – like Saudi Arabia and Pakistan – have a greater role for religion in politics as leaders are more constrained by and tied to religious groups and arguments. And more secular states, like Turkey, have corresponding politics as leaders can effectively ignore or minimize the impact of religious groups. Indeed, the manner in which religion–state connections in Muslim states have structured numerous aspects of their politics is apparent in a few examples.

One area in which they have had significant impact is on cultural policies. States with close religion–state ties found it difficult to implement policies that religious groups opposed. For example, in the 1960s, Saudi Arabia established its first television station. Conservatives strongly opposed this, as they saw television as un-Islamic. Because Saudi Arabia claimed to uphold Islam, these groups saw the move as hypocritical. And because the state had supported Islamic groups since its founding, those opposing this move gained some support. The Saudi king persisted with the initiative, but faced significant backlash and even violence when a group of conservatives – including members of the royal family – attempted to attack the television station.[2] In contrast, states with more distance between religious groups and the state could take cultural steps that religious groups opposed. As I will discuss, UAE – while a conservative officially Islamic state – maintains distance between the regime and Islamic groups. This allows it to ignore Islamic activism when it desires. This is most apparent in its attitudes toward Westerners. There has long been agitation in the country to impose a stricter dress code. While occasionally steps have been taken in this regard – such as warnings about indecent dress in malls – the state still allows the wearing of bikinis and other revealing swimwear by Western tourists on some beaches.[3]

Another area where religion–state relationships have mattered is in international forums. Pakistan has occasionally used outreach to the Organization of Islamic Cooperation (OIC) to advance its international standing and appease domestic audiences. Zulfikar Ali Bhutto, the Pakistani Prime Minister in the 1970s, used the OIC to increase his Islamic credentials and attempt to gain the support of Pakistani Islamic groups. This continued more recently, as Pakistan attempted to advance an international ban on religious defamation in the United Nations. Both countries professed dedication to Islamic causes and powerful domestic religious groups made a strong profile in international Islamic issues politically desirable. In contrast, Kazakhstan – which has a more distant religion–state relationship – is part of the OIC, but has downplayed the religious aspects of its work in the group, instead claiming its focus is on

---

[2] For discussion on this example, see Bronson, *Thicker than Oil: America's Uneasy Partnership with Saudi Arabia.*

[3] Katy Watson, "Dubai Dress Code: 'Cover up,' UAE Women Tell Foreigners," *BBC News Online*, July 5, 2012.

"security, economic and diplomatic issues."[4] Kazakhstan's distance from religious groups gives the regime little incentive to emphasize international religious issues, while it may be wary of provoking Islamic activism by actively campaigning on Islamic causes.

Moreover, the path-dependent nature of these religion–state connections is apparent. As Nasr has discussed in his work on Malaysia, Malaysia's current ties between religion and state grew out of regimes' attempts to co-opt powerful Islamic groups.[5] The state granted Muslims preferential positions in several areas of government, and implemented some laws in line with Islamic sentiment. This was motivated primarily by the state's desire to solidify its rule rather than an interest in advancing Islamic causes. Despite this initial motivation, the institutions set in place by earlier state policies have continued to affect Malaysian politics, granting Islamic groups some sway over decision-making. The most recent example of this is the ongoing controversy over the non-Muslim use of the term "Allah" in worship. While Malaysian Christians claim the term is a generic one meant to refer to God, Islamic groups successfully petitioned the state to ban its use by non-Muslims.[6] The historical legacy of these institutions is also apparent in Turkey. As I will discuss in the chapter on Turkey, Turkey's secular institutions have persisted even as Islamic activism in society became more prominent and a conservative religious party came to power. Attempts to implement more Islamic policies have met with fierce resistance; the conservative government that came to power in 2002 loosened restrictions on women wearing head scarves and tried to make it more difficult to consume alcohol in the country. While both initiatives succeeded, the government faced fierce resistance from more secular elements of society that appealed to the country's secular heritage.

ISLAMIC CONTENTION AND COUNTERTERRORISM COOPERATION

Thus, different religion–state relationships have developed over time in Muslim states, resulting in distinct effects on cultural policies and other areas. My argument in this book, however, is that religion–state

---

[4] "Kazakhstan Promotes Central Asian Interests within OIC," in *Eurasia Daily Monitor* (Jamestown Foundation, 2013).

[5] Nasr, *Islamic Leviathan: Islam and the Making of State Power.*

[6] Sophie Brown, "Malaysian Court to Christians: You Can't Say 'Allah'," *CNN Online*, June 24, 2014.

connections do not only affect domestic affairs or symbolic interactions between states but they can also affect high-stakes international security issues, like counterterrorism cooperation. Before I discuss how this occurs, however, I will provide a brief overview of US counterterrorism efforts and the controversies they have produced.

Counterterrorism Cooperation

US counterterrorism efforts have gradually expanded since the 1960s. The United States first began to combat terrorist threats in the 1960s and 1970s with the emergence of domestic terrorist threats and leftist groups in Europe and other regions. This intensified in the 1980s with the creation of the Central Intelligence Agency's Counterterrorism Center and increased concern over terrorism arising from the Middle East and the threat to the United States from al-Qaeda in the 1990s. After the 9/11 attacks, US efforts became even more intense, developing into the "global war on terrorism" that I discussed in this book's introduction.

By the 1990s, terrorism took on an Islamic salience. Early terrorist groups were leftist or nationalist, like the Red Brigades in Europe. Explicitly Islamic groups became more prominent in the 1980s, though – such as Hizballah in Lebanon and Hamas in Israel-Palestine. And this expanded in the 1990s with al-Qaeda and Islamic insurgences in countries like Algeria and Egypt. Moreover, al-Qaeda's efforts explicitly tied its terrorist activities and struggle with the United States to Islam. Osama bin Ladin appealed to Muslim solidarity following the Soviet Union's 1980s invasion of Afghanistan to try and gain support for his struggles. And after the 9/11 attacks, bin Ladin claimed the United States was pursuing a war against Muslims in order to attract recruits for its fighting in Afghanistan and Iraq.[7]

US counterterrorism efforts thus often took the appearance of campaigns against Muslim states and Islamic groups. This included pressure

---

[7] For useful overviews of the history of terrorism and al-Qaeda, see Peter Bergen, *The Longest War: The Enduring Conflict between Al-Qaeda and America* (New York: Free Press, 2011); Lawrence Wright, *The Looming Tower: Al-Qaeda and the Road to 9/11* (New York: Vintage Books, 2006); Rohan Gunaratna, *Inside Al-Qaeda* (New York: Berkley Books, 2003); Hoffman, *Inside Terrorism*; David C. Rapoport, "The Fourth Wave: September 11 in the History of Terrorism," *Current History* 100, no. 650 (2001); "Fear and Trembling: Terrorism in Three Religious Traditions," *American Political Science Review* 78, no. 3 (1983); Daniel Byman, *Al-Qaeda, the Islamic State, and the Global Jihadist Movement: What Everyone Needs to Know* (New York: Oxford University Press, 2015).

on states to take action against militant groups and their supporters and outright military offensives, such as the bombings of Iraq in the 1990s and the post-9/11 invasions of Afghanistan and Iraq. And due to this Islamic nature of terrorist groups, US efforts often focused on Islam itself. US policymakers attempted to understand Islamic contention and promote "moderate" alternatives to groups like al-Qaeda.

The nature of US counterterrorism efforts provoked two responses in Muslim countries. The first, among Muslim societies, was anger that often took on a religious tone. Some Islamic groups openly supported al-Qaeda, but most groups – and the vast majority of Muslims – did not. Yet, US counterterrorism efforts were still widely unpopular among Muslim societies. This was not just due to the perceived illegitimacy of some US actions. It also related to the perception that the United States was profiling Muslims as potential terrorists, as well as concerns that calls for "moderate Islam" represented disapproval or overgeneralization of Islam.[8] As Kull discusses in his extensive study of Muslim opinion, "one of the most powerful sources of anger toward the United States is the widespread perception that the United States is hostile to Islam itself."[9]

The second was anxiety among Muslim states. US counterterrorism efforts are a delicate issue for Muslim states. They faced very real costs for not complying with US pressure. Many of these states have been dependent on the United States for trade, security, and aid throughout the post-World War II era. Refusing to work with the United States could thus harm these countries' economies and security. And the United States has shown that it was willing to forcefully intervene in countries it deemed too supportive of al-Qaeda or terrorism. But Muslim states had to strike a balance in working with the United States. Several Muslim states experienced severe insurgencies by Islamic groups, so counterterrorism policies that either exacerbated or ameliorated this situation would have significant effects on the states' survival.[10] Moreover, actions taken that upset Islamic sentiment – such as working closely with the

---

[8] For a discussion of this, see Laila Lalami, "Islamophobia and Its Discontents," *The Nation*, July 2, 2012.

[9] Steven Kull, *Feeling Betrayed: The Roots of Muslim Anger at America* (Washington, DC: Brookings Institution Press, 2011): 72.

[10] Mohammed M. Hafez, *Why Muslims Rebel: Repression and Resistance in the Muslim World* (Boulder, CO: Lynne Reiner Publishers, 2003); Jonathan Schanzer, *Al-Qaeda's Armies: Middle East Affiliate Groups and the Next Generation of Terror* (Washington, DC: Washington Institute for Near East Policy, 2005).

United States on counterterrorism – pose a significant political risk to Muslim regimes.

Muslim States' Religion–State Relationships' Effects on Counterterrorism

Thus, US counterterrorism efforts became an incredibly contentious international religious issue. This did not lead to uniform uncooperative behavior among Muslim states, however. For every state like Pakistan, whose uncooperative behavior severely complicated US efforts, there was a state like Albania that cooperated extensively. These differing levels of counterterrorism cooperation can best be explained by varying religion–state relationships among Muslim states.

I draw on the theoretical discussion in Chapter 1 to categorize religion–state relationships among Muslim states. Some have open political systems, with large winning coalitions and relatively democratic elections. Others have closed political systems, with small winning coalitions in which an elite group like the military chooses leaders. And I use the types of religion–state ties characterized earlier. Having an official religion involves constitutional provisions establishing Islam as the state's religion. It also often involves numerous laws being based on Islam, or a specific interpretation of Islam. And it involves some sort of official deference to Islamic standards in laws, such as a requirement that no law or government policy can contradict Islam. Political ties between the regime and religious groups can take a few forms. In open political systems, it is often Islamic political parties serving in the legislature or running the government. And in closed political systems, it takes the form of Islamic groups administering some government functions, such as the judiciary. Likewise, Muslim states restrict numerous aspects of religious practice, including the activities of non-Muslim groups like Christian missionaries as well as Muslim religious practice out of line with the state's preferred form of Islam. The combination of these religion–state ties and political systems result in five categories of Muslim state religion–state relationships. I discuss each category in turn, as well as the effects of the religion–state relationship on counterterrorism cooperation (see Table 2.1).

The closest religion–state relationships are in states with relatively open political systems and extensive connections to religion. These states include Islamic parties in governing coalitions, establish official or unofficial advisory role for religious scholars and Islamic groups. They are also officially Islamic, and sometimes base their legal codes on Islamic standards. And these states are also relatively open political systems.

TABLE 2.1. *Categories of Religion–State Relationships among Muslim States*

Religious Influence	Officially Islamic	Restrictions on Religious Practice	Regime Connected to Religious Groups	Political System	Example
Strongest	Yes	Yes	Yes	Open	Pakistan
Strong	Yes	Yes	Yes	Closed	Saudi Arabia
Moderate	Yes	Yes	No	Closed	UAE
Minimal	No	No	Yes	Open	Turkey
Lowest	No	Yes	No	Closed	Egypt, Uzbekistan

Often the state is unable to control domestic opposition groups, which at times threaten to destabilize society. They also occasionally have hybrid political elements, such as legislatures. A prominent example of this type of state is Pakistan.

These states experience the greatest influence of religion on state behavior. In these states, religious issues are very salient and regimes depend on religious groups' support to stay in power. When religiously contentious international issues arise, regimes either hesitate to take actions that would upset groups, or implement unpopular policies but distract opposition through religiously charged rhetoric or symbolic stands. Often leaders' responses were determined by earlier regimes' policies, as appeals to religion in one period made it difficult for leaders to ignore religious pressure in later periods. For example, Pakistan has alternated between military rule and weak civilian governments, both of which gradually increased the level of religion–state connections. Appeals to Islam by early leaders established ties between Islam and the state and encouraged religious groups to pressure the state on policies. This led later regimes to either give in to religious pressure to maintain power – like Zulfikar Ali Bhutto – or actively promote religious groups they supported, as did Zia ul-Haq. Following Pakistani support for Islamic militants in Afghanistan and Kashmir, the state found it inconvenient or difficult to break with militants under pressure from the United States and other international actors. And the state also championed international causes in the United Nations and similar forums that resonated with religious groups as well as solidarity among developing countries.

These states will have the lowest level of counterterrorism cooperation. The extensive religion–state ties leave leaders little room to ignore or act against religious opposition to counterterrorism policies. Due to the power of religious groups in these states, leaders will often be hesitant to enact policies that upset them, and will often see uncooperative behavior as in their best interest. As a result, when the United States pressures these states to cooperate on counterterrorism they will half-heartedly implement policies to avoid upsetting domestic groups. These states may cooperate at times, however, when the United States presses greatly or they have more of an interest in implementing certain counterterrorism policies. This cooperation will often be short-lived, however, as the state backs down in the face of significant domestic opposition. These behaviors will all be apparent in the Pakistan case study.

Moderate religion–state ties are present in states with closed political systems and extensive religion–state connections; these states are influenced by religious contention but have greater control over society than states like Pakistan. These states have significant political ties to religious groups, restrict religious activity, and are often committed to supporting Islam. Yet, these states have significant control over society. They often have extensive resource bases, as well as very powerful security forces. Religious groups pressure these states to "live up to" their Islamic ideals, pushing them to act according to Islamic standards. For example, some states adopt policies intending to outbid domestic opposition – such as championing international Islamic causes – that gave religious groups more leverage to pressure the regime later on. Yet, as the states are relatively strong, they will only give in until regime survival is threatened, moving to repress religious groups that go too far.

This can be seen in the history of religion–state relations in Saudi Arabia. At several points, the regime faced pressure from strong religious groups, as in the backlash against economic modernization in the 1960s, the threat to legitimacy posed by the Iranian Revolution, and anger over support for the 1991 Gulf War. In each case, the regime attempted to outbid religious groups for legitimacy, such as officially declaring the Saudi king the defender of Mecca and Medina and getting post-hoc justification for working with the United States on Iraq from the *ulema*. But when religious groups pushed too hard, as in the *Sahwists'* – young, conservative clerics – protests against the king's legitimacy in the early 1990s, the regime responded with outright repression.

Moderate influence is also present in strong states with connections between religion and the state that are not as extensive as the previously mentioned categories. These states are non-democratic, and although some have hybrid elements – like parliaments – they remain strong vis-à-vis society. They are officially Islamic and restrict religious practice, but the regime is not politically connected to religious groups; similarly, religious scholars have less official power than in those states, and the security services are not closely tied to religious groups. This results in religious influence on behavior similar to the earlier mentioned category, but to a lesser degree. Examples of this state include Qatar and the UAE.

Counterterrorism cooperation for these types of states will be mixed. The close religion–state relationships make counterterrorism efforts politically risky, but the closed political system gives the states more control over society than in states like Pakistan. As a result, these states may initially hesitate on counterterrorism pressure from the United States but will cooperate if they come under threat or intensified US pressure. They will partially enact some policies or deny the existence of counterterrorism problems in order to avoid dealing with religious opposition. But they will more readily cooperate than the first category. When their security is threatened or the US increases pressure on them, they will crack down on Islamic groups and cooperate due to their relatively greater control over society than the earlier mentioned category.

Lower religious influence on behavior is present in states with open political systems and few religion–state connections; these states are often relatively democratic Muslim states like Senegal and Turkey. These states are officially secular but religious groups can affect politics through the electoral process. For example, in relatively democratic Senegal, a cooperative relationship developed between Sufi orders and the state, contributing to a consensual incorporation of religion into Senegalese politics and preventing the dominance of more radical groups. In these states, the power of religious groups is diffused by the relatively broad electorate and the state's security apparatus is often separate from – or even hostile to – religious groups. The state is thus less likely to adopt religious policies on important issues – like security or significant trade agreements – unless there is significant and widespread domestic contention surrounding the issue. For example, in Turkey, neither a short-lived Islamist government in the 1990s nor the aforementioned conservative religious resulted in drastic changes to the state's security relationship with the United States, due to both the broad electoral coalitions supporting each party and the power of the secular military.

These states will be rather cooperative on counterterrorism. Because religious groups' power is limited due to the lack of religion–state ties, regimes will generally be able to ignore religious pressure and work closely with the United States on counterterrorism. The open political system, however, allows religious groups to influence a state's policies and lead to some uncooperative behavior.

Finally, there are numerous non-democratic Muslim states that are generally secular; there is minimal religious influence on the behavior of these states. Some are opportunistic in regard to religion, like Egypt, which adopted ties to religion in order to co-opt religious groups but avoided substantive connections with these groups. Others remained secular, mostly formerly Communist states in Central Asia that significantly restrict religious political activity. And some are non-democratic states in Africa in which religion has never been a serious issue of contention. There is little to no religious influence on these states' behavior. These states will be the most cooperative on counterterrorism, as the regime operates independently of religious pressure. While I do not present a case study on this type of state in this book, I do discuss Egypt and Azerbaijan's counterterrorism cooperation briefly in the concluding chapter.

THEORETICAL EXPECTATIONS

Applying the general institutional theory of religion and international relations to US–Muslim counterterrorism provides specific testable implications for empirical studies. These include broad expectations for the types of behavior we should see in different states, as well as the specific means through which Muslim religion–state relationships lead to greater or lesser counterterrorism cooperation. These implications allow me to test the validity of my theory in the following quantitative analysis and case studies, as well as assess whether alternative explanations are useful in understanding this topic.

religion–state relationships correspond to lessened counterterrorism cooperation not because regimes in these states are more devoted to religious causes or societies are more pious. Instead, it is because of the heightened political power of religious groups and rhetoric in these states. I hold with other rationalist institutionalist scholars, and argue a regime's primary goal is always survival. Thus, regimes will be uncooperative on counterterrorism due to the threats to their survival cooperation poses, not for any idealistic reason. This manifests itself in two specific ways. The first is that regimes will be constrained from cooperating with the United States by *public pressure*, arising specifically from Islamic groups strengthened by the religion–state ties. The second is that regimes will be constrained from cooperating with the United States by *internal regime pressure*. As I noted, one effect of a close religion–state relationship is to increase the salience of religious issues and standing of religious groups. This increases acceptance of Islamic groups' arguments and makes it more likely that elites in society will sympathize with or be a part of these groups. As a result, members of the regime – such as members of a dominant political party or military officials – may be tied to religious groups. The regime will thus be limited in its ability to cooperate with the United States on counterterrorism, as it may face the risk of internal defection.

The first implication is that closer religion–state ties will correspond to lesser counterterrorism cooperation. Among all Muslim states, we should see the lowest level of cooperation among states with the closest religion–state relationships, and the greatest cooperation among those with the most distant. Moreover, our analysis should reveal that this correspondence is not due to other factors that may possibly drive Muslim states' counterterrorism cooperation, such as domestic issues or ties to the United States. Even when we take these into account, the religion–state relationship will still have an effect.

The remaining implications deal with the *mechanisms* I posit in my theory; that is, the specific manners in which religion–state relationships influence counterterrorism cooperation. There are specific expectations for both cooperative and uncooperative behavior.

For most of the states in my study, uncooperative behavior with the United States is not in the state's interest. It runs counter to the initiatives of the most powerful state in the international system, threatening a cut-off of aid or even a military response. Uncooperative behavior by Muslim states will thus not take the form of an ideological stand or anti-American offensive. Instead, it will resemble a careful balance of US pressure and the immediate threat of domestic backlash from cooperation.

This balance can take a variety of forms, depending on the context. It will often take the form of *hedging*, with the Muslim state failing to implement just enough of the US's preferred counterterrorism policies to satisfy religious groups. When the United States is placing great pressure on a state, it may attempt to comply. But with close religion–state ties the political power of Islamic groups will lead the state to *backtrack* after facing significant anger. Alternately, there may be instances in which uncooperative behavior is in the state's interest, such as when counterterrorism threatens a state's policy preferences. In these cases, we will see *strategic* non-cooperation. The states will refuse to cooperate, blaming pressure from religious groups in order to continue pursuing the policy it prefers.

No matter the type of uncooperative behavior, however, states with close religion–state ties will not be uncooperative in all aspects of counterterrorism or at all times. As leaders are motivated by their survival, they will factor the potential for angering the United States in to their calculations over responding to domestic opposition to counterterrorism. Similarly, because states are uncooperative not because of principles but strategic calculations, they will not wholeheartedly follow religious pressure. We will see the greatest cooperation in areas that pose the least threat to regimes due to the role of potential backlash in leaders' calculations. This may be aspects of counterterrorism the regime is most able to hide from domestic audiences, such as covert or classified initiatives. In contrast, domestic elements of counterterrorism that are highly visible to the public – such as mass arrests or legal reforms – will be the most contentious and may be the area of greater religious influence (and least cooperation).

Likewise, another implication of my theory is the ways in which religion *fails* to affect states' behavior, specifically the manner in which states cooperate on counterterrorism. Most instances of states ignoring religious pressure will not involve an actively secular state striving to remove all vestiges of religion from public life. Occasionally, of course, states' cooperation will accompany active repression campaigns against Islamic groups. More often, when states do not follow religious pressure they will still pay some lip service to religious causes or appeal to other interests to gain support for their unpopular policies. They may *justify* their cooperation on counterterrorism through appeal to state interests like security or economic issues, rather than as a blatant rejection of religious politics. Or they may keep their cooperation *hidden* from public view to avoid a backlash. And at times when states suddenly shift their behavior to become more cooperative, they will have to crack down on opposing groups, but will also often *offset* this in some way. For example, they may claim a religious justification for their non-religious policies or implement religious policies in some other area to distract society.

An additional implication deals with the role of institutions and historical processes. One may argue that states with powerful religious groups will be less cooperative on counterterrorism, but this is "just politics"; leaders will attempt to avoid upsetting domestic groups with their policies, whether they are religious or not. Instead, I argue that the heightened political pressure regimes with close ties to religion face are the *product* of these religion–state ties. This means, first, that the institutional religion–state relationships *structure the nature* of Islamic politics in these states. We would not be able to understand Islamic politics – and consequently Muslim states' counterterrorism cooperation – without focusing on these institutions. Second, it means that these institutions are the result, not of immediate decisions and actions by leaders and social groups, but rather long-term historical processes. The manner in which they structure contemporary religious politics thus depends on the nature of the institutions' founding and the direction in which they developed over time.

To sum this up, greater religion–state ties will lead to lessened counterterrorism cooperation due to the political power of religious issues and Islamic groups. This lessened counterterrorism cooperation will take a variety of forms but it will be driven by leaders' attempts to balance US pressure with potential domestic backlash. Likewise, when counterterrorism cooperation does occur in the face of minimal religion–state ties, leaders will still attempt to distract religious pressure; they are more able to do so because of the greater distance from religion. And while leaders' counterterrorism policies will be seemingly rational responses to political pressure, this political situation is produced by long-term processes arising from the institutional religion–state relationship.

These implications are what we should see if my theory is correct. If alternative explanations are correct, though, we will see different patterns. If religion affects Muslim states' directly, we will see states failing to cooperate due to society-wide religious beliefs or the principles of leaders. And if counterterrorism is driven by non-religious factors these things will influence counterterrorism and religion–state ties will not. For example, if US ties matter, then aid from and trade and diplomatic interactions with the United States will be the most important. Alternately, we may see domestic unrest or the regime type driving counterterrorism cooperation.

RESEARCH DESIGN

I use this theory to explain US–Muslim counterterrorism cooperation through a mixed-methods research design. Quantitative methods are useful in analyzing correlations between sets of variables and uncovering regularities among a large number of observations, while qualitative methods can identify the presence of mechanisms connecting independent and dependent variables. Combining the two allows the dissertation to test all of the theory's implications.[11]

---

[11] See George and Bennett, *Case Studies and Theory Development in the Social Sciences*; Mahoney and Goertz, "A Tale of Two Cultures: Contrasting Quantitative and Qualitative Research."

My explanatory variable is the religion–state relationship, which varies according to the categorization I discussed earlier. And the dependent variable – the outcome I hope to study – is the extent of counterterrorism cooperation. For the quantitative analysis, this is my original measure of counterterrorism cooperation I discuss next and in the next chapter. And in the qualitative analysis, this is an assessment of counterterrorism cooperation as high, moderate, and low. The "control variables" are variables representing alternative. This includes variables measuring international factors, like ties to the United States and regional security concerns. And it also includes domestic factors like terrorist violence and state capabilities. I address these in the quantitative analysis through variables in the statistical models. In the qualitative analysis, I address them through case selection and within-case analysis of each alternative explanation. Finally, I approach Islamic contention as a "constant," something that is present in all countries and does not influence variation in the dependent variable. In the case studies, I analyze Islamic contention to determine whether it was present in each country and I analyze differing levels of Islamic activism in the quantitative tests.

Quantitative Analysis

The quantitative tests analyze the relationship between religion–state connections and Muslim states' cooperation with US counterterror initiatives between 1996 and 2009.[12] I use an original dataset, with observations by country-year for every Muslim-majority country. The dependent variable is the Counterterrorism Cooperation Scale (CTCS), a measure of the counterterrorism cooperation between the United States and a Muslim state, which runs from $^{-}$10 to 10. The independent variable is a five-level ordinal variable of religion–state relationships. This is based on the previous discussion of different religion–state relationships in Muslim states and runs from 0 to 4. I also include several control variables. The quantitative analysis analyzes dynamics of US–Muslim counterterrorism cooperation, and lets us test whether – on average – closer religion–state ties correspond to lessened counterterrorism cooperation. It also lets us test whether religion–state ties affect some aspects of counterterrorism

---

[12] The time period is based on the availability of the source for the counterterrorism measure. While the source continued after 2009, the information included in the report decreased, making it less useful beginning in 2010. The numerous robustness checks I performed on the measures, including for several different breakdowns by time period, ensure the findings are not dependent on this time range.

greater than others. I will discuss the quantitative analysis in more depth in the next chapter.

Qualitative Analysis

The qualitative analysis focuses on the other implications of the theory I laid out earlier. This analysis consists of three case studies, allowing me to combine cross-case analysis – highlighting variation among cases – and within-case analysis, which focuses on the causal mechanisms connecting religion–state ties to counterterrorism cooperation.

Case Selection

The cases are Pakistan, the United Arab Emirates, and Turkey. These cases provide significant insight into the relationship between religion–state connections and counterterrorism cooperation due to their variation on the variables of interest, their amenability to historical analysis, and their substantive importance. The case studies divide their analysis into the pre-9/11 and post-9/11 periods; the pre-9/11 period begins in the early 1990s – when al-Qaeda and associated transnational terrorist groups were arising – and the post-9/11 period ends in the administration of the US President Barack Obama. The specific end points of the analyses vary, but all include some of the events accompanying the Arab Spring so none of the analyses are biased by truncation.

These three countries vary greatly on the explanatory and dependent variables, and cover many of the control variables. Pakistan, as I discussed earlier, has the highest-level of religion–state ties. The UAE, in contrast, has a moderate level of these ties. And while Turkey is not at the lowest level of religion–state ties, it is markedly lower than the other cases. They also differ greatly in their counterterrorism cooperation, with Pakistan's minimal, the UAE's moderate, and Turkey's higher. And they cover many of the alternative explanations. All three have significant Islamic activism, as well as close diplomatic, military, and economic ties to the United States. They vary in some other control variables, as Pakistan has faced the most significant domestic unrest and has more security concerns related to Islamic groups. Likewise, the UAE has the most closed political system. I will deal with these variations in the within-case analysis, however, as I discuss later.

Each case also allows us to assess the historical processes I posit to be important in religion–state relationships' effects. All of these states were founded in the twentieth century through abrupt departures from earlier political arrangements. Turkey formed from the breakup of the Ottoman Empire after World War I. Pakistan, in turn, formed from the independence of India from the United Kingdom after World War II. And the United Arab Emirates gained independence from the United Kingdom in the 1970s as a confederation of city-states ruled by emirs. Because each of these countries formed relatively recently, we can readily track the institution and development of their varying religion–state relationships between their founding and the beginning of US counterterrorism efforts.

Finally, these are all countries of great significance to US counterterrorism efforts and regional security issues. The United States developed close military ties to Pakistan due to its location near China and the former Soviet Union. The United States relied on Pakistan to help counter the Soviet invasion of Afghanistan in the 1980s and in its campaign against al-Qaeda and the Taliban in that country after 9/11. And Pakistan's nuclear arsenal, military strength, and international profile make it a crucial player in South and Central Asian political issues. Similarly, Turkey became a US ally after World War II due to Soviet threats to the former. The two have worked together on numerous security issues since then, and the United States has leaned heavily on Turkey to gain support for US military efforts among Muslim countries. Finally, the United States developed close ties to the UAE as part of US efforts to contain first Iran and later Iraq, and made use of UAE military facilities in its military actions in the region.

A potential issue with my case selection could be the choice of Turkey, for two reasons. The first is that a more useful comparison for a state like Pakistan might be a state like Uzbekistan, which would allow for the greatest variation in the study's explanatory variable. Yet, analysis of a case like Uzbekistan would yield little useful information on the interaction between religious contention and religion–state relationships.[13] Turkey, in contrast, can provide greater insight into the means through which the religion–state relationship affects the political effects of this contention. The second issue has to do with Turkey's politics after 2002, when the AKP – a conservative religiously aligned party – came to power. Thus, one may question whether Turkey indeed has a distant

---

[13] I do provide brief discussions of religious contention, religion–state relationships, and counterterrorism cooperation in Saudi Arabia, Egypt, and Azerbaijan in the concluding chapter, however.

religion–state relationship. Moreover, tensions between the United States and Turkey have emerged in certain areas of international relations calling into question the extent of its counterterrorism cooperation. But despite tensions in some areas, the counterterrorism relationship between the United States and Turkey remained strong. Moreover, even though a conservative Islamic party has been in power for more than a decade, Turkey's foundational religion–state relationship has remained intact. I discuss these in greater depth in the Turkey chapter and the concluding chapter.

I draw on a combination of secondary sources, English-language primary sources, and translated primary sources in the case studies. Translated primary sources are available through the Foreign Broadcast Information Service and World News Connection, and English-language primary sources are available through ProQuest and the media outlets. I used the translated primary sources for the Pakistan and Turkey case studies, which included many newspapers based in those countries. Prior to the completion of the UAE case study, the services that provided these sources became unavailable so I drew on English-language sources from ProQuest. Some of these included newspapers based in the UAE. There should be minimal concerns about bias as a result of these source changes, however. Any concerns of bias as a result of these source differences are minimal however, as – because the UAE generally has a more restrictive media environment than Turkey and Pakistan – I would likely have to rely on media sources outside of the country even if the translated news services had not become unavailable.

Qualitative Methods

I utilize a variety of qualitative methods to analyze the cases.[14] The first is cross-case comparison, which uses the differences among the cases to assess whether religion–state relationships influence counterterrorism cooperation. I use a *diverse* case selection technique to highlight the range of values on the explanatory and dependent variables, providing insight into the mechanisms connecting religion–state connections and counterterrorism cooperation.[15]

---

[14] For more in-depth discussion on the methods and findings, see the Methodological Appendix.

[15] Jason Seawright and John Gerring, "Case Selection Techniques in Case Study Research: A Menu of Qualitative and Quantitative Options," *Political Research Quarterly* 61, no. 2 (2008).

The rest of the methods involve within-case analysis, analyzing these mechanisms. The congruence method assesses whether changes in the explanatory and dependent variables correspond to my theoretical expectations.[16] I use this to analyze whether certain values of religion–state relationships occur alongside the expected levels of counterterrorism cooperation. Process tracing illustrates the mechanisms I posit in the cases by examining how the variables are connected and whether this fits with the theory's claims.[17] I draw specifically from Bennett's Bayesian version of process tracing, which assesses the likelihood of evidence being available given the theory's expectations.[18] I use this primarily to highlight evidence that is unlikely to be present if my theory were incorrect. Additionally, I use concepts of historical analysis from Pierson and Mahoney to highlight the importance of the religion–state institutions.[19] I use the concept of causal chains – a string of events over time that leads to an outcome – to analyze how historical developments led to contemporary institutions.[20] I also use path-dependent lock-in – the institutional forces that prevent actors from making significant changes to durable institutions – to emphasize the constraining effects of religion–state ties.[21]

Finally, I use a few qualitative methods to assess alternative explanations. I use the method of sequence elaboration to determine whether alternative explanations override the importance of religion–state relationships.[22] With this method, the alternative explanation can be incidental to the effects of religion–state relationship, or it could *contextualize* or *diminish* the effects. It would contextualize it when the alternative explanation contributed to the rise of the religion–state relationship and

---

[16] George and Bennett, *Case Studies and Theory Development in the Social Sciences.*

[17] Ibid.; Andrew Bennett, "Process Tracing and Causal Inference," in *Rethinking Social Inquiry: Diverse Tools, Shared Standards*, eds. Henry Brady and David Collier (Lanham, MD: Rowman and Littlefield Publishers, 2010).

[18] "Process Tracing and Causal Inference"; Andrew Bennett and Jeffrey Checkel, "Process Tracing: From Philosophical Roots to Best Practices," in *Process Tracing: From Metaphor to Analytic Tool*, eds. Andrew Bennett and Jeffrey Checkel (New York: Cambridge University Press, 2014).

[19] I should note that the tools of historical analysis I use focus on how institutional religion–state relationships persist in the face of challenges or new situations, not how they are transformed over time. Analysis of changes is beyond the scope of this book, but I discuss them briefly in the concluding chapter.

[20] Pierson, *Politics in Time: History, Institutions, and Social Analysis.*

[21] Mahoney, "Path Dependence in Historical Sociology."

[22] James Mahoney, Erin Kimball, and Kenra L. Koivu, "The Logic of Historical Explanation in the Social Sciences," *Comparative Political Studies* 42, no. 1 (2008).

the low counterterrorism cooperation, but the religion–state connections and particular cooperation issues would not necessarily arisen as a result of the alternative explanation. Alternately, it would contextualize the relationship if alternative explanations intervened between religion–state connections and the counterterrorism cooperation, and the religion–state connections gave rise to both. And it would diminish it when the alternative explanation would completely explain the rise of religion–state connections. Finally, I used counterfactuals to assess whether the logical conclusion of an alternative explanation for religion–state relationships' effects is valid.[23]

CONCLUSIONS

Thus, we can use my institutional theory of religion and international relations to understand US–Muslim counterterrorism cooperation. The widespread religious opposition to US counterterrorism efforts occurred in the context of decades-long Islamic contention in Muslim countries and vastly differing religion–state relationships. Based on this theory, we should see closer religion–state ties corresponding to lesser counterterrorism cooperation. Moreover, we should see leaders being uncooperative on counterterrorism not because of ideals but due to concerns about political survival. As a result, the greatest effects of religion–state relationships will be on areas of domestic aspects of counterterrorism that tend to be more contentious and visible. And uncooperative behavior will not be an ideological rejection of US ties, but rather a careful hedging on the part of the Muslim state to minimize both potential domestic backlash and US anger.

Moreover, this theory leads us to expect that uncooperative counterterrorism policies are not "just politics," that is, they are not just leaders responding to domestic pressure. Instead, the political dynamics that cause uncooperative behavior are the product of the institutional religion–state ties in countries. The strength (or weakness) of Islamic groups and the salience of religious issues arise from the ties between religion and the state. Additionally, the dynamics structuring leaders' incentives to comply with Islamic pressure – and not cooperate on counterterrorism – or ignore and work closely with the United States are not the result of these leaders' decisions; instead, they arose from decades-long

---

[23] James D. Fearon, "Counterfactuals and Hypothesis Testing in Political Science," *World Politics* 43, no. 2 (1991).

historical processes that gradually shaped the institutions into their current form.

Over the next four chapters, I will use the previously mentioned research design to analyze the dynamics of US–Muslim counterterrorism cooperation. In Chapter 3, I use a large-n statistical analysis to assess whether on average close religion–state relationships correspond to lessened counterterrorism cooperation, and whether this is more apparent in domestic aspects of counterterrorism. The three case studies, in turn, will assess the other implications of my theory. By looking at varied religion–state relationships among Pakistan, Turkey, and the UAE, I will further test whether differences in religion–state ties lead to different levels of counterterrorism cooperation. And by providing in-depth information on the connections between religion–state ties, Islamic politics, and the states' counterterrorism policies I can demonstrate that the correspondence between religion–state ties and counterterrorism cooperation is due to the formers' effects on Islamic politics in a state. Finally, the historical analysis of evolving religion–state relationships in these case studies will highlight how these institutions developed and structured later political dynamics.

3

Counterterrorism Cooperation and Religion–State Relationships Among all Muslim States

In Chapter 2, I presented my theory for how religion influenced Muslim states' counterterrorism cooperation with the United States. Close religion–state ties amplify the political salience of religious issues and leaders' dependence on religious groups, making it more likely they will act in line with religious pressure. Moreover, the establishment of a close religion–state relationship in a country sets in motion a path-dependent cycle; Islamic groups are able to influence state behavior because of the close religion–state ties, which result in the state adopting religious policies that further entrench the close religion–state relationship, strengthening Islamic groups, and making it even easier for them to affect state behavior. This can significantly influence a Muslim state's security policies if Islamic contention focuses on a contentious international issue, such as counter-terrorism cooperation. Because many saw US counterterrorism efforts as a religious issue – with US initiatives targeting Muslims – opposition to Muslim states' cooperation took on a religious salience. Religious groups pose a greater threat to regime survival in states with close religion–state ties; these states are thus unlikely to cooperate extensively in order to avoid domestic backlash.

In this chapter, I test some of the implications of this theory, specifically that closer religion–state relationships will correspond to lessened counterterrorism cooperation and that this is due to political pressure on regimes to not cooperate, which arises from the religion–state relationship. Using an original dataset measuring the extent of Muslim states' counterterrorism cooperation with the United States and the nature of their religion–state relationship, I assess the relationship between these two variables through a statistical analysis. I find that closer religion–state relationships do correspond to lessened counterterrorism cooperation among all Muslim states, and that this effect is stronger for domestic aspects of counterterrorism. This also provides insight into the second claim, as it indicates that Muslim states are more likely to hesitate over the most politically contentious and visible aspects of counterterrorism, and cooperate on more easily obscured counterterrorism efforts when they can.

Additionally, I assess the alternative explanations for Muslim states' counterterrorism cooperation I laid out in the previous chapter by including variables measuring the alternative explanations as control variables. I find that most of these alternative explanations are not valid, as their corresponding variables have no effect on counterterrorism cooperation. And even those that do contribute to Muslim states' cooperation – specifically alliance ties with the United States and significant aid from the United States – do not undermine the importance of religion–state relationships.

Moreover, I also provide historical context on the dynamics of counterterrorism cooperation among Muslim states. Using my original measure of counterterrorism cooperation, I demonstrate that counterterrorism cooperation was generally negative before 9/11. After the 9/11 attacks, it rose dramatically – as Muslim states came under great pressure from the United States to follow its lead – but gradually decreased as many terrorist situations proved hard to resolve and anger at US actions such as the invasion of Iraq grew. Counterterrorism cooperation varied greatly by region, with Europe having the highest overall level of cooperation and sub-Saharan Africa the lowest.

This chapter proceeds in four parts. First, I briefly discuss how I measure counterterrorism cooperation, and present my original measure. I then use this to discuss dynamics and trends in counterterrorism cooperation around the world. After that, I present my analysis on the effects of religion–state relationships, demonstrating the significant connection between closer religion–state ties and lessened counterterrorism cooperation. Finally, I present the implications of these statistical findings for this book's topic, and discuss how this chapter relates to the subsequent case studies.

MEASURING COUNTERTERRORISM COOPERATION

I measure counterterrorism cooperation through an original quantitative variable, the Counterterrorism Cooperation Scale (CTCS). This measure captures the unique nature of counterterrorism cooperation, which is complex and semi-hierarchical. It does this by measuring a variety of different types of counterterrorism-related behaviors, and producing a number for each country year representing the overall level of its cooperation with the United States.

US–Muslim counterterrorism cooperation is distinct from broader types of cooperation – like overall US-British relations – or specific issues, like the North American Free Trade Area negotiations among Canada, the United States, and Mexico in the 1990s. US–Muslim counterterrorism cooperation entails a variety of domestic and international policies, from sharing intelligence to arresting terrorist targets to legal reforms, border security, and support for international US actions like the invasion of Iraq. While some of these aspects of counterterrorism may seem more important than others, a full understanding of counterterrorism requires analysis of all aspects of these interactions. Additionally, US–Muslim counterterrorism cooperation is a pseudo-hierarchical relationship. As the dominant state in the international system, the United States exerts significant influence over most other states. As a result, US–Muslim counterterrorism cooperation did not take place with each party on an equal footing. Instead, the United States was able to set the terms of the interactions. Muslim states were able to not comply, but they had little ability to change US policies relating to counterterrorism cooperation.

The CTCS captures these aspects of US–Muslim counterterrorism cooperation by drawing on official US documents that catalog various aspects of countries' counterterrorism policies. I used the US State Department's Country Reports on Terrorism, which have been issued each year since the 1990s. The reports provide us information on counterterrorism in each country in the world by year since before 9/11. More importantly, they reflect US priorities, as they detail to what extent states are complying with what the United States deems effective and ideal counterterrorism behaviors.

I created the CTCS by quantifying a set of variables based on these reports and aggregating them into a scale measuring counterterrorism cooperation. I developed a list of variables representing different types of counterterrorism activities noted in the reports, both cooperative and uncooperative ones. Examples of cooperative behaviors include restricting terrorist financing, arresting terrorist targets, and participating in US international military actions. And uncooperative examples include failures to undertake cooperative behaviors or active steps to frustrate US efforts, such as refusing to extradite terrorist suspects. I calculated the percentage of cooperative and uncooperative behaviors a country engaged in, and took the difference between these two numbers. This gives us a measure of counterterrorism cooperation that runs from ⁻10 (completely uncooperative) to 10 (completely cooperative). By measuring the balance of cooperative and uncooperative behaviors, I was able to assess the overall level of a country's counterterrorism efforts; most states will be cooperative in some areas but not others, so a measure that includes this variation will be more accurate than one that simply states whether or not a state cooperated.[1]

COUNTERTERRORISM COOPERATION AROUND THE WORLD

Looking generally at Muslim countries' counterterrorism cooperation, it appears that the United States was successful in influencing these states' counterterrorism policies after 9/11, although this varied by region. Muslim states were not very cooperative on counterterrorism before 9/11, but after the attacks and intensified US efforts, cooperation rose dramatically. The overall level of cooperation began to dip eventually, though, returning to lower levels. Counterterrorism cooperation differed greatly by region, with Europe the most cooperative and sub-Saharan Africa and South-Central Asia the least.

Before the 9/11 attacks states were generally not cooperative on counterterrorism. While the United States was less active in counterterrorism in the 1990s than it was after the 9/11 attacks, US policymakers did pressure many states on terrorism, especially as the United States was formulating its campaign against al-Qaeda. For example, the United States pressed both Saudi Arabia and the Sudan to look into the presence of and support for al-Qaeda in their territories before 9/11. While both states did expel al-Qaeda leader Osama bin Ladin – forcing him to return to Afghanistan – they were less than fully cooperative; Saudi Arabia dragged its feet on addressing extremist voices among its religious leaders and the United States suspected Sudan of persisting in its support for various terrorist groups.

This changed dramatically after 9/11 when the United States launched its Global War on Terror and called for compliance from other states. This gave states a great incentive to go along with US efforts. The numbers bear this out. The average CTCS score among all Muslim countries rose dramatically after 2001. By the end of 2002, the first full year of the US Global War on Terror, Muslim states' cooperation *doubled* from the months immediately preceding the attacks. For example, as I will discuss

---

[1] The CTCS was valid and robust according to a series of methodological checks. For more information on the CTCS, see the Methodological Appendix.

extensively in a subsequent chapter, the United Arab Emirates passed laws strengthening limits on terrorist financing and limited many of the financial flows through the country's banks that had previously been suspected of aiding al-Qaeda.

Unfortunately (from the United States' perspective), Muslim state counterterrorism cooperation peaked in this year. Starting in 2003, Muslim states' cooperation generally decreased, dropping off sharply from the high in 2002 and decreasing nearly every year since then. This occurred as the initial goodwill toward the United States after 9/11 – and apprehension about US retaliation for lack of cooperation – faded amidst anger over the 2003 invasion of Iraq, controversial practices such as harsh interrogation techniques, and a general intractability of terrorist activity in many countries. For example, while Nigeria took some steps to cooperate after 9/11 – such as strengthening airport security and deploying counterterrorism police units – by 2009 its cooperation sagged as the government failed to pass new counterterrorism legislation due to political disputes[2] (see Table 3.1).

The aggregate counterterrorism cooperation for all countries, however, obscures interesting differences by region.[3] Generally, all regions' counterterrorism cooperation followed the previous trend; they were mostly uncooperative before 9/11, but their levels of cooperation increased significantly after the attacks, and then leveled off as time went by. But among regions, the amount of increase and decrease varied greatly. This difference is to be expected, as Muslim countries extend from Europe to Southeast-Asia, with vastly difference institutions, cultures, and ties to the United States. But these regional differences can indicate the different sorts of terrorist activity and responses to US efforts we saw before and after 9/11.

The most cooperative regions were Europe and, interestingly, the Middle East-North Africa. Even before 9/11, Europe's counterterrorism cooperation was generally positive. This is not surprising, as European states tend to be close to the United States and generally cooperative in its international efforts. Albania, in particular, has been incredibly cooperative with the United States; after 9/11, it provided overflight and landing rights to the US military, contributed troops to the international force in Afghanistan, passed new laws to crack down on terrorist financing

---

[2] "Country Reports on Terrorism 2008: Chapter 2. Country Reports: Africa Overview," (US Department of State, 2009); "Country Reports on Terrorism 2009: Chapter 2. Country Reports: Africa Overview," (US Department of State, 2010).

[3] I use the region breakdowns provided by the Correlates of War project, a commonly used data source on international conflict, for my region characterizations.

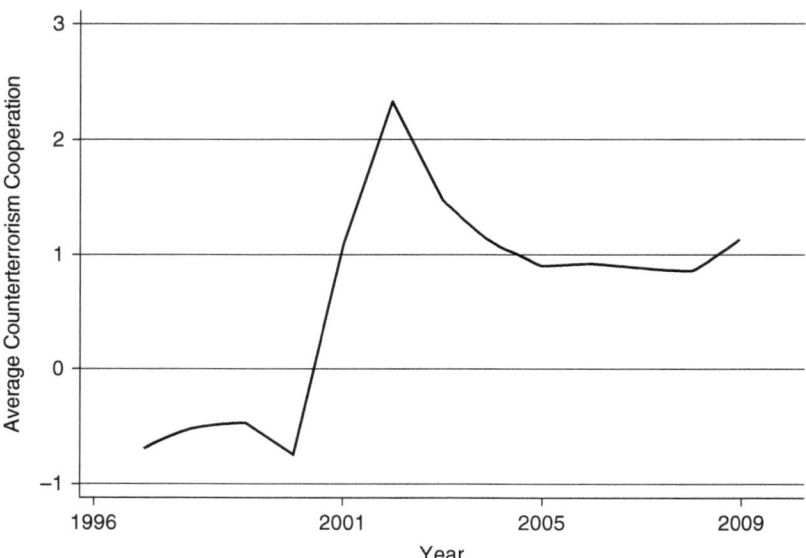

TABLE 3.1. Average Counterterrorism Cooperation among All Muslim Countries, 1996–2009

and arrested individuals suspected of terrorist activity.[4] And Azerbaijan strengthened its border security (greatly limiting the flow of militants across its territory), cracked down on terrorist financing, and arrested several suspected militants.[5]

While the Middle East-North Africa was not as cooperative as Europe, it was more cooperative than other regions. Before 9/11, the countries in this region were generally uncooperative. This changed greatly after 9/11, however, as counterterrorism cooperation spiked after 2001. While this may seem surprising, it makes sense when we take into account specific Middle Eastern countries. The Middle East includes countries like Syria and Iran, which were often not very cooperative with the United States on counterterrorism, but many states in the region were close allies. For example, Qatar hosts several US military installations – including the US Central Command Forward Headquarters (the US Central Command oversees US military actions in the region) – and passed laws restricting terrorist financing. Moreover, other countries may have initially been uncooperative, but quickly increased their cooperation on

[4] "Patterns of Global Terrorism 2002: Europe Overview," (US Department of State, 2003).
[5] "Patterns of Global Terrorism 2002: Eurasia Overview," (US Department of State, 2003).

counterterrorism after US pressure increased and they came under attack from militants. This was the case in Saudi Arabia, which faced fierce US criticism for initially doing little to stem the flow of militants from its population or undermining the appeal of extremist messaging; it cracked down on terrorist groups and sympathizers after a string of attacks in the country in 2003.

Muslim states in South/Central Asia and sub-Saharan Africa were less cooperative, although for varying reasons. South/Central Asian states were nearly as cooperative across all years as Middle East states, but they tended to drag behind those states in counterterrorism cooperation. Before 9/11, South/Central Asian states were very uncooperative; their scores did increase dramatically after 9/11, but their scores dropped off sharply after that, tending to stay lower than the Middle East's for many of the post-9/11 years. This is to be expected considering many of the states in this region, with widespread militant activity and states that often appealed to extremist sentiment for support. The most noteworthy is Pakistan, which had very tense counterterrorism relations with the United States before and after 9/11, as I discuss in a subsequent chapter.

While South/Central Asia's counterterrorism cooperation was limited due to states' policies relating to militant groups, much of sub-Saharan Africa's minimal counterterrorism cooperation was related to the weak states in this region. The CTCS scores of states in this region tended to be rather stable, hovering around 0. Most scores of 0 indicate little counterterrorism-related activity, which reflects the fact that many sub-Saharan African Muslim states had little part to play in the US Global War on Terror. For example, the Gambia – a majority-Muslim county in sub-Saharan Africa – had minimal terrorist-related activity according to US sources throughout the time period of this study. After 9/11, however, as all other regions' cooperation spiked dramatically, sub-Saharan Africa's increased only marginally. Thus, while sub-Saharan Africa's cooperation never fell to the depths seen in South-Southeast Asia, it also never had as high counterterrorism cooperation as in other regions. The lack of a significant increase under US pressure is related to the limited capacity of many states in sub-Saharan Africa. Those states that experienced terrorist activity were unable to move against terrorist groups to the extent that states with stronger militaries could, as in the Middle East. For example, Mauritania has generally attempted to cooperate with the United States, but struggled to maintain control over its borders with Algeria and Mali where al-Qaeda in the Islamic Maghreb frequently operated.

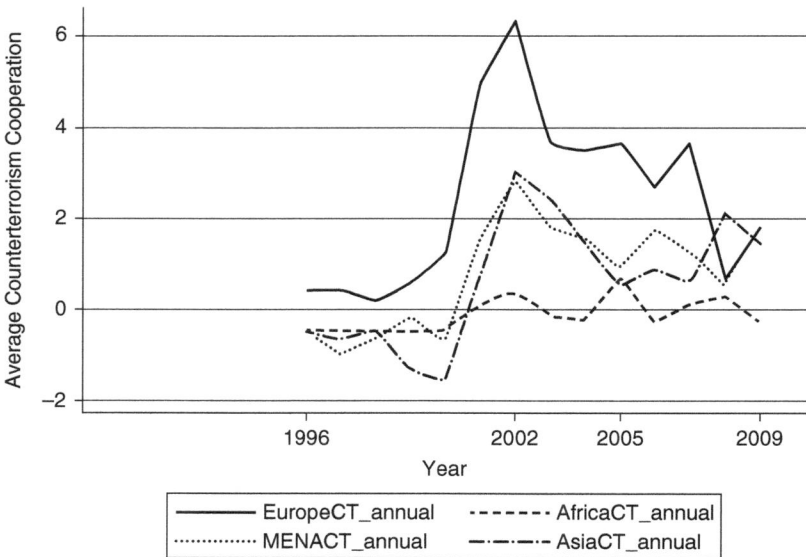

FIGURE 3.1. Counterterrorism Cooperation by Region, 1996–2009

Southeast Asia's counterterrorism cooperation fell in between these extremes. This region includes Malaysia, which had generally positive but erratic counterterrorism cooperation. After 9/11, Malaysia launched numerous counterterrorism initiatives, including regional counterterrorism coordination efforts, the arrest of numerous militants, new laws to combat terrorist financing, and the ratification of international counterterrorism convention. At the same time, the country has opposed US military actions in Afghanistan and Iraq. The region also includes Indonesia, which has taken several steps to improve counterterrorism cooperation but generally fallen short of US preferences. Indonesian forces detained numerous militants in the country, but often released many of them due to lax judicial sentencing; and Indonesia struggled to implement strong limits on terrorist financing[6] (see Figure 3.1).

THE EFFECTS OF RELIGION–STATE RELATIONSHIPS
ON COUNTERTERRORISM COOPERATION

Counterterrorism cooperation among Muslim countries varied greatly, both across time and across regions. While we can come to some

[6] Ibid.

understanding of the causes for specific states' cooperation or non-cooperation – such as Egypt's domestic terrorist threat driving cooperation, and Mauritania's weakness driving non-cooperation – it is difficult to extend these explanations to all countries or determine that they were the primary influence on counterterrorism. As I have argued, however, the varied religion–state relationships among Muslim states can account for these diverging levels of counterterrorism cooperation. In this section, I assess this claim. I first discuss my quantitative measure of religion–state relationships, before analyzing the data. Using both descriptive analysis of the data and statistical tests, I demonstrate that close religion–state relationships have a significant negative effect on Muslim states' counterterrorism cooperation, even when I address other competing explanations for differing behavior.

Religion–State Relationships among Muslim Countries

I measured my proposed explanation for varying counterterrorism cooperation, the nature of religion–state relationships, with a quantitative variable that aggregates different aspects of religion–state ties. As I discussed in the previous chapter, I categorized Muslim states' religion–state relationship according to whether or not they are officially Islamic, whether Islamic groups are connected to the regime, and how extensively they restrict religious practice. I combined this with measures focused on whether or not they had an open political system – based on the size of the country's winning coalition. I use this as the basis for the *Religion–State* variable in my quantitative analysis, which runs from o to 4 with 4 representing the closest religion–state ties. I draw on a variety of publicly available sources to measure religion–state relationships, including Fox's Religion and State dataset, the Pew Research Center's Government Restrictions on Religion data, and the US State Department's International Religious Freedom report. I also use the Polity dataset – which contains extensive information on the political institutions of states – and procedures developed by Bruce Bueno de Mesquita *et al.* to measure whether or not they have a small winning coalition.[7]

Muslim states' religion–state relationships varied significantly and were distributed across all regions. A plurality of Muslim states have

---

7 The Polity IV data are available at www.systemicpeace.org/polityproject.html. Information on winning coalition size is available at Bueno de Mesquita *et al.*, *The Logic of Political Survival*.

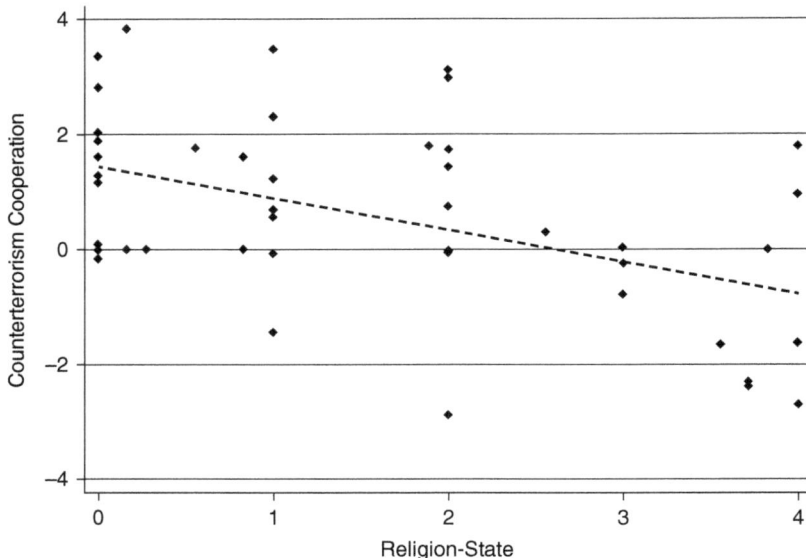

FIGURE 3.2. Counterterrorism Cooperation and Religion–State Relationships

the most distant religion–state ties (such as secular authoritarian states), although this amounted only to 30 percent of all Muslim states. Many other states had moderate religion–state relationships, relatively open secular political systems, or traditional political systems with Islamic law but little role for Islamic groups in policymakers. Fewer states had the closest religion–state ties – either strong authoritarian states that were officially Islamic or weaker Islamic states with significant role for Islamic groups in governing.

The Relationship between Religion–State Ties and Counterterrorism Cooperation

Using basic descriptive tests, there appears to be a strong connection between religion–state relationships and counterterrorism cooperation. The two are strongly and negatively correlated, indicating that an increase in one corresponds to a decrease in the other. This is apparent in a visual examination, using the countries' average scores across all years. As I show in Figure 3.2, countries with closer religion–state relationships tended to be less cooperative than those with more distant ones when we look at their average level of cooperation across all years (see Figure 3.2).

But, as I discussed in the introductory chapter, other scholars and policy analysts have advanced numerous alternative explanations for Muslim states' cooperation – or lack thereof – with the United States. It is possible, for example, that states with closer religion–state ties tended to have more severe terrorist violence or be weaker, so their lack of counterterrorism cooperation would be related to these factors. Likewise, these states may also have been more distant from the United States – with more limited aid flows or diplomatic ties – so their limited cooperation would arise from this, not their religion–state ties. Can we say, then, that this apparent connection between religion–state relationships and counterterrorism cooperation is real, or would other possible explanations be the real driving force behind US–Muslim counterterrorism cooperation?

I used a statistical test specifically designed for these types of questions to assess my claims regarding the importance of religion–state connections. As I am analyzing all Muslim countries' counterterrorism cooperation over several years, I must take into account the relationship between a country's cooperation in one year and previous years; it is likely similar factors affect cooperation across multiple years, and the level of cooperation in one year probably influences a state's level of cooperation the following year. I thus used a type of statistical test called a generalized estimating equation, in this case I specifically used a Gaussian generalized estimating equation with autoregressive within-cluster correlation; this test is uniquely designed to account for these aspects of my data.[8] I also included numerous control variables to address the various alternative explanations for counterterrorism cooperation, from severity of domestic terrorism to aid from the United States.[9]

Testing My Claims

For the first claim – on the role of religion–state relationships – the statistical tests strongly support my argument. The findings indicate that, across all majority-Muslim countries, states with closer religion–state relationships tended to be less cooperative on counterterrorism, while Islamist activity had little effect. I ran three models using the data, one that included just the religion–state relationship, one that added domestic variables to the model, and one that added international variables (see

---

[8] See Christopher J. W. Zorn, "Generalized Estimating Equation Models for Correlated Data: A Review with Applications," *American Journal of Political Science* 45, no. 2 (2001). See the Methodological Appendix for more information on the statistical analysis and the numerous robustness checks I used.

[9] I present more information on the statistical tests, the variables used, and potential limitations of the test in the Methodological Appendix.

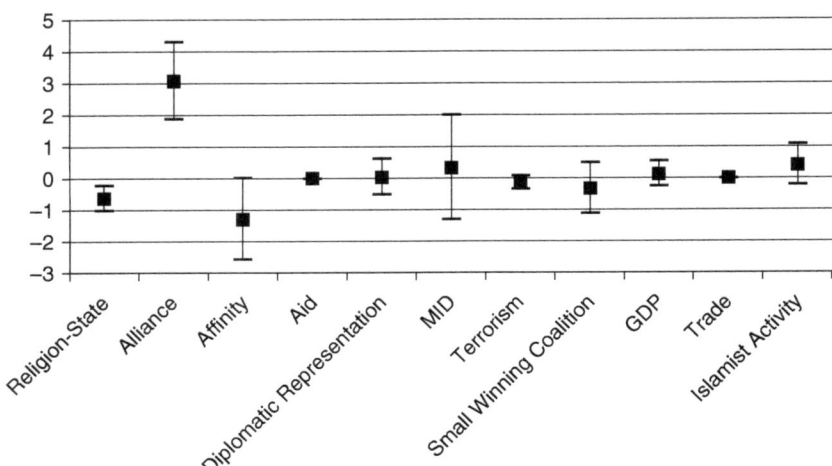

FIGURE 3.3. The Effect of Religion–State Relationships and other variables on Counterterrorism Cooperation (displaying coefficients and confidence intervals)

Figure 3.3) demonstrates the results of these tests, presenting the coefficient and confidence intervals of each variable; if the confidence interval does not cross zero the variable was statistically significant, while if the coefficient lies below zero it means the variable had a negative effect on counterterrorism cooperation. On its own, the religion–state relationship had a negative and statistically significant relationship with counterterrorism cooperation; that is, states with closer religion–state ties tended to be less cooperative on counterterrorism. This relationship held up in the other two models when I added the control variables – which I will discuss more later. Most importantly, Islamist activity did not appear to affect counterterrorism cooperation at all. That is, states with extensive Islamist activity were no more or less cooperative on counterterrorism than states with limited Islamist activity (see Figure 3.3).

The tests also provided strong evidence for my second claim, that religion–state relationships matter even if I address alternative explanations. Most of the control variables representing alternative explanations – like ties to the United States or domestic terrorism severity – were not statistically significant. The minimal effect of many of these variables casts doubt on their accompanying alternative explanations. The two control variables that were significant were US aid and alliance ties, but they did not undermine the importance of religion–state relationships; if religion–state relationships lost its statistical significance when these variables were included, this would suggest the apparent effect of

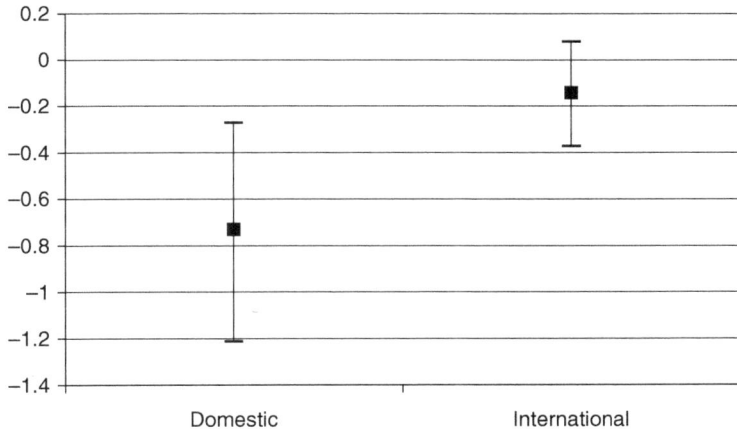

FIGURE 3.4. The Effects of Religion–State Relationships on domestic and international aspects of counterterrorism (displaying coefficient and confidence intervals of religion–state relationship with each dependent variable)

religion–state ties was actually due to these other factors. As this is not the case, we can reject that alternative explanation.

Finally, the statistical tests also supported my third claim – that religion–state relationships have the strongest effect on the most contentious aspects of counterterrorism. I ran separate tests to assess whether religion–state relationships affected different types of counterterrorism cooperation. I specifically focused on the difference between international aspects of counterterrorism – like intelligence sharing and participation in US military initiatives – and domestic aspects, like institutional reforms or the arrest of terrorist groups. Looking just at international counterterrorism, religion–state relationships had little effect. This likely indicates some states with very close religion–state relationships cooperated closely with international counterterrorism actions, while some with more distant religion–state ties did not cooperate, so the effect of religion–state relationships was muddled. This is in stark contrast to the results when I looked just at domestic aspects. In this test, religion–state relationships had a very strong negative effect on domestic counterterrorism cooperation. Figure 3.4 presents these results, with the coefficient of the religion–state relationship and confidence interval for the model using domestic counterterrorism and the model using international counterterrorism (see Figure 3.4).

This strongly suggests that the effects of religion–state relationships arise due to leaders' concerns over losing political power, not their devotion to Islamic opposition to counterterrorism. While Muslim states with closer religion–state relationships generally were less cooperative on counterterrorism cooperation, this becomes even more striking when looking just at the domestic aspects of counterterrorism. If Muslim leaders in states with close ties to religion were motivated by religious concerns, they should be uncooperative on things like US international military actions or intelligence sharing, as these are aspects of US counterterrorism efforts that have significant effects on Muslims around the world. But states are often able to shelter their international engagements from domestic audiences; intelligence sharing, for example, is often classified and hidden from public view. As a result, states are at times able to take international actions that are religiously contentious or opposed by their societies. In contrast, domestic policies are much more immediate, especially domestic aspects of counterterrorism that involve changing institutions dealing with religious fundraising and religious practices and banning groups that may have been present in a country for a long time. As a result, it is harder for a state to undertake these policies without facing significant domestic opposition. The stronger effect of religion–state relationships on domestic counterterrorism, then, indicates the political – rather than principled – motivations behind states' limited counterterrorism cooperation.

My statistical tests thus provided very strong support for the role religion–state relationships play in US–Muslim counterterrorism cooperation. Among all Muslim states, those with closer religion–state relationships tend to be less cooperative on counterterrorism. Most of the alternative explanations for this varying counterterrorism cooperation are not valid; Muslim states are not less cooperative because of tensions with the United States, their capabilities, the severity of terrorist violence, or trade with the United States. And while aid from the United States and alliance ties does lead to greater cooperation, religion–state relationships still matter even when I take these into account. Moreover, religion–state relationships have a stronger effect on domestic aspects of counterterrorism than international ones, supporting my argument that it is political motivations that drive states' limited cooperation in the face of religious opposition.

Substantive Effects

The direction and significance of religion–state relationship in the statistical tests – which I discussed earlier – can tell us whether this variable tended to matter, and in what way. But they do not tell us the magnitude of its effects on counterterrorism cooperation, which can often be as important, if not more important, than the statistical significance. Even if competing explanations for the role of religion–state relationships are rejected – due to these variables' lack of statistical significance – the substantive effect of religion–state relationships could be so small that it suggests it barely matters (and is thus not worthy of attention). Fortunately, that is not the case here. Because the CTCS is a useful measure of this overall extent of counterterrorism cooperation, we can use it to assess which variables have the biggest effect on a state's aggregate level of cooperation.

I measured substantive effects through the effects of a meaningful change in one variable on changes in counterterrorism cooperation. This varies by the specific variable. For US aid, which is a continuous variable, it is a one standard deviation change, which represents a significant change in the context of the variable's range. And for alliance, which is a dichotomous variable, it is just the presence or absence of an alliance. For religion–state, which is a multi-level ordinal variable, it is a bit more complicated. I use a 2-unit measure of change as this represent a significant shift in the religion–state relationship; for example, a 2-unit difference represents the difference between Saudi Arabia and Turkey.

Looking at substantive effects in this manner, religion–state relationships had a very large impact on counterterrorism cooperation. Based on the findings from the previous statistical tests, a 2-unit change in the religion–state relationships results in a corresponding negative 1.2-unit change in the CTCS. This change in CTCS is greater than the effect of a substantive change in aid from the United States, which is 0.5. And it is half the size of the effect of an alliance, 3 units' change in CTCS. That is, of two other variables that mattered in the models – based on alternative explanations for Muslim states' counterterrorism cooperation – religion–state relationships had a bigger effect than one of them and half the effect of the other. I present these findings in Figure 3.5, which shows the average substantive effect of a change in the variable and the range of possible effects, based on the confidence intervals from the statistical models (see Figure 3.5).

This suggests that religion–state relationships are of paramount importance in understanding Muslim states' cooperation with the United States. The United States gives out massive amounts of economic and military aid to Muslim and other countries, and this plays a huge role in US relations with these countries. So the fact that religion–state relationships had a *greater effect* on counterterrorism cooperation than US aid tells us

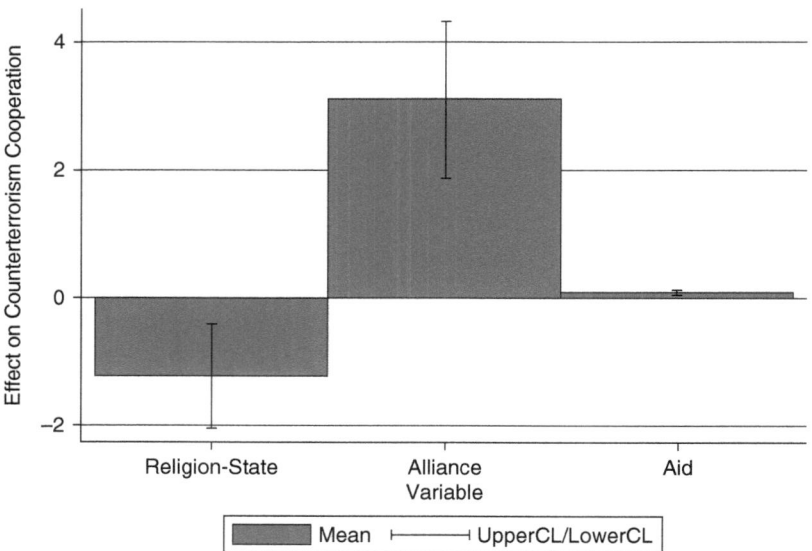

FIGURE 3.5. Substantive Effects of Religion–State and other variables on counterterrorism cooperation

something about how important these aspects of Muslim states' institutions are. And even though religion–state relationships have a smaller effect on counterterrorism cooperation than alliances, this finding also highlights the importance of the religion–state relationship. Alliances are one of the cornerstone elements of international relations. It is not surprising they affect counterterrorism cooperation, or that they have a large effect. But while alliances have a bigger effect, they do not dwarf that of religion–state relationships, suggesting how important and powerful these institutions ties are in determining Muslim states' counterterrorism policies.

CONCLUSION

As I show in this chapter, religion–state relationships among Muslim states had a strong effect on their counterterrorism cooperation with the United States. States with closer religion–state relationships were consistently less cooperative on counterterrorism, a relationship that held up under rigorous statistical analysis. This was especially the case on domestic aspects of counterterrorism, while religion–state relationships seemed to have little connection to whether or not a state was cooperative internationally. And close religion–state relationships' effects on cooperation were not trivial, as they had a greater influence on Muslim states' counterterrorism policies than did the massive amount of aid the United States provides.

This provides us with numerous insights into the causes of Muslim states' counterterrorism cooperation and the broader topic of religion and international relations, as well as strong support for my theory on the role of religion–state relationships. Close diplomatic ties, a history of tensions, or trade flows did not determine the level of cooperation with the United States. Likewise, Muslim states were neither inhibited from cooperating nor incentivized to cooperate because of how severe their domestic terrorism was. Similarly, the state's capacity to fight terrorism did not seem to matter in their level of counterterrorism cooperation. Moreover, the extent of Islamist activity in a state had little impact on its cooperation. Instead, the religion–state relationship in Muslim states has a stronger effect on whether or not a state cooperated with the United States than these non-religious and non-institutional factors. Aid from and alliance ties with the United States did promote counterterrorism cooperation, but the religion–state relationship still had a strong influence even when I included these in the statistical tests. And because the religion–state relationship had a stronger effect on domestic aspects of counterterrorism, this suggests that Muslim states' lack of cooperation was due to concerns about domestic political backlash, not principled stands on behalf of religious causes.

The statistical analysis in this chapter thus demonstrates that, on average, close religion–state relationships did seem to limit Muslim states' counterterrorism cooperation. The statistical tests, however, cannot provide insight into *how* religion–state relationships influenced cooperation. I argue that this occurs because these institutions create a path-dependent process that strengthens religious debates and groups and limits regimes' ability to cross religious sentiment without losing power. It is difficult to tell whether this is the case from the statistical analysis, which is better suited to uncovering regularities across a large number of cases. Without such insights, we will not comprehensively understand the effects of religion on counterterrorism cooperation or fully assess the validity of my theory.

The case studies I present in the next three chapters can provide the rest of the story. Case studies are particularly well-suited to uncovering the mechanisms connecting variables – such as religion–state relationships and counterterrorism cooperation – granting more nuanced analyses of a topic than statistical analysis alone. Moreover, they can delve into the historical dynamics behind an outcome, such as the development of institutional religion–state relationships I focus on here. The three case studies – Pakistan, the United Arab Emirates, and Turkey – will thus complete the analysis I began in this chapter, demonstrating how religion–state relationships developed over time in a manner that structured regimes' incentives and decisions regarding the religious opposition to US counterterrorism efforts. I turn first to Pakistan.

4

Pakistan

In May 2011, a US Navy SEALs team under the direction of the Central Intelligence Agency launched a raid from Afghanistan to the Pakistani city of Abbotabad. The target was a well-guarded compound that intelligence indicated was the hiding place of al-Qaeda leader Osama bin Ladin. Even though they were conducting a military operation in its territory, US forces were not working in coordination with the Pakistani military because of fears the Pakistani military or the Directorate of Inter-Services Intelligence (ISI) would compromise the operation. Indeed, the United States had reason to be concerned about such an occurrence, as many believed the ISI had tipped off al-Qaeda leaders about a US raid on them in Afghanistan in the 1990s. Despite the lack of local support and the difficulty of the mission, the Navy SEALs raid succeeded in killing bin Ladin and returning to Afghanistan.

This caused significant consternation in Pakistan. There was widespread public anger at the US military action in their territory, with especially strong protests from Islamic groups. For example, Muhammad Azim Randhawa – an official of the influential Islamic group Jamaat-e-Islami (JI) – claimed, "The entire nation was suffering from an acute sense of insecurity while the rulers demonstrated slavery to the United States."[1] There was also anger among Pakistani leaders. The Prime Minster of Pakistan threatened to scale back cooperation with the United States on counterterrorism, the government arrested a Pakistani doctor who had

[1] Pakistan: JI Leaders Criticize Government for Harassing Party Members, January 9, 2010; Pakistan: Jamaat-e-Islami Leader Criticizes Government for Slavish Attitude Toward US, June 4, 2011.

helped the CIA find bin Ladin, and Pakistan closed three US military intelligence liaison centers in the country.[2]

How did Pakistan and the United States – two countries with extensive and close security ties since the former's founding in the 1940s – get to the point of US raids conducted secretly for fear of Pakistan undermining them and Pakistan threatening to cut off cooperation with the country they depended on for security? Much of the answer lies in the peculiar nature of the relationship between religion and state in Pakistan and how it developed, how this promoted Islamic contention, and how it gave leaders an incentive to act in line with that pressure.

Pakistan was founded as a secular state for the Indian subcontinent's Muslims but soon developed close ties to Islam. Early leaders established a significant role for Islam in the country's laws, while the military framed its tensions with India as a religious struggle. This set in place a path-dependent process that resulted in Pakistan becoming a state with numerous laws and policies based on Islam, security policies that were often connected to Islamic groups in Pakistan and abroad, and leaders dependent on Islamic groups to stay in power. When all of these factors came together in the US war on terror, Pakistani leaders faced intense pressure from both the United States – to crack down on militant and extremist groups – and Islamic groups in the country to minimize its cooperation with the United States. Although Pakistan was a crucial partner for the United States in some areas, it mostly veered toward the latter; Islamic groups and rhetoric – strengthened by the close ties between religion and state – presented enough of a threat to Pakistani leaders that they chose to cross the United States rather than risk these groups rising against them.

This chapter will demonstrate this by presenting these pieces of the argument in reverse, discussing the outcome, and then how this outcome came to be. I first present the history of counterterrorism cooperation between the United States and Pakistan, and then discuss the nature of Islamic contention in the country and how Pakistani leaders responded to and drew on this contention. I follow this with a historical discussion of Pakistan, which demonstrates how leaders' actions and Islamic contention in the country combined to create a situation in which

---

[2] David S. Cloud, "Pakistan Shuts Down US 'Intelligence Fusion' Cells," *The Los Angeles Times*, May 27, 2011; AFP: Pakistan to Review Counter-Terrorism Cooperation with US, May 13, 2011; US Intel Head Arrives in Pakistan to Help Release Suspected CIA Agent, July 25, 2011.

leaders were hesitant to work with the United States on counterterrorism. I then conduct an in-depth analysis of this evidence, explaining how the close religion–state relationship contributed to the lack of counterterrorism cooperation and examining – and dispensing with – alternative explanations for this outcome. Thus, the first section of the chapter presents the evidence for my assertion that the religion–state relationship in Pakistan was the cause of its counterterrorism tensions with the United States, while the second section analyzes this evidence to demonstrate conclusively that this was the case. This is not intended to be an exhaustive or chronological history of Pakistan; instead I focus specifically on those aspects of Pakistan's history that relates to my argument concerning religion–state relationships and counterterrorism.

COUNTERTERRORISM COOPERATION

Most of the counterterrorism relationship between the United States and Pakistan was tense throughout the time period I cover in this book. Before 9/11, the United States repeatedly called on Pakistan to cut ties with Kashmiri militant groups and al-Qaeda. Pakistan for the most part demurred. After 9/11, US pressure intensified and expanded. Pakistan turned on its former allies in Afghanistan – the Taliban – and took some steps to limit extremist and militant influence in the country. But for the most part Pakistan continued its halting counterterrorism cooperation.

Pre-9/11

The United States placed significant pressure on Pakistan over counterterrorism before 9/11. The US called on Pakistan to cut ties with militant groups and move against al-Qaeda members in the country. While Pakistan implemented some counterterrorism policies in response to US pressure it for the most part ignored US demands, continuing its policies of supporting Islamic militants and ignoring the presence of al-Qaeda in the country and in neighboring Afghanistan.

The United States pressed Pakistan to cut its ties with Kashmiri militant groups several times in the 1990s. In 1991, a US official met with Pakistani leaders about their support for Kashmiri groups, and in 1992 the United States threatened to put Pakistan on its terrorist designation list.[3] This intensified in the mid-1990s, as some Kashmiri groups began

---

[3] Haqqani, *Pakistan: Between Mosque and Military.*

targeting Westerners. These efforts decreased toward the end of the 1990s; however, US officials did not want to exacerbate tensions with Pakistan after the dispute over its nuclear tests in 1998.[4]

The United States also pressed Pakistan to arrest individuals affiliated with al-Qaeda in the country, as well as militants who had conducted anti-US attacks. The United States worked with Pakistan to arrest both Mir Aimal Kasi and Ramzi Yousef and turn them over to the United States; Kasi attacked the CIA headquarters in 1993 – killing two and wounding several others – and Yousef helped to plan the first World Trade Center bombing.[5] The United States also called on Pakistan to expel Arab militants from the country after the formation of al-Qaeda, and to pressure the Taliban to stop harboring Osama bin Ladin.[6]

Pakistan responded positively to some US pressure. In her first term, Bhutto reached out to India to negotiate over Kashmir, and also tried to improve ties with the United States.[7] And Bhutto arrested Ramzi Yousef in response to US requests, and expelled Arab militants in the country, albeit after the Egyptian embassy in Pakistan was bombed in 1995.[8] Sharif arrested numerous non-Pakistani militants who were connected to extremist groups in Pakistan under US pressure.[9] And Sharif worked with the United States to help capture Mir Aimal Kasi.[10] Sharif also passed a controversial anti-terrorism act to control militant activity in Pakistan.[11]

---

[4] *The 9/11 Commission Report: Final Report of the National Commission on Terrorist Attacks Upon the United States* (New York: W. W. Norton and Company, 2004).

[5] Coll, *Ghost Wars: The Secret History of the CIA, Afghanistan and bin Ladin, from the Soviet Invasion to September 10, 2011*; Wright, *The Looming Tower: Al-Qaeda and the Road to 9/11*.

[6] Coll, *Ghost Wars: The Secret History of the CIA, Afghanistan and bin Ladin, from the Soviet Invasion to September 10, 2011*; John R. Schmidt, *The Unravelling: Pakistan in the Age of Jihad* (New York: Farrar, Strauss, and Giroux, 2011).

[7] Haqqani, *Pakistan: Between Mosque and Military*; October 20, 1993 – Bhutto seeks to improve ties with West, Japan.

[8] Coll, *Ghost Wars: The Secret History of the CIA, Afghanistan and bin Ladin, from the Soviet Invasion to September 10, 2011*; *The 9/11 Commission Report: Final Report of the National Commission on Terrorist Attacks Upon the United States*; Wright, *The Looming Tower: Al-Qaeda and the Road to 9/11*; May 17, 1996, Pakistan: Bhutto–No More 'Terrorist Elements' in Country.

[9] Haqqani, *Pakistan: Between Mosque and Military*.

[10] Coll, *Ghost Wars: The Secret History of the CIA, Afghanistan and bin Ladin, from the Soviet Invasion to September 10, 2011*.

[11] Pakistan: Minister: Terrorism Reduced 'Drastically' After ATA, November 15, 1997.

But neither leader durably or extensively transformed Pakistan's counterterrorism policies. Bhutto publicly supported the insurgency in Kashmir, implicitly backing ISI support for the militants.[12] Similarly, Sharif continued sponsoring Islamic militants in Kashmir. And he made numerous public pronouncements of support for Kashmir, including calling for a "Kashmir Solidarity Day Strike" in 1991.[13] Both leaders also resisted US pressure involving the Taliban. Bhutto continued Pakistan's ties to militants in Afghanistan, and reportedly lied to the United States about the extent of Pakistan's support for the Taliban.[14] Likewise, under Sharif, Pakistan hesitated to press the Taliban too strongly on turning over bin Ladin in the late 1990s.[15]

The Pakistani military, in turn, did little to respond to US counterterrorism pressure. A military caretaker government in 1996 did reportedly fire several ISI officers affiliated with Islamic groups.[16] But the same government informed the United States that, while it was not supporting terrorism in Kashmir, it would continue to provide "moral" support to Kashmiri militants.[17] Moreover, the military arranged for Pakistan to formally recognize the Taliban as the government of Afghanistan without the knowledge of then-Prime Minister Sharif.[18] And some sources indicate that Pakistan notified the Taliban of the timing and target of a US airstrike intended to take out bin Ladin, allowing him and other high profile al-Qaeda targets to escape.[19]

Post-9/11

US pressure on Pakistan increased dramatically after the 9/11 attacks. The United States continued to press Pakistan on its support for militants,

---

[12] Haqqani, *Pakistan: Between Mosque and Military.*

[13] Sharif Calls for Kashmir Solidarity Day Strike, February 5, 1991.

[14] Coll, *Ghost Wars: The Secret History of the CIA, Afghanistan and bin Ladin, from the Soviet Invasion to September 10, 2011*; C. Christine Fair, "Pakistan's Relations with Central Asia," in *Pakistan in Regional and Global Politics*, ed. Rajshree Jetly (London: Routledge, Taylor, & Francis Group, 2009); Haqqani, *Pakistan: Between Mosque and Military.*

[15] Schmidt, *The Unravelling: Pakistan in the Age of Jihad.*

[16] Pakistan: Report Says ISI Purged of Extremists on US 'Order,' July 27, 1996.

[17] Prime Minister meets US Ambassador, Denies Terrorism, May 4, 1993.

[18] Coll, *Ghost Wars: The Secret History of the CIA, Afghanistan and bin Ladin, from the Soviet Invasion to September 10, 2011.*

[19] Ibid.

but it also called on its leaders to actively disrupt militant activity and undermine the appeal of extremists in the country. While Pakistan initially became more cooperative on counterterrorism, it soon reverted to limit steps on response to US pressure.

After the 9/11 terrorist attacks, the United States pressed Pakistan to join its efforts against al-Qaeda, and other militants in the region.[20] The United States called on Pakistan to break its ties with the Taliban and cooperate in the US invasion of Afghanistan.[21] Also, following the 2001 attack on the Indian parliament by militants, the United States pushed Pakistan to break its ties with Kashmiri militant groups.[22]

The United States also pressured Pakistan to take actions against al-Qaeda members and other militants in the country.[23] The greatest tensions emerged over suspected official Pakistani ties to the "Haqqani network," the militant group started by Jalaluddin Haqqani that Pakistan and the United States sponsored in the 1980s and Pakistan continued to work with into the 1990s. The group was allied with the Taliban, and conducted attacks against US and NATO troops after the invasion of Afghanistan. For example, in 2011, US officials publicly stated that the ISI was still aiding the Haqqani network, with Admiral Michael Mullen – the outgoing Chairman of the Joint Chiefs of Staff – calling it a "veritable arm" of the ISI.[24]

In addition to these efforts, the United States also endeavored to minimize the spread of what it deemed extremist messages in Muslim countries. In Pakistan, this translated into attention to the numerous conservative religious schools throughout the country. For example, in 2005, the US State Department met with Pakistani education officials to change curriculum the United States deemed "inciteful."[25]

---

[20] C. Christine Fair *et al.*, *Pakistan: Can the United States Secure an Insecure State?* (RAND Corporation, 2010).

[21] Selig Harrison, "Global Terrorism: US Policy after 9/11 and Its Impact on the Domestic Politics and Foreign Relations of Terrorism," in *Pakistan in Regional and Global Politics*, ed. Rajshree Jetly (London: Routledge, Taylor, & Francis Group, 2009).

[22] Pakistani Analyst Sees Steps Against 'Terrorism' as Reversal of Previous Stance, January 14, 2002.

[23] Harrison, "Global Terrorism: US Policy after 9/11 and Its Impact on the Domestic Politics and Foreign Relations of Terrorism."

[24] AFP: Pakistan Stares Down US Pressure Over Action Against Haqqanis, October 3, 2011.

[25] Pakistan: Editorial Disapproves US Demand of 'Excluding Jihad' from Curriculum, August 22, 2005.

Finally, and most controversially, the United States tried to gain Pakistani assent to US military operations in Pakistani territory. Some of this involved cross-border attacks on militants who would flee to Pakistani territory after attacking US forces in Afghanistan. This also included numerous US drone strikes; unmanned US aerial vehicles would conduct reconnaissance and increasingly strike against targets in Pakistan. And the most famous example of such an effort was the US raid to kill Osama bin Ladin in 2011.

Post-9/11 US pressure on Pakistan involved high-level diplomatic pushes and even threats to cut off aid. US officials like Secretary of State Condoleezza Rice frequently visited Pakistan to pressure it on counterterrorism.[26] Similarly, in a high-profile visit in 2011, US Secretary of State Hillary Clinton, CIA Director David Petraeus, and the current Joint Chiefs Chairman pushed Pakistan to take immediate action against the Haqqani network.[27] And the United States set up several official bodies to coordinate these efforts, such as the US-Pakistan Strategic Dialogue and the Defense Consultative Group.[28] On top of these interactions, the United States made its significant aid to Pakistan conditional on Pakistani cooperation on counterterrorism, as well as nuclear proliferation and democratic reforms, after 9/11.[29]

US pressure seemed to work, for awhile. Musharraf allowed the US military some rights in Pakistani territory, as well as the use of bases in Pakistan in its campaign against Afghanistan.[30] And Pakistan began cooperating with the United States on law enforcement and counterterrorism operations in the country.[31] The Pakistani government also moved against al-Qaeda elements in the country. Pakistan arrested numerous al-Qaeda operatives in the country.[32] This included Khalid Sheikh Mohammed – an

---

[26] Rice Visiting Pakistan with Heavy Agenda, March 16, 2005.
[27] AFP: Pakistan 'Appeared' to Give Commitment to US to Dismantle Militant Havens, October 21, 2011; Clinton in Afghanistan Urges Pakistan to Act Against Haqqanis, October 20, 2011.
[28] Fair *et al.*, *Pakistan: Can the United States Secure an Insecure State?*
[29] Pakistani Daily Says Conditions for US Aid Do Not Suggest Strong Relationship, July 19, 2003.
[30] Haqqani, *Pakistan: Between Mosque and Military*; Harrison, "Global Terrorism: US Policy After 9/11 and Its Impact on the Domestic Politics and Foreign Relations of Terrorism."
[31] "Global Terrorism: US Policy After 9/11 and Its Impact on the Domestic Politics and Foreign Relations of Terrorism."
[32] Bergen, *The Longest War: The Enduring Conflict between Al-Qaeda and America*.

al-Qaeda planner responsible for the 9/11 attacks, the murder of Daniel Pearl, and other operations – and Ramzi bin al-Shibh, another al-Qaeda planner. And Pakistan worked with the United States to conduct air strikes against al-Qaeda targets, like the one that killed Hamza Rabia, an al-Qaeda operations chief.[33]

Pakistan also took broader steps against militants in the country. Pakistan banned many Kashmiri militant groups, including *Jaish-e-Mohammed*, *Sipah-e-Mohammed*, and *Lashkar-e-Jhangvi*; Musharraf froze the assets of many groups in the country as well.[34] Musharraf also conducted broader operations, arresting and expelling many suspected militants as part of his crackdown on religious schools.[35] Eventually, Pakistan launched military offensives against militants in the Afghanistan border region, and conducted several operations under US pressure, such as a 2006 raid on a religious school that provoked widespread protests by Islamic groups throughout the country.[36] Prime Minister Zardari pledged to continue these operations after he came to power.[37]

And Musharraf took steps to counter extremist voices in education. In 2002, he issued an ordinance requiring religious schools to register with the government, report on the source of donations, expel foreign students, and not teach anything that "promoted militancy"; he followed this with a 2005 bill in parliament.[38] Musharraf took similar steps outside education. He discussed changing conservative Islamic laws that disfavored religious minorities and women, planned to arrest people "promoting sectarianism" under anti-terrorism regulations, and called for the removal of all "hate materials" from markets.[39]

---

[33] Pakistan: Editorial Terms Al Rabi'ah's Death 'Major Success' in War on Terror, December 6, 2005.

[34] Imtiaz Gul, *The Most Dangerous Place: Pakistan's Lawless Frontier* (New York: Penguin Books, 2011); Pakistani Analyst Sees Steps Against 'Terrorism' as Reversal of Previous Stance, January 14, 2002; Pakistani Daily Hails Musharraf's Steps Against Extremists, Comments on Kashmir, January 13, 2002.

[35] Haqqani, *Pakistan: Between Mosque and Military*; AFP: Pakistan Arrests 800 Suspected Islamic Militants, July 30, 2005.

[36] Gul, *The Most Dangerous Place: Pakistan's Lawless Frontier*.

[37] AFP: Pakistan Prime Minister Urges US Not to Act 'Unilaterally' Against Militants, July 29, 2008; Pakistan Editorial Flays Zardari for Agreeing with US to Launch Operation in NWA, November 11, 2011.

[38] Pakistan: Government to Amend Law Regarding Registration of Islamic Seminaries, September 28, 2005.

[39] Pakistan: Government's Efforts to Reform Islamic Seminaries Achieve Little Success, May 9, 2005; AFP: Musharraf's Call for Review of Islamic Laws Draws 'Mixed' Response, May 17, 2004; AFP: Pakistan's Musharraf Launches New Fight Against Islamic Extremism, July 15, 2005.

Yet, Pakistan's counterterrorism actions were not completely cooperative with the United States. Musharraf initially hesitated to break ties with the Taliban, instead trying to negotiating with them to turn over bin Ladin.[40] When he did change policies, Musharraf justified his cooperation as being in Pakistan's strategic interests, and pointed out that the international community should be sure to also address the plight of Muslims in India and Israel.[41] He also argued that the cooperation was an alliance of convenience, and referred to an Islamic story of a short-lived alliance between Muhammad and Jews in Medina.[42]

There are also indications that Pakistan's military maintained some ties to the Taliban and other militant groups. For example, Pakistan for the most part left Taliban agents in Pakistan alone, and did little at first against al-Qaeda operatives in the border region.[43] Several sources suggest that, despite official Pakistani protestations, Pakistan gave the Haqqani network a haven in the country and may even have coordinated some of their operations to destabilize the Afghan government.[44] Beyond active ties to militants, there were also several indications that Pakistan's offensives against militants in the border region were not as comprehensive as they could have been. Some analysts claimed the military was unwilling to commit to military efforts against the Taliban.[45]

Pakistan's actions against Kashmiri militants were also half-hearted.[46] Musharraf differentiated between al-Qaeda and "freedom fighters" in Kashmir, taking less severe steps against the latter.[47] Although the government banned numerous groups, its actions were selective; for example, *Jaish-e-Mohammed* was able to mostly continue operating; Pakistan also

[40] Schmidt, *The Unravelling: Pakistan in the Age of Jihad.*
[41] Pakistani Daily Backs Musharraf's Stance on Attacks on Afghanistan, October 9, 2001; Daily Finds Pakistani Stand on Terrorism Casting Shadow on Relations with India, September 21, 2001.
[42] Harrison, "Global Terrorism: US Policy after 9/11 and Its Impact on the Domestic Politics and Foreign Relations of Terrorism."
[43] Schmidt, *The Unravelling: Pakistan in the Age of Jihad.*
[44] Gul, *The Most Dangerous Place: Pakistan's Lawless Frontier*; Indian Article Examines Reasons Behind Pakistan Intel Agency's Links with Taliban, October 16, 2011; Commentary in Indian Daily Says Islamabad Encouraging Taliban Operations in Kabul, October 15, 2011.
[45] Schmidt, *The Unravelling: Pakistan in the Age of Jihad*; UK: IISS Sees Pakistan's Zardari Possibly Facing Threat from Army, September 18, 2008.
[46] Haqqani, *Pakistan: Between Mosque and Military*; Kanti Bajpai, "Managing Ambivalence: Pakistan's Relations with the United States and China since 2001," in *Pakistan in Regional and Global Politics*, ed. Rajshree Jetly (London: Routledge Taylor & Francis Group, 2009).
[47] Haqqani, *Pakistan: Between Mosque and Military.*

did not shut down militant training camps in the country, and allowed *Lashkar-e-Taiba* to change its name and continue operating.[48] And there are some indications that the ISI maintained its links with Kashmiri groups after Musharraf's crackdown.[49]

Pakistan took similarly halting steps against extremist voices in the education system. In the 2005 negotiations over the registration of religious schools, Musharraf amended his orders so that registered schools would not have to report their donations.[50] And a US government analysis from that year found that the expulsion of foreign students was occurring intermittently, and the government was slow to implement procedures for registering educational organizations.[51]

By the time President Obama took office in 2009, US pressure on Pakistan and Pakistani half-steps on counterterrorism had escalated to recurrent tensions between the two countries. Pakistani leaders became publicly critical of US actions. Similarly, after the bin Ladin raid, Pakistani leaders publicly called for a reduction in US troops in the country.[52] Later in 2011, under pressure from the United States to act against the Haqqani network, Gilani claimed that "Pakistan cannot be pressurised [sic] to do more" on counterterrorism.[53]

The tensions over counterterrorism also degraded US-Pakistani intelligence cooperation. After the bin Ladin raid, Pakistan closed three military intelligence liaison centers in the country, which the United States used to share intelligence with Pakistan on al-Qaeda and the Taliban.[54] And in December 2010, the name of the CIA station chief in Islamabad was leaked in the Pakistani media, with US officials claiming the ISI was the source.[55]

Pakistan's counterterrorism policies also complicated US resupply efforts in Afghanistan. After numerous attacks on US supply convoys in the border region, Pakistan had to close the border in order to conduct

[48] Schmidt, *The Unravelling: Pakistan in the Age of Jihad.* Indian Daily Skeptical about Peace Bid, Says Pakistan Cannot Take on Terrorists, May 7, 2003.

[49] Indian Columnist Says Arrested Terrorist Confirms Pakistan's Role in Terrorism, February 20, 2002.

[50] Pakistan: Government to Amend Law Regarding Registration of Islamic Seminaries.

[51] FBIS Analysis, August 25, 2005: Limited Progress in Crackdown on Religious Schools.

[52] Cloud, "Pakistan Shuts Down US 'Intelligence Fusion' Cells."

[53] AFP: Gilani Says Pakistan 'Cannot Be Pressurised To Do More' in War on Terror, September 29, 2011.

[54] Cloud, "Pakistan Shuts Down US 'Intelligence Fusion' Cells."

[55] Declan Walsh, "Pakistani Media 'Name' CIA Station Chief in Islamabad," *The Guardian*, May 9, 2011.

an offensive against militants.[56] And in late 2011, a US airstrike hit a Pakistan border post, killing more than 20 Pakistani soldiers; US forces claimed they were taking fire from the position, and did not know the Pakistani military was there, but Pakistan claimed it was an intentional US attack. In response, Pakistan closed US and NATO supply routes to Afghanistan and ordered the CIA to vacate a base from which it coordinated drone strikes.[57]

Pakistan's response to US actions in Pakistani territory often took the form of public denunciation but private tacit consent. For example, in 2008, Prime Minister Gilani called US drone strikes an infringement of the country's "sovereignty" and "intolerable."[58] Yet, numerous reports indicate Pakistani leaders agreed to US military actions in private.[59]

RELIGIOUS CONTENTION

This minimal counterterrorism cooperation did not occur in a vacuum. It happened alongside widespread and often violent Islamic contention in the country both before and after 9/11. Domestic Islamic groups were very active, and pressed the state to follow religious standards. Pakistan also faced transnational pressure from Islamic groups around the world, critical of the state's ties to the United States. Much of this contention focused on as Islamic groups called on the state to support Islamic militants and avoid working with the United States. Terrorism frequently broke out across the country, targeting both the state and certain segments of society.

Pre-9/11

The 1990s represented a break with recent Pakistani history, as the military government of Zia ul-Haq transitioned to a civilian government – headed alternately by Benazir Bhutto and Nawaz Sharif throughout the

---

56 AFP: Pakistan Closes NATO Supply Route to Fight Militants, December 30, 2008.
57 Salman Masood, "In Protest Over NATO Strike, Pakistan Will Skip Afghan Conference," *The New York Times*, November 29, 2011.
58 Pakistan: PM Terms Drone Attacks Against Sovereignty; Says Government to Stop Them, October 27, 2008.
59 Gul, *The Most Dangerous Place: Pakistan's Lawless Frontier*; Schmidt, *The Unravelling: Pakistan in the Age of Jihad*. AFP: Alleged US Missile Strike Kills Four Militants in Pakistani Al-Qa'ida Stronghold, November 22, 2008; Pakistan: Report Question's Government's Silence Over Recent Missile Attack in Bajaur, May 17, 2008.

decade – but the Islamic contention that had been present throughout the country's history persisted, and possibly even intensified. Islamist groups called for Islamic law to be established in the country, and frequently attacked Pakistani leaders for failing to follow Islamic standards, not sufficiently supporting Islamist militants in Pakistan, and working too closely with the United States. Pakistan also faced pressure from international Islamic activism and violent terrorist movements within the country.

Islamic groups pushed for the implementation of Islamic law throughout the 1990s and attacked its leaders for not being committed to Islamic causes. In the 1993 election, the *Jamiat Ulema-e-Islam* (JUI), an influential Islamist party, called for an explicitly Islamic constitution.[60] And another Islamic party called for the implementation of Islamic law.[61] Islamic groups also pushed for reforms through non-electoral means; both JI and JUI often organized rallies and protests that pressured the government.[62] Many groups accused Bhutto of being anti-Islamic, or too pro-Western.[63] During 1990 debates over a shariah bill in parliament, one opposition leader said that "Shariah will be our new rallying cry in the anti-Bhutto crusade," and expressed concerns about her being a woman.[64] Similarly, in announcing their 1996 coalition with Islamic parties to remove Bhutto from power, a Muslim league spokesman accused Bhutto of trying to "confine religious parties' role in national politics to mosques and religious affairs" and removing their influence on politics.[65] Despite his generally closer ties to Islamists, Islamic groups also attacked Sharif for not following Islamic standards. Although he campaigned on adopting an Islamic law bill in his first term, he slowed its implementation once elected; this led to the resignation of an Islamist from his cabinet and Islamic groups' protests against his government.[66]

Much religious contention focused on security issues, namely the tensions with India. Islamic groups pressured the state to continue supporting Kashmiri militants. For example, in the late 1990s, the JI claimed the government must "keep to its Kashmir stand," referring at times to the fighting as a "jihad."[67] This included some appeals to international

---

[60] JUI Seeking Islamic Constitution, September 22, 1993.
[61] MDM Calls for Sunnah Laws, September 22, 1993.
[62] Pakistan: Religious Parties' 'Challenge' Discussed, October 16, 1997.
[63] Haqqani, *Pakistan: Between Mosque and Military*.
[64] Islamic Law Bill Serious Challenge for Bhutto, July 25, 1990.
[65] Pakistan: PML, Religious Parties Unite to Oust Bhutto, May 30, 1996.
[66] Nawaz Sharif Cautious on Adopting Sharia Bill, March 7, 1991.
[67] Pakistan: JI: Government Must Keep to Kashmir Stand, Islamabad The News (Internet Version) in English, June 6, 1998; Jamiyat-i-Islai Chief on Need for Nuclear Device, February 23, 1990.

Muslim audiences to support Pakistani efforts in Kashmir and oppose US counterterrorism efforts.[68]

Anti-American attitudes in the country were also connected to religion. Islamic groups claimed the United States was interfering in Pakistani politics and advancing worldwide "anti-Islam conspiracies."[69] And one editorial claimed the United States was launching a "perpetual campaign against the Islamic world," tying its efforts in Pakistan to Bosnia, Lebanon, and elsewhere.[70] This occasionally translated into acts of violence against US targets, motivated by religious sentiment. For example, after his arrest, Mir Aimal Kasi told an interviewer that he "attacked the CIA for both religious and political reasons" and that America's actions were "anti-Islamic."[71]

Islamic groups also pushed back against Pakistan's efforts to arrest al-Qaeda-affiliated militants. In April of 1993, the head of JUI attacked the government for arresting Arab nationals in Peshawar, and called on Islamic groups throughout the country to protest.[72] And the head of JI criticized the United States for trying to arrest the "Arab Mojahedins of Islam."[73] And many Islamic groups – including JI and JUI – publicly criticized Sharif for extraditing a terrorism suspect to the United States.[74]

Violent religious contention also took place throughout this time period. A failed coup occurred in 1995, an attempt by military officers aligned with Islamic groups to overthrow the government.[75] Moreover, in the late 1990s, Lashkar-e-Taiba, a Kashmiri militant group, claimed it would launch a "holy war" to establish an Islamic state.[76] Also, sectarian violence between Sunni and Shia often broke out; some of the Sunni sectarian groups reportedly had ties to al-Qaeda.[77]

---

[68] Urdu Daily Urges Muslim World to 'Wake Up,' Counter Anti-Islamic Forces, October 3, 2000; Islamic Nations Urged to Unify Against India, January 5, 1994.

[69] JUP Marks US Anti-Islam Conspiracies, February 3, 1992; JI Leader Says US Interference at Alarming Level, June 29, 1993.

[70] Pakistan: Editorial Views US, Western Anti-Muslim Posture, August 24, 1993.

[71] Quoted in Jessica Stern, *Terror in the Name of God: Why Religious Militants Kill* (New York: Harper Collins, 2003): 175.

[72] Islamic Party Chief Opposes Anti-Arab Nationals' Arrest, April 16, 1993.

[73] Religious Parties Condemn Arab Nationals' Arrest, April 16, 1993.

[74] Pakistan: Government, US Criticized for Arresting, Extraditing Kansi, June 21, 1997.

[75] Haqqani, *Pakistan: Between Mosque and Military.*

[76] Pakistan: Lashkar-i-Taiba Vows 'Holy War' for Islamic State, November 7, 1997.

[77] Gunaratna, *Inside Al Qaeda*; Vali Nasr, "International Politics, Domestic Imperatives and Identity Mobilization: Sectarianism in Pakistan," *Comparative Politics* 32, no. 2 (2000); Anwar H. Syed, "The Sunni-Shia Conflict in Pakistan," in *Pakistan: Founders' Aspirations and Todays' Realities*, ed. Hafeez Malik Malik (New York: Oxford University Press, 2001).

Post-9/11

Religious contention remained widespread after 9/11. Islamic groups continued to press for the adoption of religious standards in Pakistan. For example, in 2003, the head of JUI called on Musharraf to establish a political system like the one "pursued by the first four caliphs of Islam," and not to "present an Islam tainted with Western culture."[78] And the JI strongly opposed Musharraf's attempt to change the country's blasphemy law in 2002; Islamic parties later strongly opposed changes to the laws after deadly blasphemy-related violence in 2011.[79] This continued past the early 2000s. A conservative Islamic cleric denounced the female Minister of Tourism in 2007 for hugging French paragliders in a picture; under pressure from the cleric and other conservative groups, she was forced to resign.[80]

Islamic groups also expressed concern that Musharraf was limiting the importance of religion in Pakistani society. JI accused Musharraf of "inciting" Pakistanis against "religious parties" in 2005.[81] And in 2005 an Islamic figure called on Musharraf to stop working with the United States to minimize the role of Islam in the country; this included calls to "not promote Westernized enlightenment and liberalism" and instead "march in the right direction by harmonizing Pakistan with its fundamental Islamic ideology."[82]

Anti-Americanism persisted, in part due to the perception that America was targeting Muslims. For example, in 2005, an Islamic figure claimed that US pressure to change educational curriculum was actually aimed at "removing Quranic... verses on Jihad and fundamentals of Islam."[83] He continued, stating that the "'war against terror' was invented by Washington... to use as a garb for invading Muslim countries"; and that

---

[78] Pakistan: Opposition Leaders Demand Islamic Government, Policies Free of US Influence, September 13, 2003.

[79] Pakistan: Religious Party Leader Opposes Changes in Blasphemy Law, February 19, 2002; Pakistan: JUI Chief Vows to Resist Government's Alleged Efforts to Amend Blasphemy Law, January 17, 2011; Pakistan: PML-Q Chief Warns Government Not to Pardon Christian Woman on Death Row, November 24, 2010.

[80] AFP: Faced with Red Mosque Fatwa, Former Pakistan Minister Vows to Fight Extremism, July 28, 2007.

[81] Pakistan: JI Chief Alleges Musharraf 'Inciting' People Against Religious Parties, June 5, 2005.

[82] Pakistan: Jihadi Leader Asks Musharraf to Enforce Islam to Eliminate Extremism, August 11, 2005.

[83] Pakistani Leader: USA 'Biggest Terrorist' on Earth, Musharraf Acting as Servant, December 10, 2005.

"talk of curbing extremism" is meant to "crush [the] spirit of jihad and martyrdom."[84]

Much religious opposition to the United States focused on Musharraf's cooperation with the United States on counterterrorism. The head of JI accused Musharraf and other leaders of being "servants" in the United States' attacks on Muslims.[85] And some of this was connected to Islam, as in a 2005 protest over Musharraf's US cooperation in which an Islamic figure claimed this was "distorting the Islamic identity of Pakistan."[86] Musharraf was also attacked by Islamic groups for his raid on the Red Mosque in 2007. The United Action Front (Mutahhid Majlis-e-Amal, MMA) – a conservative Islamic political bloc – accused him of "granting eternity to Bush's anti-Muslim policies," and its chief quit parliament in protest, while Islamic groups held protests throughout the country.[87]

They also attacked Musharraf for his moves to limit support for Kashmiri militants. The head of JUI called on Musharraf to take a "courageous stand" on Kashmir, instead of giving in to US and Indian pressure to crack down on militants.[88] This was also connected to Islam; the head of one banned militant group said that "Islam, democracy and jehad [sic] are being eliminated from Pakistan and the American New World Order is being imposed."[89]

This continued into Zardari's reign as president. JI and other Islamic groups attacked him for allowing the United States to conduct military activities in Pakistan – such as the 2011 raid that killed Osama bin Ladin – and for what they deemed harassment of Islamic groups.[90] Likewise, the JI dropped out of the government in 2010, in protest against cooperation with the United States and efforts to change the blasphemy law.[91]

---

[84] Ibid.

[85] Ibid.

[86] FP: Islamic Parties Rally Against President Musharraf Over Pro-American Policies, March 20, 2005.

[87] MMA Leaders Condemn Lal Masjid Operation; Flay Government for Desecrating Seminaries, July 16, 2007; Protests in Pakistan over Red Mosque Operation, July 14, 2007; Pakistani Islamic Alliance Leader Quits Parliament, July 14, 2007.

[88] Pakistan Religious Leader Urges Musharraf to Adopt 'Courageous' Stand on Kashmir, June 14, 2002.

[89] Pakistan: Religious, Militant Groups React Adversely to Musharraf's Address, January 13, 2002.

[90] Pakistan: JI Leaders Criticize Government for Harassing Party Members, January 9, 2010; Pakistan: Jamaat-e-Islami Leader Criticizes Government for Slavish Attitude Toward US, June 4, 2011.

[91] Gul, *The Most Dangerous Place: Pakistan's Lawless Frontier*.

And political violence increased greatly. Taliban and other militant groups in the Afghanistan border region conducted numerous attacks in response to Pakistani military operations there. Other attacks occurred in the interior of Pakistan, such as a 2007 suicide bombing by al-Qaeda in the military capital of Rawalpindi, and a 2007 threat against Musharraf's life in response to the Red Mosque raid.[92] And in 2005, a Harkatul Mujahideen member was arrested for plotting to kill Musharraf.[93] Not all political violence was connected to organized militant groups, however. For example, in 2011, Shahbaz Bhatti – the Minister of Minorities – and Salman Taseer, the governor of Punjab, were assassinated for criticizing the country's blasphemy laws.

RELIGION–STATE RELATIONSHIP

This religious contention occurred in the context of close ties between religion and the Pakistani state. Both Prime Ministers in the 1990s – Bhutto and Sharif – attempted to gain the support of Islamic groups and the military through implementation of Islamic domestic and foreign policies. Pervez Musharraf initially took steps to distance the Pakistani state from Islamic groups but he soon came to rely on them for political support and scaled back on policies they opposed. And his civilian successors similarly tiptoed around Islamist groups' sentiment on security and non-security related issues.

Pre-9/11

Bhutto appealed to domestic and international Muslim audiences while in power. For example, in the early 1990s, Bhutto brought the JUI into a coalition government with her party, the Pakistan People's Party (PPP), granting JUI members significant cabinet portfolios; this enabled the JUI to establish the initial links between Pakistan and the Taliban.[94] And she tried to avoid openly challenging Islamists, such as during the aforementioned debate over a shariah bill in parliament.[95] Bhutto also made

---

[92] Ibid.; Pakistan: Local Taliban, Tribesmen Vow Revenge on Musharraf for Lal Mosque Clash, July 10, 2007; More on AFP: Pakistan Police See Al-Qa'ida Link to Bombing Near Army Office, October 31, 2007.

[93] FP: Pakistani Militant Arrested Over Terror Attacks, Musharraf Death Plot, January 17, 2005.

[94] Schmidt, *The Unravelling: Pakistan in the Age of Jihad.*

[95] Islamic Law Bill Serious Challenge for Bhutto, July 25, 1990.

several appeals to international Muslim audiences, calling for solidarity among Muslim countries.[96]

And Bhutto backed the military's support of Islamic groups in Afghanistan and Kashmir. Bhutto established ties with and support for the Taliban, at the urging of the ISI.[97] She also connected her support of the Taliban to Islam; for example, in a speech commemorating the anniversary of the Afghan invasion in 1989, Bhutto said the Afghans fought in "defense of their religion, nation and freedom" and that Pakistan took "great pride in saluting them for setting an example of Islamic valor and faith."[98]

Sharif made similar overtures to gain Islamic groups' support while he was in office. Sharif called the success of the Islamic militants in Kabul a "success of Islam"; he also connected the conflicts in Kashmir and Bosnia, calling for worldwide Muslim solidarity.[99] In addition to this, Sharif made some efforts to increase the role of Islam in Pakistan's legal code. Sharif introduced a bill in parliament that would have implemented Islamic law throughout the country, which gained him some support of Islamic groups.[100] Sharif also proposed other Islamic reforms to the legal code, such as an effort to end interest on loans, in line with Islamic beliefs.[101]

The military in turn maintained its ties to Islamic groups, and at times used them to influence political dynamics in the country. In 1992, the new chief of the ISI – Javed Nasr – was a member of the conservative Islamic group Tablighi Jamaat, and worked with Pakistani Deobandi groups to organize activities in Kashmir; the military also helped to organize the *Islami Jamhoori Ittehad* (IJI; Islamic Democratic Alliance), an Islamic umbrella party that campaigned against Bhutto in the 1989 elections.[102] Additionally, the ISI began coordinating Kashmiri militant groups' activities and funding groups.[103] This extended to Afghanistan as well.

[96] Bhutto Speaks on Foreign Policy, Investments, March 28, 1990; Pakistan: PM Asks Erbakan to Influence Pakistani Religious Parties, August 13, 1996; Bhutto Interviewed on US, Afghanistan, June 20, 1989.

[97] Coll, *Ghost Wars: The Secret History of the CIA, Afghanistan and bin Ladin, from the Soviet Invasion to September 10, 2011*.

[98] Pakistan: Bhutto Comments on Afghan Invasion Anniversary, December 28, 1995.

[99] Pakistan: Sharif: Mujahidin Rule in Kabul Success of Islam, May 5, 1992; Pakistan: Sharif Speaks of Muslim Plight in India, Bosnia, February 3, 1993.

[100] Haqqani, *Pakistan: Between Mosque and Military*.

[101] Prime Minister Agrees to Amend Shariah Bill, May 8, 1991.

[102] Haqqani, *Pakistan: Between Mosque and Military*.

[103] Daniel Byman, *Deadly Connections: States That Sponsor Terrorism* (New York: Cambridge University Press, 2007); "Friends Like These: Counterinsurgency and the War on Terrorism."

After the Soviets pulled out of Afghanistan, Pakistan continued to back Islamic militants in their attempt to take over the country; this included the Taliban, as well as other militant groups.[104] The ISI worked with the Taliban to provide security for a supply convoy in the early 1990s, and provided funding and diplomatic support as the decade wore on.[105]

Post-9/11

Similar relationships between religion and state persisted after 9/11, even though Musharraf initially attempted to limit Islamic groups' influence in Pakistan. Before 9/11, Musharraf had placed some restrictions on Kashmiri groups' ability to operate in the country. And Musharraf opposed the implementation of Islamic laws and the power of conservative Islamic voices in Pakistan. For example, in 2003, Musharraf criticized the Islamic reforms of the MMA in the Northwest Frontier Province, calling it the "Talibanisation of Pakistan."[106] He took more dramatic steps against militants as well. For example, in 2007, he ordered a raid against the Red Mosque, a prominent mosque and women's school in Islamabad that had begun harassing the community and stockpiling weapons. The raid resulted in many fatalities, and, as was noted, significant criticism of Musharraf.[107]

Musharraf continued to rely on Islamic groups for political support. For example, in the 2002 elections, his party – the Pakistani Muslim League (N) (PML-N) – formed a coalition with the MMA.[108] There are indications that Musharraf actively aided the MMA in the election, including changing the education requirements for candidates in favor of the MMA and using the ISI to undermine its rivals.[109] The ensuing victory

---

104 Pakistan Supplying Rebels with Tanks, Aircrafts, June 2, 1989; Masud Accuses Pakistan of Siding with Hikmatyar, April 26, 1993; Taleban Said Backed by Pakistan Secret Service, January 4, 1996.

105 Coll, *Ghost Wars: The Secret History of the CIA, Afghanistan and bin Ladin, from the Soviet Invasion to September 10, 2011*; Gul, *The Most Dangerous Place: Pakistan's Lawless Frontier.*

106 Pakistan: Author Views Musharraf's Criticism of NWFP's Islamization Drive, June 12, 2003.

107 AFP: Further on Pakistan Places Curfew Around 'Radical' Mosque, Warns Violators, July 4, 2007; FP: Pakistani Soldier Killed, Dozens of Students Injured in Battle at Red Mosque, July 3, 2007.

108 AFP: Pro-Musharraf Parties Reopen Coalition Talks with Islamists, November 13, 2002.

109 Harrison, "Global Terrorism: US Policy After 9/11 and Its Impact on the Domestic Politics and Foreign Relations of Terrorism"; Joshua T. White, "Pakistan's Islamist

gave these parties their greatest electoral victory, limiting the power of the PPP and granting the JUI the majority in the Northwest Frontier Province and the ability to implement Islamic law there.[110]

Musharraf made several appeals to Islam, and put in place some Islamic reforms in an attempt to gain these groups' favor. In the run-up to the 2002 elections, Musharraf claimed he would "gradually" eliminate interest in the country's banking system, in line with reforms preferred by Islamic groups.[111] Musharraf also promised to return to a democracy "based on Islamic values" after he seized power; he also said he would not change any of the Islamic laws in the Pakistani constitution.[112] And like earlier Pakistani leaders, Musharraf often appealed to international Muslim solidarity, such as pushing for greater trade among Muslim countries in 2005.[113] In addition to this, he expressed a willingness to limit perceived indecency on television in line with "Islamic values."[114]

After taking office following Musharraf's resignation, President Zardari and Prime Minister Gilani made some efforts to resist the pressure of Islamic groups, but generally attempted to appease them and maintain their support. This can be seen in the response to the 2011 blasphemy-related violence. The government initially announced three days of mourning after Taseer's death, and appointed a liberal PPP member who had previously been strongly critical of the blasphemy laws as the ambassador to the United States.[115] But initial efforts to change the country's blasphemy laws stalled; this was reportedly due to Gilani fearing protests from Islamic groups if the laws were changed.[116] Similarly, Zardari called on the United States to punish a US pastor who burned a Quran in March 2011.[117]

Frontier: Islamic Politics and US Policy in Pakistan's North-West Frontier," (CFIA Religion and Security Monograph Series, 2008).

[110] Haqqani, *Pakistan: Between Mosque and Military*.

[111] Musharraf for Gradual Islamic Banking System in Pakistan, September 18, 2002.

[112] Daily Lauds Musharraf's Pledge to Introduce Democracy Based on Islamic Values, May 4, 2002; Musharraf Assures Politicians No Plan to Amend Islamic Laws in Constitution, February 8, 2002.

[113] Pakistan: Musharraf Calls for Greater Trade Among Muslim Countries, August 10, 2005.

[114] Pakistan: Government Urged to Take Moderate Course in Formulating Media Policy, March 8, 2002; Analyst Says Domestic Problems, Renewed Terrorism Pose Threat to Musharraf's Rule, June 3, 2005.

[115] AFP: Pakistani PM Appoints New Envoy to US, November 23, 2011; AFP: Pakistan Announces 3 Days of National Mourning For Slain Minister, March 3, 2011.

[116] Pakistan: Ex-Minister Says PM Preventing Efforts to Amend Blasphemy Laws, February 4, 2011.

[117] Pakistan: Religious Leaders Appreciate President's Recent Address, March 23, 2011.

HISTORICAL OVERVIEW OF RELIGION–STATE RELATIONSHIP

Thus, Pakistan's leaders – both democratic and military – frequently appealed to Islamist groups for support and took steps in response to these groups' pressure (or avoided taking steps they would oppose). But this was not merely leaders responding to powerful social groups and beliefs and framing policies meant to avoid domestic backlash. Instead, the nature of the religion–state relationship in Pakistan structured these interactions between Islamist groups and Pakistani leaders. The close ties between religion and state provided Islamist groups with rhetorical tools and outright support for their activities, giving them greater influence over Pakistani leaders than they would have had otherwise. Moreover, the connections between Pakistani security and Islam – through its support for Islamist militants – left the military very wary of any policies taken to limit these groups' influence. These ties began with Pakistan's founding, the specific nature of which set in place a path-dependent process as successive leaders implemented policies designed to gain the support of Islamist groups, strengthening these group's sway over society and leaving future leaders even more beholden to Islamist pressure. This resulted in the situation I discussed earlier, with Islamic groups and symbols powerful in Pakistani politics and leaders dependent on Islamic groups to stay in power.

1947–1970

Muhammad Ali Jinnah, the founder of Pakistan, envisioned the state as a homeland for Muslims.[118] His early political efforts in the Indian National Congress focused on ensuring Muslims had an influential role in an independent India, and ensuring that Jinnah would serve as their leader. As his efforts progressed, he shifted focus to a separate Pakistani state that included the majority-Muslim areas of pre-independence India. Jinnah did include some Islamic appeals in his efforts, and tried to gain the support of Islamic groups by promising to implement Islamic laws.[119] Once Jinnah secured their support, though, they endeavored to

---

[118] Ayesha Jalal, *The Sole Spokesman: Jinnah, the Muslim League and the Demand for Pakistan* (London: Cambridge University Press, 1985); Cohen, *The Idea of Pakistan*.

[119] Ishtiaq Ahmed, "The Spectre of Islamic Fundamentalism over Pakistan," in *Pakistan in Regional and Global Politics*, ed. Rajshree Jetly (London: Routledge Taylor & Francis Group, 2009); Haqqani, *Pakistan: Between Mosque and Military*.

ensure the state followed Islamic standards. For example, the *Jamaat-e-Islami* (JI; Islamic Party), an influential Islamist party, was formed shortly after Pakistani independence and pushed for the adoption of Islamic laws through the state's political system.[120]

Islam took on a more prominent role in Pakistan's politics after Jinnah's death, through 1949's "Objectives Resolution."[121] This resolution, which Jinnah's successor as Prime Minister – Liaquat Ali Khan – helped to pass in the parliament, established the standards by which Pakistan would be governed. It called for an independent judiciary, minority rights, and democracy. But it circumscribed these liberal rights through reference to Islam. Early Pakistani leaders also used Islamic appeals to advance their political agendas. Pakistani leaders framed tensions with India as an assault on Islam to gain popular support.[122] Also, Pakistan's military justified its power as necessary to defend Muslims in the country and abroad.[123]

Pakistan's military rulers in the 1960s – Ayub Khan and Yahya Khan – used Islam for political gain. Ayub Khan appealed to Islam to unify the country in the face of its ethnic divisions.[124] He also framed tensions with India in a religious light, especially during the 1965 India-Pakistani War.[125] Yahya Khan continued this process as he dealt with continued tensions with India, and also intensified ties between the state and Islamic

---

[120] Ahmed, "The Spectre of Islamic Fundamentalism over Pakistan"; Ilhan Niaz, *The Culture of Governance and Power in Pakistan, 1947–2008* (New York: Oxford University Press, 2010).

[121] Haqqani, *Pakistan: Between Mosque and Military*; Ilhan Niaz, *The Culture of Power and Governance of Pakistan, 1947–2008* (Karachi: Oxford University Press, 2010); Tahir Watsi, *The Application of Islamic Criminal Law in Pakistan: Shariah in Practice* (Leiden: Brill, 2009).

[122] Bidanda M. Chengappa, *Pakistan: Islamisation, Army, and Foreign Policy* (New Delhi: A.P.H. Publishing Corporation, 2004); Haqqani, *Pakistan: Between Mosque and Military*; Lubna Saif, *Authoritarianism and Underdevelopment in Pakistan 1947–1958: The Role of the Punjab* (New York: Oxford University Press, 2011); Lawrence Ziring, *Pakistan in the Twentieth Century: A Political History* (Karachi: Oxford University Press, 1997).

[123] Mazhar Aziz, *Military Control in Pakistan: The Parallel State* (New York: Routledge, 2008).

[124] Cohen, *The Idea of Pakistan*; Ziad Haider, *The Ideological Struggle for Pakistan* (Stanford: Hoover Institute Press, 2010); Haqqani, *Pakistan: Between Mosque and Military*; Niaz, *The Culture of Governance and Power in Pakistan, 1947–2008*; Lawrence Ziring, "Weak State, Failed State, Garrison State: The Pakistan Saga," in *South Asia's Weak States: Understanding the Regional Insecurity Predicament*, ed. T. V. Paul (Stanford, CA: Stanford University Press, 2010).

[125] Cohen, *The Idea of Pakistan*; Haqqani, *Pakistan: Between Mosque and Military*.

groups.[126] He directed state resources toward Islamist political parties, in the hopes that supporting them would undermine leftist opposition groups.[127] Yahya Khan's use of Islam extended to internal Pakistani tensions, specifically between East and West Pakistan.[128] After East Pakistan (later Bangladesh) began to push for greater autonomy, the government organized Islamic groups to travel to East Pakistan to fight against Bangladeshi insurgents.[129]

1970s and 1980s

Zulfikar Ali Bhutto succeeded Yahya Khan as the leader of a civilian government under his Pakistan People's Party (PPP). He was a socialist, but made several appeals to Islam while in office. In response to Islamic opposition to his rule, Bhutto attempted to institute what he called "Islamic socialism," and passed restrictive laws on Ahmadis and drinking.[130] He also intensified restrictions on blasphemy that had been in place since the colonial period, enabling criminal prosecutions of alleged blasphemers. And he advanced Islamic causes internationally, including establishing ties with Gulf states, increasing the prominence of Pakistan in the OIC, and describing Pakistan's nuclear program as an "Islamic bomb."[131]

Bhutto's military chief of staff, Zia ul-Haq, overthrew and executed him; Zia then became president. Zia was a very devout military officer, who came from the Islam-oriented officer corps, which grew out of Ayub Khan's policies.[132] Zia intensified the importance of Islam in Pakistan's military and extended Bhutto's Islamic policies.[133] He implemented severe conservative Islamic punishments, made tithing mandatory for some

---

[126] Haider, *The Ideological Struggle for Pakistan*; Niaz, *The Culture of Governance and Power in Pakistan, 1947–2008*.

[127] Haqqani, *Pakistan: Between Mosque and Military*.

[128] Ahmed, "The Spectre of Islamic Fundamentalism over Pakistan"; Haqqani, *Pakistan: Between Mosque and Military*.

[129] *Pakistan: Between Mosque and Military*; Gul, *The Most Dangerous Place: Pakistan's Lawless Frontier*.

[130] Haqqani, *Pakistan: Between Mosque and Military*; Haider, *The Ideological Struggle for Pakistan*.

[131] Cohen, *The Idea of Pakistan*.

[132] Chengappa, *Pakistan: Islamisation, Army, and Foreign Policy*.

[133] Ahmed, "The Spectre of Islamic Fundamentalism over Pakistan"; Haider, *The Ideological Struggle for Pakistan*; Cohen, *The Idea of Pakistan*; Haqqani, *Pakistan: Between Mosque and Military*; Nasr, "International Politics, Domestic Imperatives, and Identity Mobilization: Sectarianism in Pakistan."

groups, and increased restrictions on Ahmadis and blasphemy.[134] Zia also brought the JI into the cabinet and gave conservative Islamic groups influence over the courts and education system.[135]

Zia's primary foreign policy initiative – support for insurgents fighting Soviets in Afghanistan – was oriented toward Islam as well. The Inter-Services Intelligence Directorate (ISI) – Pakistan's military intelligence service – had established ties with Afghan Islamic militants in the 1970s for use as proxies against the then-revanchist Afghan regime. Zia intensified support for these and other Islamic groups after the Soviet invasion, funneling resources from the United States and Saudi Arabia into Afghanistan.[136] He also worked with conservative Islamic groups in Pakistan to provide aid for Afghan refugees.[137] And the ISI began supporting Islamic militants in Kashmir, to fight against Indian troops.[138]

Social turmoil in Pakistan, much of it related to religion, increased in this time period. Sectarian violence broke out, some of it inspired by the Iranian revolution.[139] And conservative Islamic groups became more prominent in Pakistani politics through state support for militants in Afghanistan and reliance on these groups to aid for Afghan refugees. International events also contributed to tensions in Pakistan; for example, in 1979 a mob attacked the US Embassy in Islamabad because of rumors that the United States was responsible for the attack on the Grand Mosque in Mecca that year.

Overview: Steadily Increasing Religion–State Ties

Thus, the history of religion–state relations in Pakistan involved a steady increase in the ties between Islamic groups and the state and the importance of religion in Pakistani politics. The establishment of Pakistan as a Muslim state, and the significant role for religion in the Objectives

134 Ahmed, "The Spectre of Islamic Fundamentalism over Pakistan"; Chengappa, *Pakistan: Islamisation, Army, and Foreign Policy.*
135 *Pakistan: Islamisation, Army, and Foreign Policy*; Niaz, *The Culture of Power and Governance of Pakistan, 1947–2008.*
136 Haider, *The Ideological Struggle for Pakistan.* Haqqani, *Pakistan: Between Mosque and Military.*
137 Fair *et al.*, *Pakistan: Can the United States Secure an Insecure State?*
138 Byman, "Friends Like These: Counterinsurgency and the War on Terrorism"; Schmidt, *The Unravelling: Pakistan in the Age of Jihad.*
139 Nasr, "International Politics, Domestic Imperatives, and Identity Mobilization: Sectarianism in Pakistan."

Resolution gave Islamic groups influence over the state and led leaders to justify their policies – such as the tensions with India – through Islam. This set the stage for Zulfikar Ali Bhutto's Islamic socialism, the religious backlash against him, and his ultimate fall. Similarly, Zia ul-Haq's Islamization built on and emerged from earlier ties to Islam. These increasingly strengthened religion–state ties resulted in more intense religious contention, as religious rhetoric became common in politics and Islamic groups were actively supported by the state. And both civilian governments that followed found it difficult to take any actions opposed by religious groups due to these earlier policies and the religious groups they backed.

This increasing relationship between religion and state was not due to a dedicated mission on the part of Pakistani leaders or Pakistani society as a whole to Islamize Pakistan, however. The Pakistani state was weak from the beginning, due to economic issues, ethnic divides, and powerful Islamic opposition; as a result, leaders had to adopt policies in order to satisfy or deflect domestic audiences, even if they were not democratically accountable. Leaders often implemented Islamic laws to gain Islamic support and undermine opponents.[140] And many of the international Islamic appeals resulted in greater aid from Muslim countries.[141]

Even if they were politically expedient, the increasing religion–state ties resulted in a close connection between Islam and the Pakistani state. Both civilian and military leaders framed tensions with India in religious terms, giving that conflict an Islamic, rather than purely nationalist, salience. And state support for Islamic militants in Bangladesh and Afghanistan established this as a tool to advance the states' national security. Finally, Zia's Islamization of both domestic politics and the military increased support among military officials for Islamic groups and gave them a stake in the continued role of Islam in Pakistani politics. These connections extended beyond security issues. There were numerous laws that restricted religious practice – in favor of conservative interpretations of Islam – and set Islamic standards for government policies. Islamic groups were also politically powerful, due to their ability to mobilize followers and disrupt society; regimes were thus dependent on them for support, and wary of crossing them.

---

[140] Anas Malik, *Political Survival in Pakistan: Beyond Ideology* (New York: Routledge, 2011).

[141] Chengappa, *Pakistan: Islamisation, Army, and Foreign Policy*; Cohen, *The Idea of Pakistan*.

ANALYSIS

It is not difficult to see how this historical religion–state relationship gave rise to a situation in which religious pressure made Pakistani leaders hesitant to cooperate extensively on counterterrorism. I hope to further demonstrate this point, however – and provide support for my argument concerning the effects of religion–state relationships on Muslim states' counterterrorism policies – with an in-depth analysis of this situation. The first part of this chapter laid out the evidence for my argument, and suggested the connections between the pieces of evidence. This final section will tie the evidence together, providing analysis and further evidence connecting the previously discussed factors to demonstrate that the religion–state relationship in Pakistan produced the counterterrorism tensions between the United States and that country. In it, I will demonstrate that: (1) Pakistan's counterterrorism policies were based on leaders' concerns about domestic Islamic backlash to close cooperation, (2) the ability of Islamic groups to evoke these concerns arose from the historical religion–state relationship, and (3) while other factors mattered in this situation, the religion–state relationship in Pakistan was of paramount importance.

The Effects of the Religion–State Relationship in Pakistan on its Counterterrorism Cooperation

Pakistan's minimal and hesitating counterterrorism cooperation was connected to the extensive ties between religion and the state. Pakistan's leaders faced significant religious contention – both domestic and transnational – much of it connected to security issues. Islamic groups consistently pressed the state to implement Islamic laws and follow Islamic standards. And they opposed attempts to stop supporting Islamic militants in Afghanistan and Kashmir. This extended to opposition to US counterterrorism efforts. Much of the opposition to US counterterrorism efforts was presented in Islamic terms, while Pakistani leaders were attacked on similar terms for cooperating. Likewise, although this opposition was widespread through Pakistani society, Islamic groups were often the most visible in their attacks on Pakistan for working with the United States, and they often spearheaded protests against working with the United States.

There is evidence that Islamic laws and official appeals to Islam had, by the 1990s, intensified the political power of religious groups and the salience of religious issues. Leaders often made religious appeals to gain support, and depended on Islamic groups to stay in power. Moreover, the military supported Islamic militants in neighboring countries and had close ties to Islamic groups in Pakistan, connecting the country's security policies to Islam. There are various indications that Islamic parties – while not electorally successfully – affected state behavior, through their ability to mobilize protests and their influence over parts of society. For example, JI was regularly able to organize protests to disrupt society and influence leaders to adopt policies they favor; for example, more than 150,000 people attended an October 1998 rally by JI.[142]

Moreover, leaders' appeals to Islam were based on political calculations, not principles, indicating they responded to domestic religious pressure not their own or society's deeply held beliefs. This can be seen most clearly in the case of Nawaz Sharif, who was the closest to Islamic groups out of all the post-Zia Pakistani leaders. Even though Sharif campaigned initially for Islamic reforms, his party's manifesto in the 1993 elections focused primarily on economic development.[143] This suggests his appeals to Islam were intended to gain the support of Islamic groups. Also, many observers have claimed that his attempt to implement Islamic law in the country was designed primarily to give him more power, both by increasing the power of his office and intensifying support from Islamic groups.[144]

We can see how this situation affected Pakistani security policy from a few examples. Many of Bhutto's security policies were designed to prevent the military and Islamic groups from openly opposing her. This includes her continuation of the country's policy in Afghanistan, supporting Islamic militants in their attempt to take over the country. Bhutto reportedly attempted to change the country's Afghanistan policy, as she worried the conflict could destabilize Pakistani politics and undermine her rule.[145] But she did not proceed with this action due to her fear that it would provoke opposition from the military.[146] And Islamic opposition did weaken Bhutto while she was in power, with widespread protests and

---

[142] Schmidt, *The Unravelling: Pakistan in the Age of Jihad*. Pakistan: Editorial Examines Resurgence of Jama't-i-Islami, October 27, 1998.
[143] PML(N) Manifesto Viewed, September 22, 1993.
[144] Cohen, *The Idea of Pakistan*; Haqqani, *Pakistan: Between Mosque and Military*; Niaz, *The Culture of Governance and Power in Pakistan, 1947–2008*; Watsi, *The Application of Islamic Criminal Law in Pakistan: Shariah in Practice.*
[145] Bhutto Reportedly Changing Foreign Policy, June 7, 1989.
[146] Haqqani, *Pakistan: Between Mosque and Military.*

electoral coalitions against her in elections; likewise, as was noted, the military actively supported her opponents in elections.[147] This extended to Zardari too. Zardari reportedly faced threats from the military if he moved too strongly against militants; this suggests his public opposition to US counterterrorism activities was related to this pressure.[148]

This was evident during Musharraf's time in office as well. Musharraf's halting steps on counterterrorism were connected to the power of Islamic groups in society and the military, and his fear of these groups turning on him. Benazir Bhutto claimed that pressure from the military limited Musharraf's ability to break ties with the Taliban.[149] And others pointed out a similar dynamic concerning Islamic parties. Musharraf was hesitant to take too many actions in Afghanistan – such as moving strongly against the Taliban and al-Qaeda in the border region – that would upset these groups, as he relied on them for support.[150] This extended to Kashmiri militant groups as well, as he was afraid of losing domestic support and provoking a backlash by these groups by taking too many actions against them.[151] And the ability of Islamic groups to threaten his government limited his actions against religious schools.[152]

How Pakistan's Political Institutions Led to this Situation

Of course, one could argue that Pakistan's leaders did base their counterterrorism policies on a desire to avoid domestic backlash and stay in power but such behavior is common, even expected, among leaders and the result would be the same if the opposition was not related to religion. What is distinctive about the Pakistan case – and what highlights the crucial role of religion in this dynamic – is the fact that this political situation, in which leaders faced powerful religious groups capable of removing them from power, was not inevitable. It was the result of

---

[147] Religious Leaders to Campaign against Government, June 16, 1989; Pakistan: PML, Religious Parties Unite to Oust Bhutto, May 30, 1996.

[148] UK: IISS Sees Pakistan's Zardari Possibly Facing Threat From Army, September 18, 2008.

[149] Pakistan: Bhutto Believes Musharraf in 'Trouble', Faces 'Establishment' Pressure, September 30, 2001.

[150] Haider, *The Ideological Struggle for Pakistan*. Afghan Paper Wants Pakistan to do More in Combating Terrorism, June 26, 2003.

[151] Haqqani, *Pakistan: Between Mosque and Military*; Amin Saikal, "Musharraf and Pakistan's Crisis," in *Pakistan in Regional and Global Politics*, ed. Rajshree Jetly (London: Routledge Taylor & Francis Group, 2009).

[152] FBIS Analysis, August 25, 2005: Limited Progress in Crackdown on Religious Schools.

the decades' long development of the religion and state relationship I discussed earlier.

The historical development of the religion–state relationship in Pakistan had three interlocking effects on its politics. First, it produced a positive feedback loop, making it easier for later Islamic policies or laws to be passed. The Objectives Resolution established the importance of Islam early on in Pakistan's history, setting a precedent for other laws and policies based on Islam.[153] And the ties between Islam and Pakistan's security Ayub Khan and other early leaders established facilitated Zia's later Islamization program in both society and the military.[154]

Second, it made Islamic politics more intense, and at times violent, and gave Islamic groups more influence over policymaking. For example, after Zia supported conservative Sunni groups during his reign, sectarian violence between Sunnis and Shias intensified, due primarily to the rise of militant anti-Shia groups.[155] And some have argued that the religious rhetoric of Pakistan's leaders exacerbated Pakistan's instability, contributing to the later rise of more extreme Islamic groups.[156] One prominent example of Islamists' increasing political power due to the state's policies is the support for militants in Afghanistan, which brought Islamists into the Pakistani government, giving them greater influence over the policy process.[157] And militants supported by the ISI were able to open religious schools in Pakistan, giving them some influence over society.[158]

Finally, it constrained leaders from taking actions contrary to the state's Islamic rhetoric or Islamic sentiment in society. Zulfikar Ali Bhutto's international Islamic appeals – while politically motivated – set a precedent for later leaders like Bhutto and Sharif; these leaders were expected to similarly appeal to Islam in domestic and foreign policies by the public.[159] Likewise, many Pakistani leaders found it difficult to change Islamic laws in Pakistan, as they became accepted by society and

[153] Cohen, *The Idea of Pakistan.*
[154] Chengappa, *Pakistan: Islamisation, Army, and Foreign Policy.*
[155] Haider, *The Ideological Struggle for Pakistan*; Afak Haydar, "The Sipah-E-Sahaba Pakistan," in *Pakistan: Founders' Aspirations and Today's Realities*, ed. Hafeez Malik (New York: Oxford University Press, 2001); Ziring, "Weak State, Failed State, Garrison State: The Pakistan Saga."
[156] Niaz, *The Culture of Governance and Power in Pakistan, 1947–2008.*
[157] Malik, *Political Survival in Pakistan: Beyond Ideology.*
[158] Schmidt, *The Unravelling: Pakistan in the Age of Jihad.*
[159] Cohen, *The Idea of Pakistan*; Hafeez Malik, *Pakistan: Founders' Aspirations and Today's Realities* (New York: Oxford University Press, 2001).

Islamic groups strongly opposed any changes to them.[160] This extended to security policies; Benazir Bhutto claimed she was "slowly, slowly sucked into" Pakistan's support for the Taliban in the 1990s due to pressure from the military and social groups and the policies already in place once she assumed office.[161]

The relationship between the historical development of religion–state connections and Pakistan's counterterrorism policies is captured in an interesting example from the debate over educational reform in Pakistan. As was noted, under US pressure Musharraf attempted to increase state control over religious schools and remove supposedly extremist elements from the education. This provoked significant opposition, as it was seen as an attack on Islam and Pakistani culture, and giving in to the United States. The development of religion–state connections in Pakistan connected Islam to both Pakistani society and security, so attempts to change that provoked religious opposition. In one editorial attacking Musharraf for trying to change the educational system and remove "jihad" from the curriculum, the author claimed that jihad is not only a "basic concept of Islam," but also "part of the motto of the Pakistani Army since independence."[162] That is, the author was angry not only because Musharraf was decreasing the role of religion in the country, but also because religion was allegedly connected to the state's security since its founding.

Thus, Pakistani leaders' hesitation over counterterrorism cooperation makes sense politically, as it was a rational response to powerful domestic groups that opposed such policies. But the institutional religion–state relationship structured both the nature of the pressure they faced – religious opposition to security policies, specifically counterterrorism – and leaders' incentives to follow domestic pressure and limit cooperation with the United States. These structured political dynamics were set in place with the establishment of Islam's importance with Pakistan's founding.

Alternative Explanations

Of course, there were other things going on in Pakistan that could explain its minimal counterterrorism cooperation. Likewise, religion might have

---

[160] Schmidt, *The Unravelling: Pakistan in the Age of Jihad*.

[161] Quoted in Coll, *Ghost Wars: The Secret History of the CIA, Afghanistan and bin Ladin, from the Soviet Invasion to September 10, 2011*; 293.

[162] Pakistan: Editorial Disapproves US Demand of 'Excluding Jihad' from Curriculum, August 22, 2005.

driven its policies but it could have done so directly through the beliefs of its leaders and society. While some alternatives are valid, they do not undermine the importance of the religion–state relationship, and many cannot adequately explain Pakistan's counterterrorism cooperation.

The primary alternative explanation would be that Pakistan's resistance to US counterterrorism was due to its concerns over India. That is, Pakistan's support for the Taliban is connected to its desire to minimize Indian influence in Afghanistan.[163] And its refusal to break ties with Kashmiri militants' groups was an attempt to maintain a weapon against India. This is correct, but does not completely explain the effects of religion on Pakistan's counterterrorism policies. It was not inevitable that Pakistan would choose to oppose India by supporting specifically Islamic militant groups. Pakistan could easily have supported leftist militants in Afghanistan and Kashmir. The connections between Islam and Pakistan's security policies, however, made Islamist militants a more desirable option as they were in line with official state rhetoric. And the fact that Pakistan had supported Islamic militants made it less likely it would cooperate with the United States on counterterrorism, as there would have been less religious opposition to changing its policies if they had not been framed in Islamic terms. That is, the tension with India *contextualizes* the connection between the religion–state relationship and Pakistan's support for militant groups and its hesitation to stop doing so. Yes, tensions with India did influence Pakistan's decisions to support militant groups, but that does not explain why they chose to support specifically *Islamist* ones.

The inadequacy of this explanation is also apparent through counterfactuals. Arguing that Pakistan's minimal counterterrorism cooperation is due to tensions with India implies a few counterfactual statements. The first is that, if Pakistan had supported non-Islamic militants against India in Afghanistan and Kashmir, it would still have refused to take action in response to US counterterrorism pressure. The second is that if Pakistan had not been officially Islamic with close ties between the regime and Islamic groups it would still have supported Islamic militants. In other words, its decision to support Islamic militants was opportunistic, and not tied to the nature of the state.

---

[163] Fair, "Pakistan's Relations with Central Asia"; Fair *et al.*, *Pakistan: Can the United States Secure an Insecure State?*; Schmidt, *The Unravelling: Pakistan in the Age of Jihad*.

Neither of these counterfactuals is valid. If Pakistan had been support-ing Leftist militants in Kashmir and Afghanistan, the United States would still likely have called on it to limit its support. But Pakistan's support for these militants would have been less connected to al-Qaeda and non-violent Islamic groups, and there is little reason to expect Islamic groups would be tied to the regime as they had not played a role in its earlier poli-cies. As a result, the religion–state relationship in Pakistan would not have been as close, and it would have been easier for Pakistan to comply with US requests. Likewise, Pakistan would undoubtedly not have supported Islamic militants if it had been officially leftist or ethnically nationalist. As discussed, Pakistan's support for these groups came from earlier leaders connecting Islam to its security, so it seems unlikely the regimes would have turned to these groups without some ideological connection to their overall goals.

Some have argued that the US-Pakistani counterterrorism issues may have been the result of the weakness of the Pakistani state. That is, Pak-istan did not have the capabilities to effectively crack down on militants under US pressure. There is some validity to this.[164] Yet, this very weak-ness was partially the result of the religion–state connections in Pakistan. They increased the power of Islamic groups to the extent that the state was wary of taking actions that would upset them, while also indirectly strengthening militant activity in the country. And when the Pakistani state did feel it was under threat – as when militants seized significant territory in the country in the post-9/11 period – it was able to push them back, indicating it was not wholly incapable of acting. The weak state *contextualizes* the effect of religion–state connections, indicating they occurred alongside other factors that limited the state's ability to imple-ment strong counterterrorism policies. But the religion–state relationship still drove its halting counterterrorism cooperation.

This can be demonstrated with the attending counterfactuals. Arguing that Pakistan's hesitating counterterrorism cooperation was due to the weak state implies that if it did not have a close relationship to religion it would still be as weak. While the weakness of Pakistan was related to many historical factors, its ties to Islam did result in leaders appealing to and relying on Islamic groups that gained significant power over society,

---

[164] Niaz, *The Culture of Governance and Power in Pakistan, 1947–2008*; Ian Talbot, *Pakistan: A Modern History* (New York: Palgrave MacMillan, 2005). Byman, "Friends Like These: Counterinsurgency and the War on Terrorism."

making it more difficult to govern. A secular or communist Pakistan would be a Pakistan with weaker Islamic activist groups, and would thus have a stronger state.

Those are the two strongest, and most common, alternative explanations. Other potential alternative explanations are less effective. One would be that Pakistan's counterterrorism policies changed as its interests changed. That is, it was not in Pakistan's interest to limit ties to militants initially, although later when these groups posed a threat the state decided to act; its policies thus had nothing to do with religion. This argument is ineffective. It is difficult to assess a state's "interest," and easy to infer changing interests *post hoc* from changing behavior. Moreover, as I discussed earlier, various Pakistani leaders did attempt to take on militants and broader Islamic groups but failed due to the political pressure against them. This indicates it was not completely in Pakistan's interest to support these groups. Various other arguments suggest Pakistan's counterterrorism cooperation was connected to regime fears of domestic unrest, but this unrest was related to corruption, anti-Americanism, or ethnic tensions.[165] All of these factors did matter in Pakistani political instability.[166] Yet these factors do not explain Pakistan's counterterrorism cooperation. In this chapter, I have presented ample evidence of both Islamic opposition to counterterrorism and Pakistani leaders' concern over Islamic groups. Other factors likely motivated Pakistani society and leaders, but it is difficult to ignore the widespread religious contention.

In sharp contrast, one could argue that Pakistan's halting counterterrorism cooperation was due to widespread Islamic contention among leaders and the public. This is not accurate. There were few mass-based Islamic movements in Pakistan; no Islamist party received more than 5 percent of the vote until the 2002 elections, in which the MMA did well in the NWFP, but the MMA lost in the 2008 elections to a Pashtun nationalist party, indicating the limits of their appeals.[167] Likewise, Pakistani society as a whole is unhappy with US counterterrorism

[165] Irm Haleem, "Ethnic and Sectarian Violence and the Propensity Towards Praetorianism in Pakistan," *Third World Quarterly* 24, no. 3 (2003); Harrison, "Global Terrorism: US Policy after 9/11 and Its Impact on the Domestic Politics and Foreign Relations of Terrorism."

[166] Gul, *The Most Dangerous Place: Pakistan's Lawless Frontier*; Hamid H. Kizilbash, "Anti-Americanism in Pakistan," *Annals of the American Academy of Political and Social Science*, 497 (1988).

[167] Cohen, *The Idea of Pakistan*.

policies, but most Pakistanis are also critical of al-Qaeda and the Taliban.[168] Moreover, there were secular and liberal alternatives to the Islamists. For example, in a 2005 editorial, one of the largest newspapers in Pakistan argued that "establishing a moderate, liberal, and enlightened society" is in line with Jinnah's initial vision for Pakistan, and that a "moderate society is in Pakistan's best interests."[169] Thus, Islamists did not represent all Pakistanis and Pakistanis were not overwhelmingly supportive of the Taliban.

CONCLUSION

The story that opened this chapter was unique in the specific focus on Osama bin Ladin but hardly atypical of interactions between the two countries. Despite being dependent on the United States for security, Pakistan resisted cooperating on counterterrorism due to the widespread Islamic opposition to such cooperation and Pakistani leaders' reliance on Islamic groups to stay in power. This political situation, in turn, was the product of the decades'-long interaction between religion and state that produced a state with numerous Islamic laws, intermittent support for Islamic groups, and Islamic groups capable of crippling the government through protests and coordination with the military. Thus, religion contributed greatly to US-Pakistani counterterrorism tensions, although it did so through the mediating effects of political institutions.

Pakistan's cooperation and non-cooperation ran the gamut of the mechanisms I laid out in Chapter 2. Much of Pakistan's behavior on counterterrorism demonstrated *hedging*, adopting half-steps in line with US pressure but failing to fully cooperate. At times it attempted to go further – such as with Musharraf's education reforms – only to *backtrack* in the face of widespread anger. And some of this cooperation may have been *strategic*, such as continued support for Islamic militants, although it is difficult to tell from the evidence available. And it did cooperate at times, particularly on international aspects such as the support for the US invasion of Afghanistan or drone strikes. But it *hid* the latter and attempted to *justify* the former through appeal to Islam.

The case of Pakistan provides significant support for my argument concerning the role of religion–state relationships in US–Muslim

---

[168] "Pakistani Public Opinion" (Pew Research Center, 2009).
[169] Pakistan Daily Stresses Practical Steps to Implement 'Enlightened Moderation,' March 4, 2005.

counterterrorism tensions. Pakistan was a case of a close religion–state relationship resulting in limited counterterrorism cooperation, in line with the statistical findings from the previous chapter. Moreover, this was due to the political effects of the religion–state relationship and leaders' desire to stay in power, not a principled adherence to the Islamic issues on the part of a state. The next chapters, on Turkey and the United Arab Emirates, will further demonstrate this relationship, by showing how more distant religion–state ties gave states the freedom of movement to work closely with the United States on counterterrorism.

5

The United Arab Emirates

To some, the United Arab Emirates (UAE) seems like a country that would likely be a problematic counterterrorism partner. An officially Islamic confederation of city-states, the UAE has many laws based on Islam and a conservative Islamic populace. Indeed, this perception led to the 2006 controversy over the UAE-based Dubai Ports World. The company made a bid to manage operations at several US ports, and initially gained the US government's approval. Soon after, however, the US Coast Guard expressed concerns about potential threats to national security as a result of the deal.[1] After members of Congress publicly criticized the deal, opposition spread. US Representative Peter King argued, "Having a company right out of the heartland of al Qaeda managing those ports . . . is madness," and pointed to "reports" about "an al-Qaeda presence" in the country.[2] The backlash led to the company withdrawing its bid despite the anger of US President Bush over this slight to a country with which the US maintained close ties.

To be fair to critics of the deal, the country was one of the United States' biggest concerns about terrorist financing in the 1990s, and joined Pakistan as one of three countries to recognize the Taliban in Afghanistan. And Steve Coll pointed to reports that part of the reason the United States aborted a 1990s' air strike in Afghanistan that could have eliminated Osama bin Ladin was the presence of UAE royalty at the camp with

[1] Stephanie Kirchgaesser, "US Coast Guard Warned on Dubai Ports Deal," February 28, 2006.
[2] "Peter King: Dubai Ports Company in 'Al Qaeda Heartland'," *NewsMax Online*, February 20, 2006.

the al-Qaeda leader.[3] But after the 9/11 attacks the UAE emerged as an important counterterrorism partner for the United States. The UAE broke ties with the Taliban and made its territory available to the US military. It also arrested al-Qaeda members and sympathizers and made great strides in combating terrorist financing.

While it makes sense why the country initially was lax on counterterrorism issues, how and why did it increase its cooperation after 9/11? And given its close ties to Islam, why was it as cooperative as it was?

As with Pakistan, the nature of the UAE's counterterrorism cooperation arises from its religion–state relationship. The UAE is officially Islamic with a strong role for Islam in its laws, but it minimizes the extent to which Islamic groups can influence the regime. The country has experienced widespread Islamic activism; although much of it does not take the confrontational form seen in other countries, the state has faced pressure to act in line with religious sentiment. Due to this contention, and some regime members' affinity with the sentiment, the UAE pursued some religious policiesw – such as support for international Islamic causes – and initially did not restrict terrorist financing in the country. Under pressure from the United States to ramp up its counterterrorism activities after the 9/11 attacks, however, the UAE was able to move on these initiatives due to its specific religion–state relationship. By maintaining a hold over Islamic groups in the country, the UAE was able to crack down on these groups and ignore their opposition, facilitating its counterterrorism ties with the United States.

In this chapter, I first discuss US-Emirati counterterrorism cooperation. I then present information on Islamic contention in the UAE before moving on to the relationship between religion and state. Following this, I discuss the historical development of the religion–state relationship in the country before conducting an in-depth analysis of the effects of this relationship on the UAE's counterterrorism cooperation.

Readers may question whether Islamic contention is even present in the UAE. The UAE is a stable, closely controlled society with few hints of activism or opposition. Thus, a major alternative explanation to the UAE's counterterrorism cooperation – which I will discuss later in this chapter – is that the UAE cooperates with the United States because it has little to fear from domestic opposition. In the section on religious

---

[3] Coll, *Ghost Wars: The Secret History of the CIA, Afghanistan and bin Ladin, from the Soviet Invasion to September 10, 2011*.

contention I deal with this by presenting examples of Islamic contention in the UAE, including activism and opposition to the state. Due to the restrictive nature of the state, however, Islamic activism is only apparent when the state disrupts it. As a result, some of the evidence I give to support the presence of Islamic contention in the country involves examples of arrests of Islamist figures.

US COUNTERTERRORISM COOPERATION

The United Arab Emirates is a case of moderate counterterrorism cooperation, falling in between the two other cases in this book. Specifically, the counterterrorism relationship was marked by low cooperation on the part of the UAE before 9/11, and an increase in cooperation after the attacks, although some problems remained. Before 9/11, the UAE worked with the United States on some military issues but did not have sufficient controls on terrorist financing and other forms of support. The country also was close to other states the United States accused of supporting terrorism. After 9/11, the UAE cut ties with US targets – like the Taliban – and cracked down on terrorist financing and supporters in its territory.

Pre-9/11

Before 9/11, the United Arab Emirates was not incredibly cooperative with the United States on counterterrorism and broader international security issues. The UAE participated in some international counterterrorism events and gave the US military access to ports and air bases on its territory. But in many other areas its behavior frustrated the United States. There were persistent issues with terrorist financing, as well as some sympathy for al-Qaeda and other groups in the country. Moreover, the UAE provided support to countries and organizations that the United States was focusing its counterterrorism efforts on, such as Sudan and the Taliban.

The United Arab Emirates generally cooperated with the United States on issues of international terrorism. This included participating in international terrorism-related forums and arresting terrorism suspects. For example, in March 1996 the United States co-hosted an international summit on terrorism, which focused on opposing anti-Israeli terrorist attacks; the event occurred in Egypt, which at the time was suffering from an Islamist insurgency. The UAE was one of the attendees, even though the conference was rather controversial and other invitees – including Syria and Lebanon – boycotted the event.[4]

More significant than its work in this area, however, was the UAE's military cooperation with the United States. Due to fears over its long-standing territorial dispute with Iran, the UAE provided refueling facilities for US ships traveling in the region, which proved useful during the investigation into the 2000 bombing of the US naval ship the USS *Cole*.[5] Moreover, while the UAE opposed many aspects of US policies toward Iraq – as discussed next – it did assist the United States in some areas. For example, the UAE granted the United States use of its air bases for the US 1998 air strikes on Iraq, although it did so discreetly to avoid backlash.[6]

Besides these examples of cooperation, however, there were many aspects of UAE counterterrorism-related policies that went against US preferences. Some of this involved support for regimes that the United States suspected of terrorism ties. For example, by the late 1990s the United States had exerted pressure on numerous countries to cut ties with Sudan due to that country's hosting of Osama bin Ladin. Despite this, the UAE continued to support the government in Khartoum, although it did not offer any material assistance.[7] At the time, some believed this was because of the international prestige of the Sudanese leader, Hassan al-Turabi, among Muslims.[8] Moreover, the UAE was one of three countries to recognize the Taliban government of Afghanistan.

The UAE similarly provided support to Iraq against the United States' wishes. For example, Barzan al-Tikriti – a half-brother of Saddam Hussein who was prominent in the regime – lived for a time in the UAE.[9] The UAE joined much of the rest of the Gulf Cooperation Council countries

---

[4] Derek Brown, "Anti-Terrorist Summit Points to Middle East Fault Lines," *The Guardian*, March 12, 1996: 11.

[5] Robin Allen and Stephen Fidler, "Inside Knowledge Suspected in Attack: Aden Bombing Yemen Port Had Been Off-Limits to US Ships Until Last Year," *Financial Times*, October 13, 2000: 9.

[6] Mark Huband, "Protests Erupt Across the Middle East: Arab Reaction," *Financial Times*, December 21, 1998: 2.

[7] Mark Huband, "Sudan Pays the Price for Backing Radicals: Islamic Extremist Support Has Isolated Khartoum from Arabs and the West, Says Mark Huband," *Financial Times*, January 29, 1997: 4; Khalid Duran, "A Factory of Terrorism," *Wall Street Journal*, September 10, 1998: 10.

[8] Khalid Duran, "A Factory of Terrorism," *Wall Street Journal*, September 10, 1998: 10.

[9] Ian Black, "Henchman Free to Fly Tyrant Class for Now Western States are Being Urged to Arrest Men like Saddam Hussein's Half-Brother Barzan If They Come Visiting," *The Guardian*, October 28, 1991: 1.

to strongly oppose US-led sanctions on Iraq, and was reportedly not following them due to the strong reaction against them among Muslims.[10] Additionally, there were reports that oil from Iraq – whose sale was restricted due to US sanctions – was smuggled through the UAE.[11] And the UAE reestablished diplomatic ties with Iraq – reopening its embassy in July 2000 – despite these sanctions and the general attempts by the United States to isolate Hussein's regime.[12]

The UAE also actively opposed the United States' general policy toward Iraq. Throughout the 1990s, the UAE was critical of the apparent US policy of removing Saddam Hussein from power, instead calling for dialogue with the regime.[13] For example, in 1999 US Secretary of State Madeline Albright said the United States was "working actively" to remove Hussein from power during a speech in Saudi Arabia; the UAE joined Saudi Arabia and others in the region to oppose this. And an influential newspaper in the UAE argued US efforts were a "surefire recipe for civil war in Iraq," while UAE President Shaikh Zayed bin Sultan al-Nahyan "called for conciliation and lifting of sanctions."[14]

Another area of frequent tensions between the UAE and the United States over terrorism was terrorist fundraising. For example, in 1997, Israel reported that funds from the UAE were sent to a UK group that then contributed to Hamas.[15] And in 1999, Canadian authorities revealed they had uncovered a car theft ring in Canada that moved stolen cars through the UAE and other countries, which ultimately funded militant groups in

[10] Robert Marquand, "A Muslim Sense of Betrayal Islamic World's Reaction to Bombings: The US Treats Us as Second-Class Citizens," *The Christian Science Monitor*, August 24, 1998: 1; "Supplicant Saddam," *Wall Street Journal*, December 10, 1996: 8; Khalaf Roula, "Fallout from US Strike on Iraq Leaves Arabs Counting the Cost," *Financial Times*, September 9, 1996: 4; William A. Rugh, *Diplomacy and Defense Policy of the United Arab Emirates* (London: Emirates Center for Strategic Studies and Research, 2002).
[11] Robert Kilborn, Cynthia Hanson, and Debbie Hodges, "The News in Brief: ALL 02/13/97 Edition," *Christian Science Monitor*, February 13, 1997: 2.
[12] "Iraq Seen Making Progress in Rebuilding Arab Ties," *Mideast Mirror*, July 4, 2000; Nimah Mazaheri, "Iraq and the Domestic Political Effects of Economic Sanctions," *The Middle East Journal* 64, no. 2 (2010).
[13] Rugh, *Diplomacy and Defense Policy of the United Arab Emirates*.
[14] Michael Jansen, "Saudi Arabia Rejects US Plea to Help Overthrow Saddam The Gulf Governments are Particularly Wary of US Intentions, Stated Forcefully by the Secretary of State, to Bring Down the Iraqi Regime, Michael Jansen Reports," *Irish Times*, January 30, 1999: 14.
[15] Julian Borger, "Close Trust, Israel Pleads Britain is Being Asked to Clamp Down on Palestinian Fundraisers. Julian Borger in Jerusalem Reports," *The Guardian*, August 7, 1997: 1.

Lebanon.[16] Additionally, the United States frequently expressed concern about the lack of UAE control over illicit goods in its territory. In 1996, the United States listed UAE as a prominent country implicated in drug money laundering.[17] And in 1997, the US Secretary of State called for "stronger efforts to curb donations to [terrorist] groups by individuals, and increased sharing of intelligence about the flow of money."[18]

There were also concerns about funding going specifically to bin Ladin and the al-Qaeda network. As US efforts against bin Ladin increased in the late 1990s, the United States identified the UAE as a prominent hub for his al-Qaeda networks' fundraising.[19] Specifically, the United States pointed to the Islamic Bank in Dubai as a conduit for funds to flow from al-Qaeda's donors to the group.[20] These concerns were compounded when it became apparent that some of the 9/11 hijackers were from the UAE. An al-Qaeda operative based in the UAE received funds from al-Qaeda and transferred it to the 9/11 cell in the United States through Sharjah.[21] Moreover, the 9/11 cell members transferred excess funding back to al-Qaeda through the UAE; this includes a $15,000 transfer sent by the cell leader – Muhammad Atta – to a recipient in the Emirates.[22]

Post-9/11

After 9/11, the UAE became more cooperative on counterterrorism. The UAE broke its ties with the Taliban and offered support for US military actions. The state also arrested terrorist targets in the country and cracked down on terrorist financing. While concerns about terrorist financing and some terrorist ties in the country remained, overall the country's cooperation increased.

---

[16] Jim Bronskill, "Terrorists Netted Car-Theft Cash: RCMP: Ring Operating in Quebec is Believed to Have Funneled Proceeds Back to Group in Lebanon," *The Gazette*, March 2, 1999.

[17] Hillel Kuttler, "Syria, Iran Included on List of Those Not Fighting Drug Production, Transit," *Jerusalem Post*, March 30, 1996.

[18] Thomas W. Lippman, "Albright Urges Arabs: Don't Bankroll Terror: Expanded Role for Women Advocated," *The Gazette*, September 15, 1997: B1.

[19] James Risen with Benjamin Weiser, "US Officials Say Aid for Terrorists Came Through Two Persian Gulf Nations," *New York Times*, July 8, 1999: A6; Ian Brodie, "US Traces bin Laden Funds to UAE Bank," *The Times*, July 9, 1999: 16.

[20] Steven Edwards, "Bin Laden 'is a Magnet in World of New Terrorism': He Acts as a Lure to the Dangerous Loners who Populate the Ranks of Terrorists," *National Post*, August 20, 1999: A14.

[21] Gunaratna, *Inside Al Qaeda*.

[22] Ibid.

This increased cooperation was apparent in the UAE's actions in the immediate aftermath of the 9/11 attacks. The country began sharing intelligence with the United States and expressed support for US and NATO actions against al-Qaeda.[23] In an official pronouncement after the attacks, UAE President Sheikh Zayed bin Sultan al-Nahyan called for "a strong international alliance to eradicate terrorism, and all those who provide assistance to it or harbor [sic] it."[24]

Much of this cooperation was apparent in its responses to US international military initiatives. The government severed its diplomatic ties with the Taliban before even Saudi Arabia or Pakistan.[25] After the US invasion, it quickly established ties with the post-invasion Karzai government and contributed some troops to the international military force in the country.[26] The UAE also allowed the United States to use its territory for operations, although not offensive actions.[27] For example, about 500 US military personnel were located in the UAE after the 9/11 attacks and the country allowed the United States to use its ports and air bases for travel to and from Iraq and Afghanistan.[28] Moreover, while the UAE was hesitant about US calls for an invasion of Iraq, it did call for Iraqi leader Saddam Hussein to relinquish power and offered him amnesty.[29]

In addition to its international actions, the UAE also took steps against potential domestic terrorist threats. For example, after the United States

[23] David Reevely, "The New World Order: On the Eve of a Possible War, David Reevely Looks at how Major Nations are Choosing Sides," *The Ottawa Citizen*, September 17, 2001: A4; Hugh Pope, "Attack on America: Forging an Arab Coalition May Be Tough for Bush – His Father's Success in '90 Will Be Hard to Copy," *Wall Street Journal*, September 18, 2001: 3.

[24] David Reevely, "The New World Order: On the Eve of a Possible War, David Reevely Looks at how Major Nations are Choosing Sides," *The Ottawa Citizen*, September 17, 2001: A4; Michael Janse, "Arabs Give Support – On Condition," *Irish Times*, September 18, 2001: 10.

[25] Yaroslav Trofimov, "UAE Breaks Off Diplomatic Ties with the Taliban – Afghan Regime Keeps Support from Pakistan, Saudi Arabia," *Wall Street Journal*, September 24, 2001: 4.

[26] Kristian Coates Ulrichsen, "The Persian Gulf States and Afghanistan: Regional Geopolitics and Competing Interests," *Asia Policy* 17 (2014).

[27] Yaroslav Trofimov, "Disharmony Over Iraq Extends to Arab League," *Wall Street Journal*, February 21, 2003: A2.

[28] Rajiv Chandrasekaran, "Anti-American Sentiment Grows in Persian Gulf; Kuwait Says Attack on US Marines Plotted by Cell Linked to Al Qaeda," *Toronto Star*, October 13, 2002: B05; Christopher M. Davidson, *Dubai: The Vulnerability of Success* (New York: Columbia University Press, 2008).

[29] Ibid.; Guy Chazan and Hugh Pope, "Turkey Says No to US Troops – Vote Ignites Political Crisis Showing Cost to Friends of America's Iraq Stance," *Wall Street Journal*, March 3, 2003: A2.

provided information to the UAE on a French Algerian in the country suspected of planning attacks on European targets, the UAE moved to arrest him.[30] And the government detained Qari Saifullahd Akhtar, leader of a banned Pakistani militant group, after 9/11.[31] The government also took steps against its citizens participating in al-Qaeda operations abroad. One official in the country said he would "kick the butt" of any terrorist recruiters in the country.[32]

The UAE took even more dramatic efforts on terrorist financing.[33] The government shut down several bank accounts tied to terrorist groups and individuals the US designated as connected with terrorism.[34] The government also moved against the *hawala*, informal money exchange systems the United States claims were used to fund al-Qaeda and shut down at least one of the exchanges.[35] As a result of these efforts, by 2002, the Financial Action Task Force determined the country was no longer a risk.[36] UAE efforts continued; in 2007, the government ordered numerous accounts frozen due to suspicion of terrorist connections.[37]

There were still a few issues on counterterrorism with the United Arab Emirates, however. Despite its progress, concerns persisted about terrorist financing. As late as 2010, leaked US embassy cables revealed the United States believed the Haqqani network in Pakistan received "significant funds" through the UAE, primarily through extortion of the country's

[30] James Barry, "EU Calls Emergency Summit on Terrorism," *International Herald Tribune*, September 18, 2001: 4.
[31] "Pakistani Militant Freed Despite Al Qaeda Links," *The Hindustan Times*, May 22, 2007.
[32] Yaroslav Trofimov, "Border War: Would-Be Holy Warriors Can't Fight Their Way to Afghan Battlefields – Arab Governments Won't Let Potential Soldiers Leave Home," *Wall Street Journal*, November 16, 2001: 1.
[33] "Officials Move to Halt the Easy Movement of Money in Dubai," *The Irish Examiner*, November 7, 2001; Michael Jansen, "How Region Lines Up Behind US Campaign," *Irish Times*, October 8, 2001: 6.
[34] Michael Jansen, "How Region Lines Up Behind US Campaign," *Irish Times*, October 8, 2001: 6; Roula Khalaf and Robin Allen, "Arabia Bridles at Americans' Insistence on al-Qaeda Cash: Saudi Arabia and the Gulf Have Become the Focus of US Efforts to Track the Money Driving Islamic Militancy," *Financial Times*, February 21, 2002: 10.
[35] Robin Allen, "UAE to Tighten Rules for 'Terrorist' Cash System," *Financial Times*, November 6, 2002: 12; John Willman, "Trail of Terrorist Dollars that Spans the World: Suitcases of Cash, Informal Money Transfers, Standard Banking Procedures – al-Qaeda Used Them All to Pay the Bills of Terrorism, Reports John Willman," *Financial Times*, November 29, 2001: 11.
[36] Davidson, *Dubai: The Vulnerability of Success*.
[37] Janardhan Meena, "UAE: Dirty Money a Worry," *IPS-InterPress Service*, March 19, 2007.

Pashtun community.[38] The US reportedly saw the UAE as a "strategic gap" that terrorist groups could leverage to gain funds.[39] These issues, however, did not represent the same level of official neglect as did earlier terrorist financing concerns.

RELIGIOUS CONTENTION

This counterterrorism cooperation occurred as the country experienced widespread, if muted, Islamic contention. The UAE's populace holds very conservative Islamic values, and numerous Islamic groups are active in the country. While many of these groups are tied to the state, some groups operate – or attempt to operate – independently. There have been instances of contention over religious issues, including some criticism of the state's ties to the United States. And some in the country were supportive of al-Qaeda and affiliated groups.

Pre-9/11

General religious sentiment was apparent in the UAE before 9/11. Emirati society is marked by conservative Islamic beliefs, including an emphasis on modesty in dress – especially among women – and limits on public religious activity by non-Muslims. And some noted that there appeared to be greater expression of conservative Islamic values in the 1990s and later than when the country was formed, as seen with the veiling of women and conservative dress among men.[40] Moreover, several Islamist groups were present in the country; many of these are connected to the regime but still undertake religious activities in society. And at least one Islamist group existed that was independent of the regime, al-Islah. This group emerged in the 1970s and was still active as of 2012 when the UAE government began arresting its members; for example, in October of that year, an al-Islah official wrote an op-ed in the *Guardian* decrying the state's actions against the group.[41]

---

[38] Declan Walsh, "The US Embassy Cables: Middle East: Saudi Arabia is Cash Machine for Islamist Groups, Says Clinton: Riyadh Failing to Act Against Rich Donors Bankrolling Terrorism," *The Guardian*, December 6, 2010: 4.

[39] Eric Lichtblau and Eric Schmitt, "US Faults Arab Allies on Terror Financing," *International Herald Tribune*, December 7, 2010: 6.

[40] Vania Carvalho Pinto, *Nation-Building, State and the Genderframing of Women's Rights in the United Arab Emirates (1971–2009)*, (Reading, UK: Ithaca Press, 2012).

[41] "Islah 'Does Not Represent UAE Interests,'" *The National*, October 5, 2012.

While political activism is rare and limited in the UAE, there were several incidents before 9/11 that indicated the presence of religious contention in the country. For example, in 2000, Islamist groups around the world called for a boycott of Coca-Cola due to US support for Israel. The sale of Coca-Cola products dropped 20 percent in the UAE, indicating support for the boycott.[42] Similarly, a large group from the UAE attended a major Deobandi conference – the form of Islam arising from Pakistan that influenced the Taliban – in Pakistan in 2001.[43] The presence of UAE citizens at the conference thus indicates some Islamist presence in the country.

There were also indications of support for the al-Qaeda and Taliban, as well as participation in those groups. During the 1990s, numerous donors from the UAE reportedly funded the Taliban during its efforts to seize all of Afghanistan.[44] Moreover, Said Mokhles, a prominent member of the Egyptian terrorist group Gemaah-Islamiyah that was tied to al-Qaeda, reportedly had numerous connections in the UAE.[45] Indirect evidence of support for al-Qaeda and the Taliban in the UAE comes from reports concerning the near US air strike on an al-Qaeda training camp in Afghanistan before 9/11; the United States apparently called off the attack partly because of the possibility of members of the UAE royal family being in the camp.[46] Assuming this report is credible, it suggests support or at least interest in the activities of al-Qaeda among prominent UAE citizens.

Post-9/11

Various expressions of religious contention continued after the 9/11 attacks. Islamic activism occasionally occurred, and the arrest of some Islamists suggests their presence prior to government action. Moreover, there is some evidence that Emiratis were critical of the UAE for its ties to the United States and connections between some in the country and

---

[42] Khaled Dawoud and Brian Whitaker, "Sainsbury's on Egyptian Boycott List," *The Guardian*, December 7, 2000: 1.

[43] Dietrich Reetz Reetz, "The Deoband Universe: What Makes a Transcultural and Transnational Educational Movement of Islam?," *Comparative Studies of South Asia, Africa, and the Middle East* 27, no. 1 (2007).

[44] Seth Jones, "The Rise of Afghanistan's Insurgency: State Failure and Jihad," *International Security* 32, no. 4 (2008).

[45] David Leppard, Chris Hastings, Jessica Berry and Marie Colvin, "The Global Terrorist," *Sunday Times*, February 7, 1999: 19.

[46] Coll, *Ghost Wars: The Secret History of the CIA, Afghanistan and bin Ladin, from the Soviet Invasion to September 10, 2011*.

al-Qaeda affiliated groups persisted. Additionally, the UAE came under criticism from international Islamist groups for its cooperation with the United States.

There were continuing indications of Islamists being present in the country, as well as general religious sentiment in society. Several Islamist websites were based in the UAE, including one – Mohajroon – that the government shut down in 2007.[47] Similarly, shortly after the 9/11 attacks, the UAE government arrested a judge on an Islamic court and other citizens in the Emirate of Sharjah, who it accused of being Islamists.[48] And there was significant contention in the UAE over the Danish cartoon controversy. For example, a columnist in the UAE paper *al-Bayan* claimed "the disaster of the Danish cartoons is that this is the West . . . ridiculing and insulting the Prophet Muhammad."[49] And some Islamist media outlets in the UAE called for a boycott of Danish goods over the cartoons.[50]

There was also widespread anger – some tied to religion – at the United States, particularly its counterterrorism operations. The United States is very unpopular in the UAE; a 2009 poll put disapproval of the US at 87 percent.[51] This was particularly apparent in anger over the US invasion of Iraq in 2003. *Al-Khaleef*, a UAE newspaper, called the war a "total defeat for the values of humanity."[52] And there were reports of anti-US protests in the country over the war, which is very rare for the UAE.[53] Moreover, professional associations in the UAE discussed plans for a

47 Steve Coll and Susan B. Glasser, "Terrorists Turn to the Web; Al Qaeda, Its Offshoots Get 'Virtual Sanctuary,' Tactical Agility," *Asian Wall Street Journal*, August 8, 2005: A7; Stewart Bell, "Terror Suspects in Canada, UK Made Plans Online; Aim to Become 'Martyrs'; Son of Moroccan Diplomat on Trial in Britain," *National Post*, April 26, 2007: A7.

48 Yaroslav Trofimov, "UAE Money Firm Likely Was a Hub for Terror Attacks – Believed bin Laden Cohort Got Funds from Another in US," *Wall Street Journal*, November 2, 2001: 2.

49 Anthony Brown, "Muslim Ire Increases, but 'Day of Anger' Has Few Takers," *The Times*, February 4, 2006: 8.

50 Andrew Higgins, "Cartoon Puts Danish Firms on the Spot; Hit by Muslim Fury, Businesses Weigh Sales Against Values," *Wall Street Journal*, February 14, 2006: 6; David Rennie, "How Clerics Spread Hatred over Cartoons," *The Daily Telegraph*, February 7, 2006: 12.

51 "Saudis Insist US Cannot Use Facilities for Iraq Attack," *Irish Times*, November 4, 2002: 9; Mona Yacoubian, "Bridging the Divide: US Efforts to Engage the Muslim World," *The Middle East Journal* 63, no. 3 (2009).

52 Gerald Butt, "Arab Press Plays Down Progress of Allied Forces," *The Daily Telegraph*, March 22, 2003: 12.

53 Richard Breeston and Stephen Farrell, "Tehran Protesters Stone Embassy in Anti-British Riot," *The Times*, March 29, 2003: 13.

boycott of US goods over the war.[54] Similarly, there were reports of
anger in the UAE over US counterterrorism initiatives following the 9/11
attacks, particularly efforts that affected "traditional attitudes to religion
and culture and on business methods," such as financing restrictions.[55]
And some in the country saw US foreign policy as an attempt to "kill off
the Muslim countries."[56]

Various pieces of evidence suggest many in the UAE were critical of the
government for failing to live up to its conservative ideals and working
too closely with the United States. For example, Islamic groups in the
country reportedly "accused the rulers of permitting the construction of
churches, of actions contradicting shariah, and of allowing women to
wear jewelry."[57] The regime was also criticized for hosting US troops
and naval vessels.[58] Moreover, some in the country were angered at the
state's moves against fundraising, as it made it difficult for individuals to
act on what they saw as their religious beliefs.[59]

Several individuals tied to militants appeared to have remained in the
country after 9/11. In 2010, the UAE government arrested two Pakistanis who were accused of fundraising and recruitment for militants in
the country.[60] Similarly, Abu Taha al-Sudan, the reported leader of al-
Qaeda's operations in East Africa, reportedly operated out of both the
UAE and Somalia.[61] And in 2008 the UAE arrested Naji Hamdan, a US
citizen, who they claim had ties to Ansar al-Sunnah, an Iraqi militant
group.[62] Similarly, an associate of the Haqqani network in Pakistan and

---

[54] Lachlan Carmichael, "US Firms Fear Stronger Boycott: If Iraq War Erupts, Organizers
of the Boycotting of American Products in Mideast Are Ready," *The Arab American
News*, January 10, 2003: 2.

[55] Roula Khalaf and Robin Allen, "Arabia Bridles at Americans' Insistence on al-Qaeda
Cash: Saudi Arabia and the Gulf Have Become the Focus of US Efforts to Track the
Money Driving Islamic Militancy," *Financial Times*, February 21, 2002: 10.

[56] Wanda Krause, *Women in Civil Society: The State, Islamism, and Networks in the UAE*
(New York: Palgrave MacMillan, 2008).

[57] James Brandon, "As Dubai Thrives, an Eye on Political Reform; The City-State's Leader
Died Wednesday, Leaving a Legacy of Economic Growth but Political Inflexibility," *The
Christian Science Monitor*, January 6, 2006: 10.

[58] James Brandon, "As Dubai Thrives, an Eye on Political Reform; The City-State's Leader
Died Wednesday, Leaving a Legacy of Economic Growth but Political Inflexibility," *The
Christian Science Monitor*, January 6, 2006: 10.

[59] Krause, *Women in Civil Society: The State, Islamism, and Networks in the UAE*.

[60] "UAE Tries Two Pakistanis on Qaeda Links: Report," *Al-Arabiya*, December 27,
2010.

[61] "Somalia: Most Wanted Al-Qaida Suspects," *The Guardian*, January 10, 2007: 5.

[62] "UAE Prosecutor Claims American Man on Trial Had Ties to Al-Qaeda," *The Daily
Star*, August 25, 2009.

Afghanistan, Amir Abdullah, reportedly traveled frequently to the UAE to fundraise for the group.[63]

There was also some indication of outright support for al-Qaeda in the country. There were several reports of UAE citizens fighting with al-Qaeda and the Taliban in Afghanistan, as well as general sympathy with the movement.[64] In addition to this, non-governmental "welfare associations" in the UAE reportedly contributed money to militants in Afghanistan and Pakistan.[65] There are also some signs of connections to outside militant movements; for example, after the deadly attacks on a Moscow theater by Chechen militants in 2002, the militants reportedly made phone calls to the UAE, which may indicate they had contacts there.[66]

In addition to apparent ties between UAE citizens and militant groups, the state experienced a few threats from militants. In 2002, the UAE government arrested an al-Qaeda member reportedly planning attacks.[67] And in 2009, a terrorist cell affiliated with al-Qaeda was reportedly planning to attack several targets in Dubai, including Dubai Towers, before UAE authorities arrested the group.[68]

RELIGION–STATE RELATIONSHIP

Thus, the UAE regime faced Islamic contention throughout the 1990s after 9/11, including activism over religious issues, criticism of its ties to the United States, and outright support for al-Qaeda and other groups. This Islamic contention occurred in the context of a unique religion–state relationship. The UAE regime generally shared its populace's conservative values and concerns about international Islamic issues, and implemented policies in support of this sentiment. But the government was wary of Islamic activism; it often attempted to co-opt groups and, if this failed, to actively repress them.

---

[63] "US Blacklists Taliban Associates," *Al-Jazeera.net*, July 23, 2010.
[64] David Pugliese, "How the War Will Be Fought: Military Experts Warn that the Enemy is Ready to Send Wave after Wave of Body Bags Back to the West." *The Ottawa Citizen*, October 3, 2001: A6; Davidson, *Dubai: The Vulnerability of Success*.
[65] Ibid.
[66] Nick Paton Walsh, "Threat of War: Chechen Rebels Phoned Gulf During Siege: Moscow Says Theatre Hostage Takers Were Funded from Saudi Arabia," *The Guardian*, December 5, 2002: 1.
[67] Davidson, *Dubai: The Vulnerability of Success*.
[68] "UAE Authorities Nail Qaeda Terror Ring Plotting to Blow Up Dubai Targets," *Asian New International*, September 17, 2009.

Much of its support for Islamic causes is apparent in its policies toward the 1990s' crises in the Balkans involving Muslims. These crises generated significant attention among Muslims due to the fact that the primary victims of each conflict were Muslims. Calls for international action by Islamic figures were common in this era. Along with other Muslim countries, the UAE moved in response to this religious sentiment. During the conflict in the former Yugoslavia in the 1990s, the UAE sent significant amounts of aid to the country. During a 1995 telethon, the UAE raised $43 million for Bosnians.[69] The UAE also operated airlifts for wounded Bosnians during that conflict.[70] Similarly, the UAE sent numerous relief planes to Kosovo during the conflict over that country's independence from Serbia.[71] The UAE also set up refugee camps in Albania for Kosovars driven out by the fighting, and built numerous mosques throughout the country during its reconstruction.[72] And the UAE was the only Arab state to participate in the NATO military action against Kosovo.[73]

The UAE also undertook humanitarian actions on other causes important to Muslims. The UAE contributed heavily to the reconstruction of Kuwait after the Iraqi invasion in the early 1990s.[74] The UAE also sent military engineers to Somalia as part of the United Nation's mission there in the early 1990s.[75] This continued even after 9/11. The UAE was very active in relief efforts for several natural disasters and wars that occurred after 2001. For example, the country pledged $100 million in aid after a 2005 Iranian earthquake, and sent $20 million in aid to Indonesia after the tsunami there in the same year.[76] Similarly, the country provided aid to Lebanon and the Palestinian territories after conflicts in those areas with Israel. In 2006, the UAE – along with Kuwait and Saudi Arabia – sent

---

[69] Peter Waldman, "Growing Support: Islamic States Move Warily to Help Bosnian Brethren," *Asian Wall Street Journal*, August 14, 1995: 1.

[70] Davidson, *Dubai: The Vulnerability of Success.*

[71] Michael Binyon, "Iraq Stands with Milosevic: Other Islamic Nations Condemn Ethnic Cleansing in Kosovo." *The Ottawa Citizen*, April 6, 1999: A7.

[72] Janine di Giovanni, "The Rape of Kosovo," *The Times*, June 19, 1999: 17; Jeff Heinrich, "Pullout of International Resources Rankling Kosovars," *The Gazette*, May 23, 2003: A1; Michael B. Bushku, "Albania and the Middle East," *Mediterranean Quarterly* 24, no. 2 (2013).

[73] Davidson, *Dubai: The Vulnerability of Success.*

[74] Ibid.

[75] Ibid.

[76] Ibid.; Nasir Malick, "Fighters Rescue Children from the Rubble," *The Daily Telegraph*, October 11, 2005: 004; Neil MacFarquhar, "Disaster Aid Ignites Controversy among Arabs: Are They Stingy?" *International Herald Tribune*, January 5, 2005: 4.

$90 million in aid to Hezbollah in Lebanon and promised to help rebuild the Nahr al-Bahred refugee camp in Lebanon that was destroyed in fighting with Israel in 2008.[77] The UAE also promised to help the Gaza Strip recover from fighting with Israel in 2009.[78] And the UAE set up a region-wide education initiative in 2007.[79]

The UAE's aforementioned support for some regimes suspected of harboring terrorists is another example of its religion–state ties. As was noted, the UAE was one of three countries to recognize the Taliban government in Afghanistan. This was partially strategic, as a way to foster close ties with a state adjacent to their sometimes-rival Iran.[80] It was also, however, partly tied to their support for religious causes. A political analyst in the region noted after 9/11 that the UAE support for the Taliban was due to UAE officials' perception of the group as "young devout Muslims who are on the way to clean Afghanistan from the mess it is in."[81]

The UAE also took action on some domestic and international issues in line with religious sentiment. The government often acted to enforce the conservative religious values of the populace, especially when criticism arose over the regime's handling of issues. For example, in the 1990s the UAE government arrested an Indian theater group for putting on a play some in the country saw as blasphemous.[82] Similarly, in 2006, the UAE justice minister called the Danish cartoons depicting Muhammad "cultural terrorism."[83] And in 2009, the government decided to not issue a visa to an Israeli tennis player for a tournament being held in the country in order to avoid criticism from religious conservatives.[84]

Several of the country's policies also reflect an attempt to act on or spread religious sentiment. While the UAE arrests people for political

---

[77] "Region," *The Amman*, July 22, 2006; "Funding Shortage Fuels Credibility Gap over Nahr al-Bared," *The Daily Star*, December 31, 2008.

[78] "Gulf States Launch Arab Aid Plan to Rebuild Gaza," *Al-Arabiya*, February 21, 2009.

[79] Davidson, *Dubai: The Vulnerability of Success*.

[80] Ibid.

[81] Yaroslav Trofimov, "UAE Breaks Off Diplomatic Ties with the Taliban – Afghan Regime Keeps Support From Pakistan, Saudi Arabia," *Wall Street Journal*, September 24, 2001: 4.

[82] Salman Rushdie, "Islamic Curses: The World is Outraged by the International Terrorism of Muslim Extremists. But, from the Gulf to Pakistan, a Swathe of Retribution Against Dissidents Cries out for the West's Attention," *The Guardian*, July 13, 1993.

[83] "Knock, Knock. Who'll Dare?" *The Hindustan Times*, February 10, 2006.

[84] Ross Oakland, "Emirate Lobs Middle East Politics onto Tennis Court; Tournament Organizers Insist Israeli Barred over Safety Worries, not Gaza," *Toronto Star*, February 20, 2009: A13.

opposition or membership in certain religious and political groups, the government often releases prisoners if they can recite the Quran, indicating a religious element to their justice system.[85] The government also funded large Islamic conferences; for example, in 2004 it funded one with the subject of the "Prophet's Way of Dawa and Guidance."[86] And in 2008, Sheikh Mansour al-Nahyan, a high-level government minister, stated that the UAE would try to maintain "adherence to the national and indigenous traditions which are rooted in Islamic and Arab values" at a "National Identity Conference."[87] This extended to international affairs as well; for example, the UAE provides significant amounts of funding to several large French Islamic organizations.[88]

While the UAE did support religious causes and maintained official ties to Islam, the government was wary of Islamic activism and attempted to keep religious groups from being too influential. The regime has co-opted religious groups and limited their ability to operate independently throughout the country's existence. After 9/11, the government moved more actively against religious groups or avoiding policies that would increase their influence. For example, in 2007 the government moved against some Islamist web forums such as *Mohajroon*, which was shut down and its director threatened with arrest.[89] And some argued that the UAE government has been hesitant to crack down on what some see as inappropriate dress by tourists in the country in part because it "might send a message" to Islamists that the government was acting based on their demands.[90] The government has also made many terrorism-related arrests that may be connected to broader crackdowns on religious groups. Much of this involved charges of fundraising or providing other types of support. This includes the aforementioned two Pakistani men arrested for al-Qaeda links in 2010, and the American man arrested for ties to Ansar

[85] Davidson, *Dubai: The Vulnerability of Success.*

[86] Ibid.

[87] Pinto, *Nation-Building, State and the Genderframing of Women's Rights in the United Arab Emirates (1971–2009)*: 63.

[88] Ian Johnson and John Carreyrou, "Islam and Europe: A Volatile Mix: As More Muslims Settle Throughout Europe, Ominous Trend Emerges; As Isolation Develops, France Sees 'Political Islam' Urging Intolerance; A Push Toward Virginity Certificates," *Wall Street Journal*, July 11, 2005: A1.

[89] Stewart Bell, "Terror Suspects in Canada, UK Made Plans Online; Aim to Become 'Martyrs'; Son of Moroccan Diplomat on Trial in Britain," *National Post*, April 26, 2007: A7.

[90] Watson, "Dubai Dress Code: 'Cover up', UAE Women Tell Foreigners." Available at www.bbc.com/news/world-middle-east-18720920.

al-Sunnah in 2008.[91] Other examples include eight individuals tried for allegedly supporting terrorism in 2009.[92]

This was especially apparent after the Arab Spring uprisings, as the UAE government became concerned about Islamist activism threatening its survival. The government moved against several individuals and groups it claimed were tied to the Muslim Brotherhood. The UAE took away the citizenship of six people in 2011 for alleged ties to the Muslim Brotherhood.[93] In early 2013, the government arrested more than ten people it accused of recruiting Egyptians and fundraisers on behalf of the Muslim Brotherhood; this broadened to 30 by the time the individuals were put on trial later that year.[94] The government also claimed the Muslim Brotherhood was attempting to "weaken" the UAE by "defaming its institutions" over Twitter.[95]

The UAE also moved against the aforementioned al-Islah movement and other Islamists in the country. In 2013, the government rounded up nearly 70 members of the group, accusing them of plotting a coup against the state.[96] The government attempted to do so in a subtle manner, however. For example, after the arrest of several Islamists in 2012, the government said it did not represent "a security crackdown but a limited measure to advise and help those who 'deviated' and attempted to harm their country."[97]

HISTORICAL BACKGROUND

These domestic dynamics behind the nature of the US-UAE counterterrorism relationship arose from the historical development of the religion–state relationship in the country. The UAE is made up of conservative Islamic city-states, with domestic and foreign policies that reflect the

---

[91] "UAE Tries Two Pakistanis on Qaeda Links: Report," *Al-Arabiya*, December 27, 2010; Barbara Surk, "UAE Prosecutor Claims American Man on Trial had Ties to Al-Qaeda," *The Daily Star*, August 25, 2009.

[92] "UAE Tries Eight for Supporting 'Terrorism', Says Paper," *Daily News Egypt*, September 9, 2009.

[93] "UAE Strips Six 'Islamists' of Citizenship," *Al-Shorfa*, December 22, 2011.

[94] "UAE Busts Cell Linked to Egypt's Brotherhood, Report" *Khaleej Times*, January 1, 2013; "UAE Opens Trial of Muslim Brotherhood Suspects," *The New Zealand Herald*, November 6, 2013.

[95] "Dubai Says Islamists Trying to Weaken UAE via Twitter," *Al-Akhbar*, March 28, 2012.

[96] "UAE Islamists Convicted for Plotting Government Coup," *BBC News*, July 2, 2013.

[97] "UAE Official Says Islamists Arrested for 'Advice,' not Punishment," *BBC Monitoring Middle East – Political*, August 4, 2012.

country's Islamic sentiment. At the same time, the regime maintains strict control over society through its rentier system, and limits actions by Islamic groups that challenge the regime.

The UAE was formed in 1971 out of a group of British-ruled princely states. These emirates, referred to at the time as the Trucial States, had been a British protectorate since the late 1800s. After World War II, as occurred with many of the territories it possessed, the United Kingdom was increasingly struggling to maintain its role. Moreover, it faced some nationalist opposition in the Trucial States, with the Dubai National Front forming against British rule in the 1960s and 1950s.[98] In response to this pressure, the UK set up a federal system containing the seven emirates in the Trucial States, with the UAE gaining independence by the early 1970s.[99]

The UAE's society was very conservative, based on strict tribal customs and Islamic beliefs. The UAE society had, prior to statehood, been a tribal one strongly influenced by Wahhabism from Saudi Arabia.[100] Women often dressed traditionally, with full covering, in line with both the culture and religious law.[101] And there had been intermittent Islamist activity.[102] This includes some mainly expatriate groups, like the Muslim Brotherhood, and Tablighi Jamaat, the latter of which was particularly focused on the South Asian community.[103] And other groups focused on religious education or proselytism abroad, such as Murabitun and the Deen Intensive Program.[104] Other Islamist groups occasionally ran afoul of the state. Al-Islah, the aforementioned Islamist group, had been active in the country since the 1970s. And Ahmed Abu-Laban, an Islamist involved in the Danish cartoon protests, had originally operated from the 1980s but was expelled.[105] This is also apparent in more violent activism emanating from the country. There were reports of UAE citizens

[98] Davidson, *Dubai: The Vulnerability of Success.*

[99] Ibid.; Rosemarie Said Zahlan, *The Origins of the United Arab Emirates* (New York: St. Martin's Press, 1978).

[100] Mohamed Zayani, "Civil Society and Democratic Change in the Arab World: Promises and Impediments," *Comparative Studies of South Asia, Africa, and the Middle East* 32, no. 3 (2012).

[101] Noor al-Qasimi, "Immodest Modesty: Accommodating Dissent and the 'Abaya-as-Fashion in the Arab Gulf States," *Journal of Middle East Women's Studies* 6, no. 1 (2010).

[102] Krause, *Women in Civil Society: The State, Islamism, and Networks in the UAE.*

[103] Ibid.

[104] Ibid.

[105] Andrew Higgins, "News in Depth: How Cartoons Sparked an Outcry; Danish Paper's Drawings Showing Muhammad United Islamic Clerics and Secular Arabs in Protest," *Wall Street Journal*, February 8, 2006: 14.

fighting in Afghanistan against the Soviets in the 1980s.[106] And in 1981 the Hyatt Regency in Dubai was bombed in protest of its serving alcohol to Emiratis.[107]

The government of the UAE reflected this religious sentiment. The government incorporated many elements of Islam into its functioning; Islam was the state religion and its legal system is made up of shariah law and qadi courts.[108] It began actively pressing religious laws in the late 1970s.[109] The government also pushed Islam domestically, building mosques and supporting numerous Islamic charities.[110] And the government supported some of the aforementioned Islamist groups; for example, it reportedly funded the Murabitun's activities in Spain in order to spread Islam in that country.[111] The government also funded the activities of Islamic scholars from a variety of countries.[112]

The UAE state was rather strong with significant control over society. The state set up what Davidson calls a "ruling bargain" characterized by oil wealth, a patrimonial network, government employment, and the aforementioned Islamic aspects.[113] The state's control over society is a classic example of an oil-facilitated rentier state. The UAE has significant oil reserves, which it has drawn on to facilitate its economic development.[114] The country's oil wealth allows it to provide significant support to the populace, including jobs and economic benefits.[115] It is also able to maintain a repressive capacity to control domestic unrest.

[106] Samina Ahmed, "The United States and Terrorism in Southwest Asia: September 11 and Beyond," *International Security* 26, no. 3 (2002).

[107] Christoper M. Davidson, *The United Arab Emirates: A Study in Survival* (Boulder, CO: Lynne Reiner Publishers, 2005).

[108] Ibid.; Vali Nasr, "Regional Implications of Shi'a Revival in Iraq," *The Washington Monthly* 27, no. 3 (2004).

[109] Davidson, *The United Arab Emirates: A Study in Survival*; Pinto, *Nation-Building, State, and the Genderframing of Women's Rights in the United Arab Emirates (1971–2009)*.

[110] Davidson, *Dubai: The Vulnerability of Success*.

[111] Krause, *Women in Civil Society: The State, Islamism, and Networks in the UAE*.

[112] Ibid.

[113] Davidson, *Dubai: The Vulnerability of Success*: 103.

[114] Frauke Heard-Bey, "The United Arab Emirates: Statehood and Nation-Building in a Traditional Society," *Middle East Journal* 59, no. 3 (2005); Ross. Michael L., "Does Oil Hinder Democracy?," *World Politics* 53, no. 3 (2001); Gerald Butt, "Oil and Gas in the UAE," in *United Arab Emirates: A New Perspective*, eds. Ibrahim al-Abed and Peter Hellyer (London: Trident Press, 1997).

[115] Davidson, *Dubai: The Vulnerability of Success*; Heard-Bey, "The United Arab Emirates: Statehood and Nation-Building in a Traditional Society." John Willoughby, "Segmented Feminization and the Decline of Neopatriarchy in GCC Countries of the Persian Gulf," *Comparative Studies of South Asia, Africa, and the Middle East* 28, no. 1 (2008).

There have been some political and economic reforms, most of them since 2000, but the regime has remained primarily in place. In 2006, the UAE set up the National Federal Council, a parliamentary body with 40 elected members, to allow more input into its decision-making.[116] Some of the emirs also added intermediaries to hear petitions from citizens – which the emir had previously handled alone – to allow for greater input into the government.[117] And in 2001, the Sharjah emir appointed five women as consultants to the government.[118] The government also implemented some economic reforms to diversify the economy, by focusing on shipping, finance, and other sectors; by 2008, 90 percent of the UAE's Gross Domestic Product came from non-oil industries.[119]

The UAE's foreign policies are marked by its Islamic values as well as its desire for regional stability. Sheikh Zayeb bin Sultan al-Nahyan, the UAE's first president who passed away in 2004, laid out the state's foreign policy priorities in a 1972 speech: the UAE's goals would involve: "maintaining good relations and cooperation" with neighboring states, "settling disputes that arise" in the region, a "commitment to the Arab world," "improving Islamic solidarity" worldwide, and "fruitful cooperation with all nations."[120] The government often focused on securing oil markets and regional stability.[121] As part of this, it has become dependent on the United States for defense.[122] But the government has also emphasized Islamic and Arab causes in much of its foreign policy.[123] It joined the Arab League and Organization of the Islamic Conference shortly after it gained independence.[124] The government gave significant aid to Egypt and Syria during the 1973 war with Israel, as well as a good amount of aid to the Palestinian Liberation Organization.[125] And the UAE was active

[116] Anoushiravan Ehteshami and Steven Wright, "Political Change in the Arab Oil Monarchies: From Liberalization to Enfranchisement," *Royal Institute of International Affairs* 83, no. 5 (2007).

[117] Davidson, *Dubai: The Vulnerability of Success.*

[118] Ehteshami and Wright, "Political Change in the Arab Oil Monarchies: From Liberalization to Enfranchisement."

[119] Davidson, *Dubai: The Vulnerability of Success.*

[120] Rugh, *Diplomacy and Defense Policy of the United Arab Emirates*: 5.

[121] Peter Hellyer, "Evolution of UAE Foreign Policy," in *United Arab Emirates: A New Perspective*, eds. Ibrahim al-Abed and Peter Hellyer (London: Trident Press, 1997).

[122] David A. Lake, "Legitimating Power: The Domestic Politics of US International Hierarchy," *International Security* 38, no. 2 (2013).

[123] Hellyer, "Evolution of UAE Foreign Policy"; Davidson, *Dubai: The Vulnerability of Success.*

[124] Rugh, *Diplomacy and Defense Policy of the United Arab Emirates.*

[125] Davidson, *Dubai: The Vulnerability of Success.*

in Islamic causes outside the region. It developed close ties to Pakistan and Afghanistan, and tried to promote Islamic causes in Central Asia and elsewhere.[126]

Domestically, the UAE's policies represent a balance between its rentier-driven control over society and conservative values. While the government promotes conservative Islamic values, it exerts a strict control over non-governmental organization activities.[127] Much of its efforts focus on Islamist groups. The state generally supports Islamic-oriented activities, but takes steps to ensure what these groups are doing does not threaten the state or go against its interests.[128] The government also has numerous limits on the Muslim Brotherhood's activities. Members are not allowed to contact other members outside the UAE, and the government does not allow Muslim Brotherhood members to participate in other groups.[129] And welfare organizations require licenses from the Ministry of Labor and Social Affairs, and cannot include non-Emiratis.[130] This extends to cultural organizations. For example, the Emirates Association for the Revival of Folks Arts formed in 1980, with its budget under the complete control over the government.[131] The control over these groups may be due partly to a desire to promote Emirati involvement in social groups or encourage cultural activities, but they are also likely related to a desire to control all social organization and limit outside influence.

ANALYSIS

Thus, dynamics in the UAE are distinct from those in Pakistan. When the United States began pressing states on counterterrorism in the 1990s, the ties between religion and state in the UAE made it hesitant to reverse policies like enabling terrorist financing and supporting some states the United States accused of terrorist sponsorship. After the US intensified its pressure after 9/11, though, the distance the UAE state kept from Islamic groups – despite its official support for Islam – allowed it to implement

---

[126] Shireen T. Hunter, "Religion, Politics, and Security in Central Asia," *SAIS Review* 2, no. 1 (2001); Brahma Chellany, "Fighting Terrorism in Southern Asia: The Lessons of History," *International Security* 26, no. 3 (2002).

[127] Zayani, "Civil Society and Democratic Change in the Arab World: Promises and Impediments"; Davidson, *The United Arab Emirates: A Study in Survival*.

[128] Krause, *Women in Civil Society: The State, Islamism, and Networks in the UAE*.

[129] Ibid.

[130] Davidson, *The United Arab Emirates: A Study in Survival*.

[131] Ibid.

counterterrorism policies in line with US efforts despite religious opposition.

As in other chapters, though, I will move beyond hinting at the connections between the UAE religion–state relationship and its counterterrorism cooperation and present in-depth evidence through a variety of qualitative methods validating the claims I made in Chapters 1 and 2. Specifically I will show that the UAE's religion–state relationship explains both its *weak counterterrorism cooperation* in the 1990s and the *rise in cooperation* after 9/11. This change happened not because of a change in the religion–state relationship, but because of the peculiar nature of this relationship. Specifically, I will demonstrate that: (1) the UAE regime initially followed religious sentiment on its counterterrorism policies, but effectively ignored religious sentiment after US pressure increased after 9/11, (2) this was possible because its political institutions limited the power of Islamic groups despite official ties to Islam, and (3) while other factors – like security concerns – mattered, the religion–state relationship in the UAE was the driving force behind its counterterrorism cooperation. Because the UAE is such a closed society, it is difficult to get insight into leaders' decision-making or even the presence of Islamist activity absent official crack downs. As a result, I rely on inferences I draw from the primary evidence I presented earlier and insights from secondary studies to a greater extent than in the Pakistan and Turkey case studies.

Religion–State Effects

As the previous discussion shows, the UAE's counterterrorism cooperation with the United States was connected to the nature of its religion–state relationship. Initially, the UAE was minimally cooperative with the United States. The government maintained ties to regimes that the US accused of supporting terrorism, like the Taliban in Afghanistan and Sudan. It also tolerated support for al-Qaeda among its citizens, and allowed financial flows that benefited al-Qaeda and other terrorist groups to flow through its banking system. While the US protested many of these policies – or lack of policies – the UAE did little to address US complaints.

This was due to the nature of the UAE's relationship with religion. As an officially Islamic state, with numerous roles for Islam in its laws and functioning, the UAE had some affinity with similarly Islamic regimes. As I noted earlier, some of the UAE's support for the Taliban and Sudan were due to the UAE leaders' perceptions of these regimes as pious Islamic organizations. Likewise, while there is no indication the UAE was actively supporting al-Qaeda, the conservative Islamic views of much of its populace would frown on restrictions on financial support to Islamic movements abroad. Limiting fundraising for al-Qaeda and terrorist use of its banking system, then, would have produced some popular discontent, which the regime likely hoped to avoid. The UAE faced backlash from some in society over its crackdown on terrorist financing after 9/11, and it is likely the regime foresaw a similar reaction in the 1990s. At the same time, there may have been more active support, or at least sympathy, for al-Qaeda among UAE. Thus, positive views of al-Qaeda among some in the regime, enabled by its official Islamic strictures, would also make the UAE less likely to crack down on financing.

This all changed after 9/11. As with all other Muslim states, the UAE faced a stark choice as the United States began its Global War on Terror; those who did not actively cooperate in the struggle against al-Qaeda would be viewed as enemies of the United States. The UAE, dependent on the US for security assistance, could hardly afford to be placed in the latter camp. The UAE thus moved to bring its counterterrorism policies in line with US efforts, cracking down on terrorists in the country, restricting financing for al-Qaeda and other groups, and ending diplomatic support for regimes like the Taliban.

Of course, all Muslim states endeavored to avoid negative repercussions from crossing the United States. What distinguished the UAE from countries like Pakistan was its greater freedom of action vis-à-vis religious groups, thanks to its religion–state relationship. While the UAE had affinity for Islamic causes it was not willing to follow religious sentiment to the point of threatening its hold on power, as would have happened if it had crossed the United States. Moreover, because it had always limited the influence of religious groups, it was able to implement policies unpopular with them – and actively repress them – without fearing a widespread backlash.

Historical Processes

This is not just a case of a government responding to domestic pressure when it threatens the regime, however. The specific situation in which the regime was able to ignore religious opposition to counterterrorism cooperation after earlier acting in line with religious sentiment arose from the historical development of the UAE's religion–state relationship. The UAE's ability to ignore and repress religious opposition was due to the type of system set up on its founding. By establishing a confederative system that centralized power within each Emirates' ruling elite, it limited the ability of opposition groups – including religious ones – from openly acting and threatening the regime. But because the regime was also closely tied to Islam, it did engage in some religiously influenced policies, in contrast to other states that restricted religious groups but were more secular in nature, like Turkey. Analyzing the UAE's counterterrorism policies as "just politics" – giving in to domestic pressure when it did not matter, and acting against when it was able and willing to do so – would leave us unable to understand both why the UAE initially was uncooperative and so quickly became cooperative, even as it followed some religious policies.

The religion–state relationship of the UAE had three overlapping effects on its Islamic politics over time, which contributed to the nature of its counterterrorism cooperation. The first is the UAE regime's incentive to adopt religious policies, both domestic and international. As discussed earlier, the UAE's authority arises from a combination of its rentier policies and support for Islamic causes. Thus, the regime implemented religious policies partly to shore up its domestic legitimacy even if they did not directly benefit the regime or advance its interests. This extended to international affairs through its support for Muslim victims of conflicts and other initiatives. Likewise, I noted some observers who believe the UAE's lax terrorist financing regulations were motivated by a desire to avoid upsetting religious sentiment.

The second, closely related effect increased the likelihood of religious policies through affinity between UAE elites and religious sentiment. The official Islam of the UAE and support for religious causes made it more likely elites would emerge that shared the preferences and goals of some Islamic groups. This does not mean UAE royal members were in league with al-Qaeda. But just as some members of Emirati society were opposed to counterterrorism policies they saw as targeting Islam even though they did not support terrorism, it is possible some UAE elites did not see lax counterterrorism policies or outreach to suspected terrorist sponsors a major problem because of their shared religious affinity. For example, the ties between UAE royals and the Taliban – including the reported presence of UAE elites at an Afghanistan camp with bin Ladin – likely arose from this process.

And the third, countervailing, historical process is the weakness of these Islamist groups through increasingly restrictive UAE policies. Because of the UAE regime's minimal ties to religious groups, there was a lock-in effect in which the regime's fears of Islamist opposition led them to restrict Islamic political activity, weakening these groups and making it unlikely they would have the power to influence the regime in the future. As I discussed earlier, there are reports of the UAE expelling Islamist figures as early as the 1980s. And when Islamic contention became a serious concern for the regime after the Arab Spring uprisings, the state arrested mass numbers of activists it charged with supporting terrorism. The regime also developed institutions to prevent the rise of widespread Islamic contention, such as the limits on Muslim Brotherhood members' international contacts or interactions with other domestic groups.

These three processes combined to create the situation in which the UAE was at first minimally, and later extensively, cooperative on counterterrorism. Because the UAE political institutions incentivized religious policies and made it likely individuals who support these policies will be influential, the UAE was initially uncooperative on terrorism as its leaders were hesitant to upset religious opinion by cracking down on terrorist financing and were supportive of states that the United States deemed terrorist sponsors. Yet, the regime did not face as extreme pressure from Islamic groups or widespread social unrest as in Pakistan due to the limits it placed on these groups' political activity. As a result, in contrast to Pakistan, the UAE did not experience a lock-in effect from its institutions in which earlier policies made it difficult for leaders to change course. When the United States pressed the UAE to reform its counterterrorism policies after the 9/11 attacks, the regime's freedom of movement enabled it to dramatically increase its cooperation.

Alternative Explanations

Granted, there are several alternative explanations for the nature of the UAE's counterterrorism cooperation. While the religion–state relationship in the country did figure prominently in its counterterrorism policies, the strength of the UAE state, its security situation, and relative stability are all also plausible explanations for its counterterrorism policies. As with the other countries I discuss in this book, however, these alternative explanations are either invalid or actually related to the religion–state relationship.

One obvious alternative explanation is the strength of the UAE state. The UAE had such significant control over society that it was able to crack down on terrorist financing and presence without fear of religious backlash. But the UAE was such a strong state in part because it had limited religious groups' ability to oppose the regime. If the religion–state relationship of the UAE had been different, it would be likely that the state would not be so strong. Thus, the strength of the UAE state contextualizes the role of the religion–state relationship, but does not undermine it.

The importance of the religion–state relationship even in the face of the strong UAE state is also apparent through comparison to Saudi Arabia. Saudi Arabia is similar in many respects to the UAE and arguably has an even stronger state. But Saudi Arabia had long actively supported Islamic groups both domestically and abroad, and thus had a different religion–state relationship then the UAE. When the United States began pressuring Saudi Arabia after 9/11, the state initially resisted cooperating with the United States and only moved on terrorist groups after it came under their attack. Thus, despite having a strong – or stronger – state than the UAE, Saudi Arabia was not equally cooperative, due partly to its differing religion–state relationship.

Another alternative explanation is that the UAE did not support Islamic militants as part of its foreign policy – as did Pakistan – and thus had no security reason to limit its cooperation with the United States. This is also accurate, but misleading. Part of the reason the UAE did not support Islamic militants was because it attempted to minimize the influence of Islamic groups in its society. As discussed earlier, it was wary to even crack down on Western dress to avoid appearing as if Islamists drove its policies. So the lack of support for Islamic militants is connected to the religion–state relationship, and this – like the previously discussed alternative explanation – serves to contextualize the role of the relationship.

An additional alternative explanation for the UAE's counterterrorism cooperation involves leadership change. Zayed bin Sultan al Nahyan ruled the UAE from its formation until his death in 2004, when his son – Khalifa bin Zayed bin Sultan al Nahyan – succeeded him. This leadership change roughly corresponded to the increase in the UAE's counterterrorism cooperation after 9/11, so one could argue that this change was due to the new leader of the state. Such a leadership change undoubtedly did affect many of the countries' policies, but this alone did not explain all aspects of the country's counterterrorism policies. Even if the impetus to increase the UAE's counterterrorism cooperation came from the new leader, the opportunity to do so arose from the institutional configurations that limited Islamic backlash to this policy change.

Finally, one could argue that the UAE simply lacked the religious contention present in a state like Pakistan. As a result, it was under less pressure from religious groups to limit its counterterrorism cooperation.

Hopefully the previous discussion of religious contention in UAE demonstrates that this was very much present. It is true that the country experienced less turmoil from religious groups than in Pakistan. But, as with the previous discussion, this related to its religion–state relationship, which limited these groups' activities from the country's founding. The attending counterfactual would be that if the UAE experienced stronger religious opposition it would have limited its counterterrorism cooperation. This is not tenable, however. As can be seen during the Arab Spring uprisings, the UAE came under greater threat of Islamist activism. But it did not alter its policies; it cracked down on religious groups. This is because its religion–state relationship gave it continued freedom of action even in the face of religious opposition. Moreover, as the chapter on Turkey will demonstrate, the presence of widespread religious contention is not enough to cause limited counterterrorism cooperation.

CONCLUSION

The United Arab Emirates thus falls in between Pakistan and the next case study, Turkey. It has a rather close religion–state relationship – an officially Islamic country with Islam-based laws – that nevertheless limits the political influence of Islamic groups. While Islamic contention occurs in the country, the state co-opts or represses groups when they become too powerful. As a result, the UAE follows religious sentiment in many areas, such as support for international religious causes, but is able to ignore religious pressure when it threatens the regime. In the case of counterterrorism, the UAE initially looked the other way in cases of terrorist financing and supported states that the United States accused of supporting terrorism due to their international religious prestige. After the 9/11 attacks, the United States pressed the UAE to reform its counterterrorism policies and the UAE was able to comply – increasing its cooperation – due to the regime's freedom of movement vis-à-vis Islamic groups in society.

The UAE's counterterrorism behaviors took on a few distinct forms. In the 1990s, when the UAE's enforcement of terrorist financing was lax, this primarily took the form of *hedging*. As I discussed earlier, the UAE cooperated with some international US counterterrorism efforts and US supported US military actions in the region, but this did not extend to cracking down on suspected domestic support for terrorism. After 9/11, when counterterrorism cooperation increased dramatically, this still involved some – maybe implicit – attempts to *justify* the UAE's cooperation as it continued its support for Islamic causes and values abroad and at home.

Thus, the case of the UAE provides further support for my claims regarding the role of religion–state relationships in counterterrorism cooperation. Its religion–state relationship falls in the moderate range of scores, as did its counterterrorism cooperation; this fits the general pattern I discovered in the quantitative analysis. Moreover, the specific connection between the religion–state relationship and its counterterrorism policies is in line with the claims I made in Chapter 3. The ties between religion and state in the UAE made its leaders amenable to some religious policies, either active ones – like its support for Sudan and the Taliban in the 1990s – or passive ones, such as enabling terrorist financing. Yet, the specific nature of its religion–state relationship – which minimized the power of Islamic groups – also allowed the state to dramatically increase its counterterrorism cooperation under US pressure. Moreover, it can help to deal with the counterargument that it is conservative Islamic contention, not the religion–state relationship, which affects counterterrorism cooperation as the conservative Islamic UAE proved cooperative on counterterrorism after 9/11.

6

Turkey

In 2002, the AKP – a conservative religious party with Islamic roots – won Turkey's parliamentary elections. This came as a shock to most Western observers, as Turkey was seen as a Westernized Muslim country long ruled by secularist parties and a military antagonistic toward Islamists. A year later, the AKP government under Prime Minister Recep Tayyip Erdogan refused to cooperate with the US invasion of Iraq, seriously complicating US plans. Numerous observers saw the combination of a religious party's electoral victory and the lack of cooperation on Iraq as a significant breach in the previously close US-Turkish security relationship.

A focus on these two events, however, obscures the aggregate relationship between the United States and Turkey, which was marked by close counterterrorism cooperation. Turkey joined in numerous international counterterrorism efforts, most notably the US-led mission in Afghanistan. It also reformed domestic policies like money-laundering restrictions, and took action against al-Qaeda supporters in the country. Moreover, despite the religious nature of the AKP, Turkey was not transformed into an Iran-style theocracy after 2002. The AKP did broaden the role of religion in Turkey's politics, such as loosening restrictions on the wearing of head scarves, but often came under attack from Islamic groups for not being sufficiently dedicated to Islamic causes.

Turkey, then, is nearly the opposite of Pakistan. Turkey maintained close counterterrorism cooperation with the United States despite both the rise of Islamic political groups and some very real tensions emerging. While there are vast differences between Turkey and the other countries

I discuss in this book, the same factor explains its close counterterrorism relationship in spite of religious pressure. Whereas Pakistan had extensive ties between religion and state and the UAE was an officially Islamic state that kept Islamic groups at bay, Turkey's political institutions established and maintained an official secularism that kept religion and state separate.

Turkey was founded in the 1920s as an officially secular state. The country's political institutions codified a Western secularism that restricted the public expression of religion and charged the military with maintaining this system. This established path-dependent processes that led to gradually increasing distance between religion and state, gave secular actors political and rhetorical tools to uphold the distant religion–state relationship, and limited the rise of widespread Islamist contention. By the 1990s, the Turkish regime had significant freedom of movement on contentious issues due to the limited influence of Islamic groups. As a result, it could cooperate with the United States when it began its international campaign against al-Qaeda. The durability of the institutional religion–state relationship persisted even after the AKP was elected.

As with the other case studies, I will first present the history of counterterrorism cooperation between the United States and Turkey, and then discuss the nature of Islamic contention in the country and how Turkey's leaders responded to and restrained this contention.[1] I follow this with a historical discussion of Turkey, which demonstrates how its foundational distant religion–state relationship was perpetuated throughout the twentieth century, creating a situation in which leaders were able to ignore opposition to working with the United States on counterterrorism. I then conduct an in-depth analysis of this evidence, explaining how the distant religion–state relationship facilitated this cooperation and why alterative explanations for US-Turkish counterterrorism ties are insufficient without attention to the religion–state relationship. As with other case studies in this book, this is not intended to be an exhaustive study of Turkey, but a survey of the relevant events in its history.

Before I begin, one question that may occur to readers of this chapter involves the AKP, the political party that ruled Turkey from 2002 to the time of writing. This party arose from Islamist political movements and

---

[1] Primary sources in this chapter were accessed through the Foreign Broadcast Information Service and World News Connection unless the full media outlet is cited, in which case they came directly from the outlet.

has advanced numerous religious policies. I follow many other observers of the AKP and refer to them as a conservative religious party – a party advancing the values and interest of conservative religious segments of Turkey's populace – rather than an Islamist party as the AKP has not been actively endeavoring to implement Islamic law.[2] Undoubtedly, however, the AKP has challenged Turkey's official secularism, so it may be confusing to think of Turkey as having a distant religion–state relationship under this party. Despite this, it is still accurate to discuss Turkey as having a distant religion–state relationship. As I will discuss next, for the time period of this study the AKP challenged but also accepted Turkey's official secularism. Moreover, while one could argue the AKP attempted to change Turkey's religion–state relationship in its first decade in power, I argue – and present evidence to support this argument – that the religion–state relationship persisted due to the powerful effects of these institutional arrangements on a country's politics. That being said, as time went on, the AKP became more assertive in controlling society. I will address these issues in this book's concluding chapter, however, where I will discuss the prospects for change in religion–state relationships and how this argument extends to events following the Arab Spring.

COUNTERTERRORISM COOPERATION

While there was tension in some aspects of their relationship, counterterrorism cooperation between the United States and Turkey was rather close. Before 9/11, the United States was critical of Turkey's tough stance against Kurdish separatist groups, but called on Turkey to move against al-Qaeda. And after 9/11, the United States relied on Turkey to both disrupt al-Qaeda networks in its territory and back US international efforts. For the most part, Turkey complied. It eliminated numerous al-Qaeda-connected cells in the country and intensified efforts to limit terrorist financing. Turkey also participated in the US-led mission in Afghanistan and supported international counterterrorism initiatives. That being said, tensions emerged in a few areas – notably Turkey's refusal to join the 2003 invasion of Iraq – and disagreement on issues outside of counterterrorism affected the US-Turkish relationship.

---

[2] For a similar approach, see M. Hakan Yavuz, *Secularism and Muslim Democracy in Turkey* (New York: Cambridge University Press, 2008); Kuru, *Secularism and State Policies Towards Religion: The United States, France and Turkey.*

Pre-9/11

Before 9/11, much of US pressure on Turkey actually criticized its extensive counterterrorism efforts. Turkey had been conducting campaigns against Kurdish separatists – notably, from the 1990s on, the Kurdistan Workers' Party (Partiya Karkeren Kurdistane, PKK) – since the 1980s. Many international observers viewed Turkish actions as overly aggressive with little consideration for human rights. Several US officials and activists were openly critical of Turkey in the early 1990s.[3] In 1994, the US Congress tried to make aid to Turkey conditional on its activities in the southeast, although it dropped these conditions under pressure from the US Secretary of State.[4]

Turkey did not completely comply with US pressure on the Kurdish issue. Turkey continued to pursue aggressive counterterrorist actions against the PKK throughout the decade, and US pressure produced a backlash in Turkey. A prominent Turkish politician claimed in 1995 that there were "double standards" in place, and called on support for Turkish efforts against the Kurds.[5] And Turkish officials claimed they would "reconsider" their ties with the United States due to its criticism.[6]

The two countries became closer on counterterrorism by the late 1990s, however. The United States gradually decreased its criticism of Turkey's counterterrorism activities and came to support its actions against the PKK. In 1999 the United States noted that Turkey had improved its human rights record.[7] And the United States took a stronger stance against the PKK in the late 1990s.[8] By 2000, the US State Department praised Turkey as a "model country" for its counterterrorism activities.[9]

These improved ties occurred alongside Turkish cooperation on US efforts against al-Qaeda. Turkey supported US air strikes against purported al-Qaeda targets in Afghanistan and Sudan in 1998.[10] Turkish

---

[3] James Brown, "The Turkish Imbroglio: Its Kurds," *Annals of the American Academy of Political and Social Science*, 541 (1995); Columnist Views 'New Snag' With US Relations, March 29, 1994.

[4] 'Discontent' Over Proposed Rejection of US Aid, May 30, 1994; Ciller Welcomes US Decision on Military Aid Article Type, July 1, 1994; Columnist Views 'New Snag' with US Relations, March 29, 1993.

[5] Ozal on Antiterror Stand, April 21, 1995.

[6] Turkey: Ankara 'Reconsidering' Relationship with US, July 9, 1996.

[7] Turkish Envoy Notes 'Giant Leap' in Human Rights, June 24, 1999.

[8] Turkey: Turkish Envoy Lauds US Stand Against PKK, November 20, 1998.

[9] United States Praises Turkey, Criticizes Greece on Terror, May 1, 2000.

[10] Turkey: Turkey Expresses Support for US Air Strikes, August 21, 1998.

officials also expressed support for US counterterrorism efforts in 1999, and called for continued cooperation.[11] Additionally, there were reports that Turkey was supporting anti-Taliban forces in Afghanistan.[12]

Turkey also took actions against al-Qaeda elements in Turkey. In 2000, regional authorities increased security at the US air base at Incirlik in response to a potential al-Qaeda threat.[13] And in early 2001, Turkish authorities worked with US and UK officials in response to potential threats against Western targets in Turkey.[14] Likewise, in 1999, Turkish authorities arrested a senior al-Qaeda official who attempted to travel through the Istanbul airport.[15]

Post-9/11

The US-Turkish counterterrorism relationship became much closer after the 9/11 attacks. US officials requested Turkish participation in the military action against Afghanistan.[16] The United States also requested broader help from Turkey in Afghanistan, such as with intelligence and humanitarian operations.[17] And the United States hoped to gain Turkish support in its 2003 invasion of Iraq, particularly the permission to move US troops through Turkish territory to invade Iraq from the north.[18] The United States also put some pressure on Turkey involving its domestic policies, such as establishing counterterrorism standards for police and addressing concerns about terrorist financing.[19]

Additionally, the United States hoped to leverage Turkey's status as a powerful Muslim democracy to advance its broader efforts to fight terrorism. In his second term, US President Bush called for a widespread

---

[11] Demirel Notes Turkey's Role in NATO Southern Wing, November 7, 1999.

[12] Afghanistan: Anti-Taleban Leaders in Turkey to Get Support, September 9, 1998.

[13] Adana Security Director Says Measures Taken at Incirlik Against Terror Threat, October 25, 2000.

[14] Turkish Security Alerts US, UK, Israel Embassies Against Bin-Ladin Attacks, March 29, 2001.

[15] Turkish Police Arrest Senior Aide of Bin-Ladin, September 16, 1999.

[16] Douglas Frantz, Turkey Says Troops to Join US Campaign and Train Anti-Taliban Forces, *The New York Times*, November 2, 2001, B1.

[17] Turkish Government Tasks 90-Person Special Force in Response to US Request, November 1, 2001.

[18] "Turkey Rejects US Troop Proposal," *CNN Online*, March 1, 2003. Available at www.cnn.com/2003/WORLD/meast/03/01/sprj.irq.main/.

[19] US Requests Help From Turkish Police in Fight Against Fundamentalist Terrorism, November 11, 2001; Eric Lichtblau and Timothy L. O'Brien, Efforts to Fight Terror Financing Reported to Lag, *The New York Times*, December 12, 2003: A1.

effort to promote democracy in the Middle East and surrounding regions, as a means to undermine support for al-Qaeda and other groups. Turkey was a major aspect of this, as the United States hoped to point to Turkey as an example of a Muslim democracy. This involved Turkey taking the lead in advocating for democratic reforms and counterterrorism activities in the region and around the world.[20]

For the most part, Turkey complied with US counterterrorism pressure after 9/11. Several Turkish officials expressed strong support for the United States after the 9/11 attacks.[21] The defense minister in 2001 praised US support for Turkey on terrorism while criticizing Europe's inaction on Kurdish groups.[22] And after the Bush administration announced democracy promotion efforts intended to undermine support for terrorism, Erdogan publicly called for a strong role for Turkey in this initiative.[23]

One example of Turkey's international counterterrorism efforts was the launch of the Global Forum on Counterterrorism. In September 2011, the United States and Turkey launched this initiative as an information platform intended to promote international cooperation on counterterrorism.[24] The organization provides funds for governmental programs around the world that are intended to counter violent extremism. It also promotes legal reforms focused on counterterrorism and disseminates counterterrorism-related information.

Turkey also enacted domestic reforms. In 2002, Turkey and the United States established information-sharing capabilities and shared intelligence relating to al-Qaeda and its supporters with the United States.[25]

---

[20] Turkey's Vision, Role in 'Greater Middle East Project' Viewed, March 2, 2004.

[21] Turkish Justice Minister Addresses International Conference on Terrorism in Warsaw, November 6, 2001; Turkey's Cem Vows to Combat Terrorism in UN Anniversary Message, October 23, 2001; Turkey's Sezer Sends Messages to Bush 'Harshly' Condemning Terrorist Strikes, September 11, 2001; Anne Dismorr, *Turkey Decoded* (London: Saqi, 2008); Dan Tschirgi, "Turkey and the Arab World in the New Millenium," in *Turkey's Foreign Policy in the 21st Century*, eds. Tareq Y. and Mustafa Aydin Ismael (Burlington, VT: Ashgate, 2003); Joshua Walker, "Turkey and Israel's Relationship in the Middle East," *Mediterranean Quarterly* 17, no. 4 (2006).

[22] Turkey: Cakmakoglu Thanks US for Support in Fight Against Terror, Warns EU, December 18, 2001.

[23] Turkey's Vision, Role in 'Greater Middle East Project' Viewed, March 2, 2004; Ayegul Sever, "Turkey's Constraining Position on Western Reform Initiatives in the Middle East," *Mediterranean Quarterly* 18, no. 4 (2007).

[24] "Fact Sheet on the Global Counterterrorism Forum," www.cfr.org/counterterrorism/fact-sheet-global-counterterrorism-forum/p28460.

[25] Turkey: Column Gives Details from Testimony of Militants with Al-Qa'ida Links, June 20, 2002; Turkey's Cicek Comments on Al-Qaida, Security Measures Against Possible Attacks, May 3, 2011.

Turkey also implemented policies at several points relating to terrorist financing – freezing the assets of designated terrorist groups and individuals connected to terrorist groups – after international observers expressed concerns.[26] For example, Turkey passed a law in 2013 that strengthened money-laundering enforcement and addressed these concerns.[27]

Turkey also took actions against al-Qaeda targets. Shortly after the 9/11 attacks, Turkish forces moved against militant groups operating in the country's southeast.[28] They arrested a top al-Qaeda operative and extradited him to Tunisia in 2003.[29] Likewise, in 2005 Turkey disrupted a plot to attack Israeli ships via a speedboat by a man affiliated with Abu Musab al-Zarqawi, the leader of al-Qaeda in Iraq.[30] And Turkish forces arrested al-Qaeda operatives in numerous cities in 2009 and 2010.[31] This continued in 2011, with a large operation against al-Qaeda elements in the southeast city of Gaziantep and other cities.[32]

Moreover, Turkey took an active role in the US-led invasion of Afghanistan. Turkey sent troops as part of the international coalition and established a special task force with the United States to assist with intelligence and humanitarian operations.[33] This continued under the AKP. Erdogan opposed the invasion but did express support for an "international joint fight against terrorism."[34] Turkey remained involved in the international coalition throughout the Bush and Obama administrations, even taking on the crucial – and difficult – task of attempting to mediate

---

[26] Turkish Cabinet Freezes Assets of 9 More Persons, Organizations Funding Terror, April 12, 2002; Turkish Government Decides to Freeze Assets of Terrorist Organizations, December 30, 2001.

[27] "Turkish Parliament Approves Anti-Terrorism Financing Law," *Reuters*, February 7, 2013.

[28] Turkey: Adana Police Carry Out Operation on Hizb-ut Tahrir; 7 Arrested, October 16, 2001.

[29] Fundamentalist Sources Cited on Prominent Al-Qa'ida Figure's Arrest in Turkey, June 23, 2003.

[30] Suspected Top Terrorist Arrested in Turkey Lived in Germany, August 14, 2005.

[31] Turkey: Five Al-Qa'ida Suspects Detained in Izmir, October 22, 2010; Turkey: 16 Al-Qaeda Suspects Remanded in Custody in Adana, January 22, 2010; Turkey: AA Reports on Al-Qa'ida Suspects Arrested After Nationwide Operations, October 19, 2009.

[32] Turkey: 13 Al-Qa'ida Suspects Detained in Southeastern City, December 19, 2011; Turkey: Suspected Head of Al-Qa'ida's Local Branch Detained in Southeast, April 12, 2011; AFP: Turkey Arrests Instanbul's Al-Qa'ida Chief, April 12, 2011.

[33] Turkey Said to Assume Key Role in Afghanistan as Member of International Group, November 16, 2001; Turkish Government Tasks 90-Person Special Force in Response to US Request, November 1, 2001.

[34] Turkey's Islamist Parties, Press Said Divided Over Strike on Afghanistan, October 9, 2001.

between Pakistan and Afghanistan as tensions broke out over the former's alleged tolerance of militants.[35]

Differences did emerge over the US invasion of Iraq in 2003. As was noted, the United States tried to gain Turkish support for its effort against Iraq and the use of bases in Turkey to launch a northern front as part of the invasion. The Turkish people, including both Islamic and secular groups, were widely opposed to the invasion.[36] The AKP, caught between public opposition to the US invasion and concern over upsetting Turkey's longtime ally, decided to have the Turkish parliament vote on it. The legislature voted against the measure, preventing Turkey from cooperating. Many Turkey observers believe the AKP thought parliament would approve, thus sparing the AKP from making a politically difficult decision.[37] Others suggest the AKP was opposed to working with the United States, but hoped the parliament would vote down cooperation rather than the government rejecting it outright.[38] Whatever their motivations, this failure to work with the United States in its invasion of Iraq angered numerous US policymakers.[39]

Other points of contention arose. Some of this involved the nature of US counterterrorism activities. Erdogan opposed the use of the term "Islamic terrorism" to describe al-Qaeda and its affiliates.[40] Other leaders, such as Gul, argued that the manner in which the United States pursued its international counterterrorism efforts implicitly linked Islam and terrorism.[41] Counterterrorism cooperation issues also involved resistance to a more active part in US military actions. In 2004 Gul expressed

---

[35] Turkey Reaffirms Commitment to Contribute to Stability in Afghanistan, March 20, 2012; Turkey: Ankara Said Trying to Revive Dialogue Between Pakistan, Afghanistan, September 17, 2008.

[36] Ioannis N. Grigoriadis, "Friends No More? The Rise of Anti-American Nationalism in Turkey," *Middle East Journal* 64, no. 1 (2010); Philip H. Gordon and Omer Taspinar, *Winning Turkey: How America, Europe, and Turkey Can Revive a Fading Partnership* (Washington, DC: Brookings Institution Press, 2008).

[37] Yavuz, *Secularism and Muslim Democracy in Turkey*; Philip Robins, "Confusion at Home, Confusion Abroad: Turkey between Copenhagen and Iraq," *International Affairs* 79, no. 3 (2003).

[38] Soner Cagaptay and Mark Parris, "Turkey after the Iraq War: Still a US Ally?," in *Policy Analysis* (Washington Institute for Near East Policy, 2003).

[39] F. Stephen and Ian O. Lesser Larrabee, *Turkish Foreign Policy in an Age of Uncertainty* (Santa Monica, CA: The RAND Corporation, 2003); Metin Munir, "Principles Come at a Price," *Euromoney*, April 2003.

[40] Turkey's Erdogan Opposes Use of Term 'Islamic Terror,' July 27, 2005.

[41] Gul Comments on Syria, Austria, Says Bin Ladin's Death 'Significant Development,' May 4, 2011.

hesitation over US requests to send more troops to Afghanistan, pointing to incidents of US troops killing civilians in Afghanistan and Iraq, and the continued conflict between Israel and Palestinians.[42] And after the invasion of Iraq, Erdogan stated Turkey would assist with the stabilization of Iraq but would not "go to Iraq as police."[43]

Turkish authorities were also concerned about the lack of US pressure on the PKK.[44] In 2005 a top military official claimed that "merely putting them on a list [of designated terrorist groups] meant nothing," and called for strong action against the group.[45] A major controversy erupted in 2003 when Turkey sent commandos into Iraq to take action against Kurdish targets; US troops arrested the Turkish commandos, causing significant anger among Turkish leaders and public.[46] While calling for an "international platform to combat terrorism," Erdogan claimed that other countries were not sufficiently interested in fighting terrorism due to their minimal action against the PKK.[47] And while noting Turkey's extensive intelligence sharing on terrorism, a Turkish official complained that other countries did not reciprocate with information on Kurdish groups.[48]

Other areas of tension involved broader regional issues. Erdogan was critical of both Israel and the "Western world's . . . double standards."[49] Turkish anger over US support for Israel, as well as opposition to the invasion of Iraq, contributed to tensions between the two and a reported sense on the part of Turkey that the two countries had different interests

---

[42] Turkey's Gul Expresses 'Extreme Concern' over Recent Mideast Developments, May 21, 2004.

[43] Erdogan Says Turkey Not to be Police Force in Iraq; Wants to Expand Ties with US, September 13, 2003.

[44] Columnist Opposes Erdogan's Remarks on Strategic Relationship Between Turkey, US, June 9, 2005; Angel Rabasa and F. Stephen Larrabee, *The Rise of Political Islam in Turkey* (Washington, DC: The RAND Corporation, 2008).

[45] Turkey: Gen Basbug's Speech Said Shows Turkish-US Policies Mostly Overlapping, June 8, 2005.

[46] Gordon and Taspinar, *Winning Turkey: How America, Europe, and Turkey Can Revive a Fading Partnership*; F. Stephen Larrabee, *Troubled Partnership: US-Turkish Relations in an Era of Global Geopolitical Change* (Washington, DC: The RAND Corporation, 2010).

[47] Turkey-Fight Against Terrorism: Turkish Premier Says World Not Interested in Turkey's Proposal to Establish International Counter-Terrorism Platform," May 10, 2011.

[48] Turkey's Cicek Comments on Al-Qaida, Security Measures Against Possible Attacks, May 3, 2011.

[49] Turkey: AKP Leader Erdogan Comments on Death Penalty, Other Issues, February 27, 2002; Gareth Jenkins, "Muslim Democrats in Turkey?," *Survival* 45, no. 1 (2003).

in the region.[50] And as the Arab Spring uprisings broke out, Turkey's attempts to influence the outcome of these protests led to some tensions with the United States. It often pursued these efforts in a manner not completely in line with the United States, acting – according to a 2011 *New York Times* piece – as a "crucial if imperfect partner."[51]

These areas of difficulty did not prevent the two from cooperating closely on counterterrorism. Turkey continued to participate in the international coalition in Afghanistan throughout the decade, and cooperated with the United States on disrupting al-Qaeda elements in Turkey. And even though Turkey did not participate in the invasion of Iraq, Erdogan did agree to work with the United States after the invasion; Turkey granted the United States overflight rights and allowed the United States to use its airspace and bases in its territory for resupply and emergency landings.[52] In 2005, Erdogan's foreign policy advisor noted that the two countries worked closely on numerous issues, and that "the only problem in those issues was seen in Iraq."[53]

RELIGIOUS CONTENTION

This close counterterrorism cooperation did not occur absent significant domestic opposition and religious contention. Islamic groups were active throughout the country, placing significant pressure on the state to increase the role of religion and minimize its official secularism. These groups were also strongly critical of the government for its secular policies and close ties to the United States. This continued even after the election of the religious AKP in 2002; while this group took some actions Islamic groups favored, they continued to be critical of its US ties and relative moderation. In addition to nonviolent activism, Turkey faced recurring threats from Islamic militants, including several devastating attacks.

[50] Graham E. Fuller, *The New Turkish Republic: Turkey as a Pivotal State in the Muslim World* (Washington, DC: United States Institute of Peace Press, 2008); Ted Galen Carpenter, "Estrangement: The United States and Turkey in a Multipolar Era," *Mediterranean Quarterly* 21, no. 4 (2010).

[51] Steven Lee Myers, "Tumult of Arab Spring Prompts Worries in Washington," *The New York Times*, September 17, 2011.

[52] Turkey: Gen Basbug's Speech Said Shows Turkish-US Policies Mostly Overlapping, June 8, 2005; Joshua Walker, "Reexamining the US-Turkish Alliance," *The Washington Quarterly* 31, no. 1 (2007/2008); Robins, "Confusion at Home, Confusion Abroad: Turkey between Copenhagen and Iraq."

[53] Turkey: Erdogan's Foreign Policy Adviser Details AKP's 'Active' Foreign Policy, December 1, 2005.

Pre-9/11

Following political and social openings in the late 1980s and early 1990s – which I will discuss later – Islamic groups increased in political power. Islamic foundations proliferated, many of which had ties to political parties.[54] Islamic media outlets also increased in prominence.[55] And the Islamist Welfare Party (*Refah Partisi*, RP) performed well electorally beginning with the 1994 elections.[56] This culminated in the premiership of the RP's Necmettin Erbakan in 1996 as part of a coalition government with the leftist Tansu Ciller.[57]

These groups actively campaigned for the application of Islamic law. One third of RP supporters wanted Islamic law, according to a 1995 poll.[58] And in 1994, the RP Deputy Chair called for the application of "Koranic law."[59] There were also broader calls to respect Islamic beliefs, even though they fell short of explicitly calling for Islamic law to be put in place. For example, in 1993, Erbakan argued that "no one has the right to insult and provoke religious sensibilities" in a Muslim country.[60]

Many Islamic figures, however, argued not for the application of Islamic law but an increased role for Islam in Turkish politics. In a 2001 interview with a secularist paper, Recep Tayyip Erdogan said he was against "a state based on Islamic principles," and instead wanted a country "where the community can live like a Muslim."[61] Moreover, several members of the Virtue Party (*Fazilet Partisi*, FP) – which succeeded the banned RP – claimed they did not want to set up an "Islamic state" and instead emphasized "religious freedom."[62] Also, Abdullah Gul stated that he saw Islamic law "as a matter of view of piety and religious freedom," not actions by the state.[63] A leader of the FP expressed similar sentiments, and called for an "Anglo-Saxon" style of secularism.[64]

These groups also were intensely critical of Turkey's official secularism. In 1995, a RP member called Ataturk an "illegitimate child," in effect

---

[54] Islamic Foundations Grow in Number, Influence, March 10, 1995; Yavuz, *Secularism and Muslim Democracy in Turkey*.

[55] Turkey: Islamic Publishing Press Market Control Viewed, March 15, 1996.

[56] Welfare Party's Increase in Popularity Viewed, November 1, 1994.

[57] The Welfare Party is sometimes also referred to in English as the Prosperity Party.

[58] Pro-Islam Prosperity Party Voter Profiled, January 22, 1994.

[59] Welfare Party Official Calls for Koranic Law, November 10, 1994.

[60] Opposition Leader Comments on Government Plan, July 7, 1993.

[61] Turkey's Erdogan on Political Views, AK Party's Objectives, August 28, 2001.

[62] Turkey: Islamists Seen Turning Away from Political Islam, February 16, 2000.

[63] Virtue Party's Abdullah Gul Interviewed on Split, Sharia Istanbul, February 9, 2000.

[64] Turkey: FP Leader Kutan on Freedom of Expression, Secularism, July 1, 1998.

calling his legacy in Turkish secularism into question.[65] Other Islamic groups argued that the state was "built on the blood of Muslims."[66] Of course some of this took on a more moderate tone. Abdullah Gul gave an interview when he was an official with the RP in 1994. He pointed out that Islam is a unifying force in Turkey, but claimed he was not opposed to secularism, only "anti-Islamic" secularism.[67]

This Islamic activism did not just focus on domestic issues, however; many Islamic groups pressured Turkey over its foreign policy. In the 1990s, a good amount of this activism focused on the plight of Bosnian Muslims, who were targeted in the conflicts over the breakup of Yugoslavia. Gul called for action to defend Bosnian Muslims and pointed to the fact that they were attacked because of their religion.[68] And a demonstration in 1994 over Serbian attacks on Muslims turned into an Islamic protest that involved attacks on a UN building.[69] Similar calls to support global Muslims focused on other conflicts as well, including the civil war in Afghanistan prior to the rise of the Taliban, and the brutal civil war in Algeria between the government and Islamic groups.[70] And protests by Islamic groups broke out at several points, including a 1992 protest in response to the Algerian coup in which the Algerian military removed an Islamist party from politics.[71]

A significant portion of Islamic agitation over Turkey's foreign policies focused on the United States. As I will discuss in more depth later, Turkey has had extensive ties to the United States since the end of World War II. This led to anger among both some secular nationalists and Islamists. Many Islamic groups believed the United States was manipulating Turkey.[72] After Islamists were purged from security forces in the early 1990s, some accused the United States of interfering in Turkish politics.[73] Erbakan argued Operation Desert Storm was a Western campaign against Muslims, and that the United States pressured Turkey to participate in this and later operations in Iraq in order to

---

[65] PKK, Islamic, Left-Wing Terrorism Viewed, January 27, 1995.

[66] Diversity Among Islamic Groups Observed, September 4, 1992.

[67] Prosperity Party Official Interviewed, August 16, 1994.

[68] Prosperity Party Official Interviewed, August 16, 1994.

[69] PKK, Islamic, Left-Wing Terrorism Viewed, January 27, 1995.

[70] Prosperity Party Official Interviewed, August 16, 1994; Diversity Among Islamic Groups Observed, September 4, 1992.

[71] Pro-Islamic Demonstrations Reported in Istanbul, February 24, 1992.

[72] Diversity Among Islamic Groups Observed, September 4, 1992.

[73] Prosperity Member Scores ANAP for 'Purges,' September 9, 1991.

advance its interests in the region.[74] Erbakan also claimed NATO "regards green [representing Islam] as a hostile color" and "equates Islam with terrorism."[75]

Turkey also faced violent Islamic contention. Much of it was domestic. Hizballah – a militant group unconnected to Lebanon's Hezbollah – fought with the PKK in the southeast, and also targeted numerous intellectuals.[76] Other militant groups endeavoring to establish an Islamic state operated outside the southeast. One particularly violent group was the Greater Eastern Islamic Raiders-Front, which conducted attacks against bars and Jewish cemeteries.[77] The group also claimed credit for killing a prominent journalist in 1993.[78] There were other acts of violence connected to Islamic movements, although the specific groups responsible were unknown. For example, numerous secularist intellectuals were murdered in the 1990s, reportedly by Islamic groups.[79] There was also a plot by extremists to fly a plane into Ataturk's mausoleum in Ankara.[80]

International terrorist threats arose as well. In 1990, "Islamic terrorists" with Kuwaiti passports reportedly attempted to enter Turkey and attack it in retaliation for its cooperation with the United States.[81] Al-Qaeda planned attacks against US targets in Turkey as well, including a failed 2000 plot against the US Consulate in Istanbul and a threat against the US Embassy in Ankara in 2001.[82] Additionally, some militants in Turkey were connected with foreign groups. For example, in 2000, the Turkish Interior Military claimed the Turkish Hizballah had ties to both a militant group in Iraq and al-Qaida.[83] The international connections of

---

[74] Erbakan Claims US Involvement, March 30, 1995; Erbakan Seeks Expulsion of Multilateral Force, January 14, 1992.

[75] Erbakan Comments on Visit to Washington, October 26, 1994.

[76] Islamic Organization's Link With Iran Reported, February 14, 1995; Cost of Fight Against Terror, Casualties Seen, January 27, 1995; Turkey: 3 Bodies Uncovered in Ankara Hizbullah Operation, January 20, 2000.

[77] PKK, Islamic, Left-Wing Terrorism Viewed, January 27, 1995.

[78] Islamic Group Claims Credit, January 27, 1993.

[79] Cost of Fight Against Terror, Casualties Seen, January 27, 1995; 'Islamic Movement,' October 7, 1990; Nicole Pope and Hugh Pope, *Turkey Unveiled: A History of Modern Turkey* (Woodstock, NY and New York, NY: The Overlook Press, 1997).

[80] Coll, *Ghost Wars: The Secret History of the CIA, Afghanistan and bin Ladin, from the Soviet Invasion to September 10, 2011*.

[81] Alert on for Terrorists with Kuwaiti Passports, October 31, 1990.

[82] Terror Alert at US Consulate General In Istanbul; Three Bin-Ladin Men Sought, November 17, 2000; Turkey: US Embassy Road-Block Against Possible Suicide Attacks Reported, July 7, 2001.

[83] Turkish Sources: Hizbullah Has 'Close Ties' to UBL, February 6, 2000.

some Turkish militant groups are also apparent in the presence of some Turkish citizens fighting with militants in Kashmir.[84]

Post-9/11

A similar situation existed after 9/11. Even after the AKP's election, Islamic groups continued to push for an increased visibility of religion in Turkey. Much of this focused on the ban on women wearing headscarves in government buildings and universities. Several protests broke out in 2004 calling for an end to the headscarf ban.[85] And groups also wanted the government to increase support for religious schools in the country.[86] At a 2009 election rally, Erbakan called for an end to interest rates and a "just order" based on Islam, while also calling on Turkey to leave NATO and turn away from the EU.[87] Moreover, in 2010 an Islamic writer attacked secularists for expressing concern about religious individuals serving in the judiciary, education, and military while not being critical of "freemasons, Sabbateans" and "atheists" in these positions.[88]

Islamic groups also protested US counterterrorism efforts for targeting Muslims. In 2003 a member of the Felicity Party (*Saadet Partisi*, SP) attended an international meeting of Islamists in Pakistan that called for the formation of an international Muslim bloc to oppose the United States.[89] In 2010 an Islamist writer claimed that the "covert target" of the US and NATO actions against terrorism was "Islam," which would eventually target the "entire Islamic geography."[90] And after the formation of South Sudan, an Islamist figure argued that this was the result of the US "Greater Middle East Project," which he claimed was an effort to reshape Muslim countries.[91]

---

[84] Pakistani Article Cites Six Turkish Fighters Martyred in Kashmir, August 30, 2001.

[85] Turkish Islamist Press Review, October 11, 2004.

[86] Turkey: Imam-Hatip Assembly Criticizes Government Education Policies, Headscarf Ban, May 23, 2005.

[87] Turkey: Felicity Party Rally Features Islamic Rap, Erbakan's Rhetoric, March 2, 2009.

[88] Highlights: Turkish Islamist Press, October 9, 2010. The three groups named are often the targets of criticism by conservative Islamic voices for their supposed secretive nature and anti-Islamic activities. "Sabbateans" are the followers of a heretical seventeenth-century Jewish rabbi who later converted to Islam.

[89] Pakistan: Islamic Movements Call for Creation of Muslim Bloc Against US Designs, August 23, 2003.

[90] Highlights: Turkish Islamist Press, November 28, 2010.

[91] Turkey: SP Leader Kamalak Says 'Sudan Victim of Greater Middle East Project,' April 29, 2012.

A significant amount of this opposition focused on Iraq and Afghanistan. While many protested the US invasion of Afghanistan in moderate terms, a few used more extreme language. For example, one figure branded the United States the "Great Satan" and calling the invasion a "crusade."[92] The Iraq invasion attracted even more significant opposition. In 2003, Islamic groups organized several protests in Turkey against the US military operations in Fallujah, Iraq, attacking the United States for its "Crusader spirit"; the protesters also criticized the Turkish government for its "silence."[93] And in 2004, a column claimed that US operations in Fallujah were a "Crusade . . . bent on the massacre of the billion-strong Islamic world."[94]

Islamic groups also criticized the AKP. For example, in 2005, some attacked the party for failing to move quickly enough on ending the headscarf ban.[95] Some attacked the AKP for trying to join the European Union – which they called the "crusader union" – and not focusing on the "Islamic world."[96] Islamic groups also attacked the AKP for not doing enough to protect Turkish citizens during the 2010 Gaza flotilla incident, and for not taking a stronger stance against the Danish cartoon controversy.[97] They also opposed the AKP electorally; the SP ran against the AKP in parliamentary elections, forming an alliance of Islamist parties in 2011.[98]

Some Islamic groups specifically attacked the AKP's counterterrorism policies and US ties. In a 2010 interview, a SP member claimed the AKP "has surrendered to the International Monetary Fund and the Greater Middle East Project"; the official also attacked the AKP for allowing the United States to use Incirlik Air Base to conduct operations in Iraq.[99]

---

[92] Turkey's Islamist Parties, Press Said Divided Over Strike on Afghanistan, Turkish, October 9, 2001.

[93] Turkey: Idealist Hearths Protest US Operations in Al-Fallujah, November 12, 2004.

[94] Turkey: Column Sees Neo-Cons as Delusional Devil-Worshiping Crusaders, November 11, 2004.

[95] Highlights: Turkish Islamist Press, November 23, 2005.

[96] Turkey: SP Leader Kamalak Says 'Sudan Victim of Greater Middle East Project,' April 29, 2012.

[97] Turkey: Felicity Party Faults Government for Not Protecting Aid Flotilla, June 4, 2010; Turkey: Felicity Party Calls on Erdogan to Reveal 'True Stand' on Caricatures, February 9, 2006.

[98] Turkey: SP, DP, TP, BBP to Continue with Erbakan's Election Alliance Plan, March 1, 2011; Turkey's Birand Says Anti-AKP Circles Surprised with Outcome of Elections, July 24, 2007.

[99] Turkey: SP Leader Kurtulmus Interviewed on Differences Between SP, AKP, February 18, 2010.

In 2008, an Islamic writer criticized the AKP for its counterterrorism activities, claiming its actions against "al-Qaeda and Hizballah suspects who have nothing to do with those organizations" were conducted to appease the United States.[100]

But Islamic political activity in Turkey – even with an Islamic-oriented party in power – did not take as extreme a form as in many other Muslim countries. While Islamist groups were active and pushed conservative interpretation of Islamic law, many Islamic groups took a more moderate and pluralist stance. A prominent example of this is the Gulen movement, which has extensive media, business, and cultural contacts and emphasizes interfaith dialogue and a greater role for religion in public life. The Gulen movement had been closely allied with the AKP. By 2012, a split emerged over Gulen criticism of Erdogan's governing style and Erdogan's accusations of a Gulenist conspiracy against him. Nevertheless, Gulen remains prominent in Turkey and his attitudes are telling about perceptions of Islamic activism in the country. For example, in a 2004 interview, Gulen argued that there is not a major threat of "reactionism" in Turkey, and that the "clamor about reactionism" is more threatening to society than Islamic activism.[101] This attitude was shared among other Islamic intellectuals. On a 2001 television show an Islamic intellectual argued that there was a difference between Turkish Islamism and that "influenced by radical Arab Islam."[102] Another argued that Islamists who supported the 9/11 attacks were "marginal" in the country.[103]

Although religious terrorism was not as widespread in this period, al-Qaeda was present in Turkey and conducted a few attacks against Turkish targets. Al-Qaeda elements in Turkey helped to coordinate activities in the Balkans.[104] And in 2003, al-Qaeda launched attacks against synagogues in Istanbul, killing 27 and injuring more than 300.[105] Later in the year, the group launched another series of attacks against a bank and the British Consulate in Istanbul, killing 40 and wounding hundreds. And

---

[100] Highlights: Turkish Islamist Press, January 10, 2008.
[101] Turkish Religious Leader Comments on 'Reactionism,' Charges Against Him, March 25, 2004.
[102] Turkey 'Islamists,' 'Liberals' Said Split in Reaction to September 11 Events, October 21, 2001.
[103] Ibid.
[104] Gunaratna, *Inside Al Qaeda*.
[105] UK Paper: Al-Qa'ida Claims Istanbul Bombings, Threatens Attacks in US, Elsewhere, November 17, 2003.

transnational connections among militants emerged; after the US invasion of Afghanistan, numerous Turkish citizens who had travelled to fight with al-Qaeda were arrested.[106] And Turkish counterterrorism operations reportedly revealed al-Qaeda had a presence in Istanbul, the southeast, and other parts of the country.[107]

RELIGION–STATE RELATIONSHIP

This Islamic contention occurred in the context of a durably distant religion–state relationship. The election of an Islamist Prime Minister in the 1990s and the dominance of a conservative religious party in the 2000s did not result in widespread changes to the country's political institutions. And the military remained committed to the official secularism, continuing to intervene in politics when it believed things were moving in an unfavorable direction.

Pre-9/11

Despite the increased prominence of Islamic groups, religion and state remained separate in the 1990s. Secularists frequently criticized Islamists, and government actors took steps against religious elements of society. The military also maintained policies opposed by religious groups. And even though the country had an Islamist Prime Minister for a short period – Necmettin Erbakan – he was forced to moderate his views in the face of secularist pressure and was ultimately removed from power.

Erbakan's rise and brief tenure did result in some changes to Turkey's foreign policies that demonstrate the effects of the political expression of religion. Upon taking power, Erbakan moved beyond the state's limited outreach to Muslim states; he emphasized Turkey's Muslim identity in his foreign relations, meeting with Iran, Libya, and Muslim Brotherhood

---

[106] Turkey: Column Gives Details from Testimony of Militants with Al-Qa'ida Links, June 20, 2002.

[107] Turkey: Authorities See Possible Al-Qa'ida Link to Ammonium Nitrate Seized, August 31, 2012; Turkey: 8 Al-Qa'ida Suspects Detained in Simultaneous Operations in 4 Provinces, March 29, 2012; Turkey: 13 Al-Qa'ida Suspects Detained in Southeastern City, December 19, 2011; Turkey's AA Reports Police Detain 15 Persons in Al-Qa'ida Operation in Konya, November 22, 2011; Turkey: Agency on Police Raids Against Al-Qa'ida Suspects in Several Provinces, July 10, 2010; AFP: Turkey Arrests Istanbul's Al-Qa'ida Chief, April 12, 2011.

members from Egypt.[108] He also mirrored popular dissatisfaction with Turkey's ties to Israel by publicly criticizing the state.[109]

Yet, secular forces in society limited the impact of Islamic groups. The military, judiciary, and civilian secular elites were frequently critical of Islamists and the influence of religion on politics.[110] In 1995 a military official said that "antisecularist propaganda" was a threat to the state, and warned against electing the RP.[111] Military officials in 1996 said that Islamists represented "separatist and extremist" forces trying to disrupt society.[112] And after an outbreak of political violence in the early 1990s, the prime minister called on religious leaders to keep their mosques out of political activities.[113]

The state also took actions against religious members of the security forces and individuals who were critical of Turkey's secularism. In 1991, numerous people deemed too religious were removed from security positions.[114] And the military discharged more than 1,000 troops for ties to Islamic groups in 1991.[115] The state also took actions against individuals who were critical of Turkey's secularism. The judiciary barred Erdogan from political participation for his political activities.[116] And the aforementioned religious leader who claimed an earthquake was punishment for secularism was arrested by the state for "inciting hatred."[117]

In addition to this, the state exerted strict control over religious activity in the country. The state attempted to use a counterterrorism law to influence the activities of religious foundations.[118] Security forces also took several steps to control what it called "antisecular" education in schools, and attempted to censor Islamic publications.[119] In 2001, the

[108] M. Hakan Yavuz, *Islamic Political Identity in Turkey* (New York: Oxford University Press, 2003); Dietrich Jung and Wolfango Piccoli, *Turkey at the Crossroads: Ottoman Legacies and a Greater Middle East* (London: Zed Books, 2001); Lenore G. Martin, "Turkey's Middle East Foreign Policy," in *The Future of Turkish Foreign Policy*, eds. Lenore G. and Dimitris Keridis Martin (Cambridge, MA: MIT Press, 2004).

[109] "Turkey's Middle East Foreign Policy."

[110] US Stand Said 'Changed' After Cold War End, May 6, 1990.

[111] Military Prosecutor Warns Against RP Victory, December 1, 1994.

[112] Turkey: Military Presents Views 'Diametrically Opposed' to RP, July 25, 1996.

[113] Demirel Warns Muftis on Political Involvement, March 8, 1993.

[114] Prosperity Member Scores ANAP for 'Purges,' September 9, 1991.

[115] Military Discharges Linked to 'Reactionary Views,' November 16, 1991.

[116] Sabah Columnist Says Legal Efforts Against Erdogan Politically Motivated, August 22 2001.

[117] Nur Sect Leader Kutlular Arrested by Ankara Court, October 19, 1999.

[118] Islamic Foundations Grow in Number, Influence, March 10, 1995.

[119] 'Important Decisions' of Security Council Reported, August 8, 1995; Fikret Bila Views NSC Decision on Private Islamic Schools, October 28, 1999.

state closed an Islamic youth foundation it claimed had ties to militant groups.[120] The state also tried prominent Islamic leader Fethullah Gulen, claiming he had formed an organization to implement Islamic law.[121]

Turkey continued its close ties to Israel despite significant protest from Islamic groups. The military maintained its ties with Israel throughout the 1990s.[122] The two countries held joint training in 1996; Turkey gave Israel access to its airspace for training, and negotiated arms deals.[123] And the military conducted naval maneuvers with Israel against the wishes of Erbakan, who was then the prime minister.[124]

The strongest example of secular forces' power is the "soft coup" that removed Erbakan from power in 1997. Erbakan faced increasingly strong secularist protests during his rule. On February 28, 1997, the top officials of the Turkish military implemented several policies that further restricted religious activities in Turkey.[125] The military then increasingly minimized Erbakan's power, excluding him from security-related decision-making in an attempt to push him to quit.[126] He stepped down in June of that year, and the state soon banned the RP.[127]

Post-9/11

The religion–state relationship in Turkey changed significantly with the rise of the religious conservative AKP in 2002, although the country's official secularism remained. The AKP – a coalition of Islamists, conservative voters, and business interests – won in the 2002 parliamentary elections, and stayed in power for the rest of the decade. The party increased the role of religion in Turkish politics, but maintained a commitment to the

[120] Turkey: Closure of National Youth Foundation Halts Support to Islamic Terrorism, January 27, 2001.
[121] Turkey: Fethullah Gulen Trial to Start on Oct 16 at Ankara State Security Court, September 7, 2000.
[122] Turkey: Military Said Firmly Behind Agreement with Israel, May 23, 1996.
[123] Suha Bolukbasi, "Behind the Turkish-Israeli Alliance: A Turkish View," *Journal of Palestine Studies* 29, no. 1 (1999); Gulnur Aybet, *Turkey's Foreign Policy and Its Implications for the West: A Turkish Perspective*, Rusi Whitehall Paper Series (Dorset: Roal United Services Institute for Defence Studies, 1994); Jung and Piccoli, *Turkey at the Crossroads: Ottoman Legacies and a Greater Middle East.*
[124] Turkey: Turkish Army Defies Erbakan in Bid To Force Him to Quit, May 15, 1997.
[125] Kuru, *Secularism and State Policies Towards Religion: The United States, France, and Turkey.*
[126] Turkey: Turkish Army Defies Erbakan in Bid To Force Him to Quit, May 15, 1997.
[127] Turkey: Diplomat' Cited on Army Plan to Ban Welfare Party, July 13, 1997; Kepel, *Jihad: The Trail of Political Islam.*

country's secularism. And the military continued to exert influence over politics to avoid secularism being undermined.

When the AKP came to power in 2002, the country had a religiously oriented party in charge of a single-party government for the first time in decades. After the FP was banned, the party split into two factions. The more hard-line Islamists in the party formed the SP. The "moderate" wing, in turn – combining Islamic-oriented figures like Recep Tayyip Erdogan and Abdullah Gul with business interests – became the AKP.[128] The party benefited from economic problems and widespread anger at the ruling parties to win in the 2002 elections.[129]

Once in power, the AKP pushed for an increased public role of religion. Erdogan, as prime minister, tried to criminalize adultery and increase the ability of women to wear headscarves.[130] And the AKP attempted to make it easier for students to study in religious schools.[131] Erdogan also advocated for Muslim causes internationally. He was critical of European states' restrictions on Muslim women's ability to wear headscarves, arguing that this was a decision for a "Muslim theologian," not secular courts.[132] And he was also critical of the idea of "moderate Islam," stating that "there is no need to place a word before or after Islam."[133] This continued throughout his tenure. In 2011, the Turkish minister for EU accession claimed Turkey was an example of a state combining "Islamic culture together with democracy."[134] After the controversial 2012 film that was sharply critical of Muhammad – which some saw as blasphemous – Erdogan called for "Islamophobia" to be recognized as a "crime against humanity."[135]

Erdogan changed Turkey's foreign policy as well. The AKP broke with many long-standing security policies, including relations with Middle Eastern states, Cyprus, and Armenia.[136] He increased outreach to other

---

[128] Yavuz, *Secularism and Muslim Democracy in Turkey.*

[129] Robins, "Confusion at Home, Confusion Abroad: Turkey between Copenhagen and Iraq."

[130] Fuller, *The New Turkish Republic: Turkey as a Pivotal State in the Muslim World.*

[131] Ibid.; Highlights: Turkish Islamist Press, December 16, 2005.

[132] Turkey's Erdogan: Muslim Theologian, Not ECHR, Authorized to Rule on Headscarf, November 16, 2005.

[133] Turkey's Erdogan on 'Moderate Islam,' Iraq, EU, Israel-Palestine Conflict, PKK, April 26, 2005.

[134] Minister Bagis Says Turkey Example of State Combining Islamic Culture, Democracy, March 5, 2011.

[135] Turkey's Erdogan to Comment More on 'Innocence of Muslims' at UN 25 Sep Assembly, September 17, 2012.

[136] Yasin Aktay, "Politics at Home, Politics in the World the Return of the Political in Turkish Foreign Policy," *Mediterranean Quarterly* 21, no. 1 (2010).

Muslim countries. This included a peacekeeping trip to Iraq to resolve Sunni-Shia tensions, increased economic and diplomatic ties to Syria, and relations with Iran.[137] Erdogan also took more steps to support Palestinians, leading to some tensions with Israel. And Turkey increased its visibility in the OIC; it hosted an OIC meeting for the first time in 2003, and became chairman in 2004.[138]

Moreover, Islamic groups had some influence over the party due to the makeup of its electoral coalition. The AKP appealed to conservative working and middle-class voters, many of whom the Islamist parties also courted. And Islamist members of the AKP helped it to maintain its electoral power. As a result, the AKP did have to partially answer to Islamists. For example, a 2003 article argued that some AKP supporters are hesitant to acknowledge that the 2003 attacks in Istanbul were conducted by religious groups, resulting in Erdogan having to hedge in his responses.[139]

And the AKP took action against secularist forces. The government ordered the arrest of several former government officials involved in the 1997 overthrow of Erbakan.[140] And in 2012 the government tried hundreds of Army officers for purportedly planning the aforementioned 2003 plot against the AKP government. The government also launched the controversial investigation into the "Ergenekon" movement. The government claims this movement is a coalition of military officials, journalists, and government employees that had been working to harass Islamic groups and keep them from participating in politics. As part of the investigation, the AKP has arrested numerous journalists, military officials and other members of civil society on suspicion of belonging to the movement. While the veracity of the claims is unclear – as some argue the AKP is using this to harass opponents – it does indicate the AKP's efforts to combat secularist forces in society.

Yet, the AKP repeatedly emphasized it was not going to implement Islamic law and said it would uphold secularism. In a 2001 interview with a secular paper, Erdogan said he was against "a state based on Islamic principles," and instead wanted a country "where the community can live like a Muslim."[141] Erdogan also discussed Turkey as a "model

---

[137] Fuller, *The New Turkish Republic: Turkey as a Pivotal State in the Muslim World*; Rabasa and Larrabee, *The Rise of Political Islam in Turkey*.

[138] Fuller, *The New Turkish Republic: Turkey as a Pivotal State in the Muslim World*.

[139] Turkey: Writer Cites AKP Government's Difficulties Combatting 'Religious Terrorism,' November 23, 2003.

[140] Turkey: Former Education Board Members Detained in 28 February Probe, June 23, 2012.

[141] Turkey's Erdogan on Political Views, AK Party's Objectives, August 28, 2001.

country" that "[fused] the culture of Islam with that of democracy."[142] And at a 2004 conference, Erdogan argued that the "AKP does not believe it is right to pursue politics on the basis of religion," but does hold to the "importance of religion as a social value."[143]

Instead of pushing Islamic reforms, the AKP often emphasized economic and political development. Some have noted that the AKP focused primarily on democracy, human rights, and economic liberalization.[144] For example, in a 2007 interview, Gul pointed to Turkish support for EU accession and economic and political liberalization, continuing, "Why would we do this is if we were trying to Islamize Turkey?"[145] And in 2008 Erdogan announced a massive project to develop the economy and infrastructure of southeastern Turkey as a way of preventing terrorist violence there.[146]

Moreover, the AKP kept its distance from more extremist elements in Islamic groups both in Turkey and abroad. Some observers have noted the minimal links between the AKP leadership and more hard-line Islamist followers.[147] Also, the party adopted some policies to combat extremism. For example, shortly after the US invasion of Afghanistan, Turkey's Religious Affairs Department claimed it would send clergy to Afghanistan and rebuild a religious school it had constructed in Afghanistan before the Taliban rose to power. The head of the Religious Affairs Department said this was intended to "promote real Islam" in Afghanistan and combat the Taliban.[148] Turkey also sent religious advisors to promote tolerance among Turkish communities in Europe.[149]

And the military maintained its support of state secularism, with frequent clashes with the AKP. The military expressed concern about AKP efforts to end the ban on headscarves and facilitate religious

---

[142] Turkey's Vision, Role in 'Greater Middle East Project' Viewed, March 2, 2004.

[143] "Turkish Premier Says Party Against Religion-Based Politics," BME-P, January 10, 2004.

[144] Ihsan Dagi, "Turkey's AKP in Power," *Journal of Democracy* 19, no. 3 (2008); Tepe Sultan, "Politics between Market and Islam: The Electoral Puzzles and Changing Prospects of Pro-Islamic Parties," *Mediterranean Quarterly* 18, no. 2 (2007).

[145] Gordon and Taspinar, *Winning Turkey: How America, Europe, and Turkey Can Revive a Fading Partnership*: 9.

[146] Turkey: GAP Action Plan for Southeast Anatolia Outlined, May 27, 2008.

[147] Sultan, "Politics between Market and Islam: The Electoral Puzzles and Changing Prospects of Pro-Islamic Parties."

[148] Turkey Said Decided to Send Muslim Clergymen to Afghanistan to Fight Fanaticism, December 13, 2001.

[149] Religious Affairs Official Asserts Turkey's Secular Trait, Condemns Terrorism, April 25, 2004.

education.[150] Also, in 2005, a top military official publicly opposed US efforts to support "moderate Islam" and said that "the secular state and moderate Islam cannot coexist."[151] The most prominent example of this was the tension in 2007 over the appointment of Abdullah Gul as president. The president had traditionally been seen as guardian of Turkey's secularist system, and many secularists – especially in the military – were concerned about Gul due to his Islamic leanings. During debates in Parliament over his appointment, the military placed an article on its Website discussing its commitment to secularism and hinting it might take action to protect the country's secular system. Many saw this as a warning that it would intervene if Gul became president, and the incident became known as the "e-coup." Despite the warning, however, Gul's appointment went through and he became president.[152]

HISTORICAL RELIGION–STATE RELATIONSHIP

Turkey's leaders for the most part did not follow the lead of Islamic pressure in domestic and foreign affairs, even when the leaders were generally sympathetic to or in league with these groups. This manifested itself in counterterrorism cooperation with the United States. But this was not merely leaders ignoring social groups that had little political sway. Instead, Turkey's religion–state relationship structured the interactions between the regime and Islamic groups just as Pakistan's and the UAE's did. But in contrast to those countries, the distant religion–state relationship limited the power of Islamist groups and made it difficult for them to make significant changes to the state's behavior.

The Founding of the Turkish Republic to the 1980s

The early years of the Turkish Republic involved the removal of Islam from its formerly official status under the Ottoman Empire. Mustafa Kemal – a military officer also known as Ataturk – created modern-day Turkey. After the Ottoman Empire's defeat in World War I, Ataturk led the Turkish nationalist movement to defeat Allied forces and gain

---

[150] Selection List: Turkish Press, June 27, 2005.
[151] Turkey: Gen Basbug's Speech Said Shows Turkish-US Policies Mostly Overlapping, June 8, 2005.
[152] Ibon Villelabeita, "Ex-Turkish Army chief says "E-coup" justified," *Reuters*, May 8, 2009. Available at www.reuters.com/article/2009/05/08/us-turkey-military-general-idUSTRE5471UQ20090508.

Turkey's independence. Ataturk accelerated the secularizing reforms that began in the latter days of the Ottoman Empire.[153] He abolished the Ottoman-era Caliphate and removed Islam as the state religion; he also required the adoption of Western dress and script.[154] In addition to this, the Turkish state restricted the role of Islam in schools, limited the ability of women to wear headscarves, and restricted the practice of Sufi orders.[155] The military committed itself to strongly defending this "Kemalism" against changes by society or political leaders.[156]

Turkey's early foreign policy was marked by defensiveness over losing territory. Some discuss this as the "Sevres Syndrome"; this refers to the Treaty of Sevres between the Allied powers and the Ottoman Empire after World War I, which broke up the Ottoman Empire. Early disputes with Iraq and Syria over borders, and Stalin's expansionary behaviors after World War II further increased these worries. As a result, Ataturk desired to avoid becoming too entangled in European contests, and adopted a policy of "active nuetrality"; this translated into Turkey remaining on the sidelines during World War II, declaring war on Germany only when it was clear the Axis powers would lose.[157]

Turkey's first multi-party elections, held shortly after World War II, resulted in the election of the conservative religious Democratic Party. Significant segments of the rural population and business community were upset with the ruling secular Republican People's Party (*Cumhuriyet Halk Partisi*, CHP) and there was greater demand for an increased visibility of Islam.[158] This led to multi-party elections in 1950, in which a combination of pious conservative voters and business interests helped Adnan Menderes' Democratic Party come to power.

These elections brought into power a religiously leaning government that was overthrown by the military and followed by a series of weak successors. Menderes increased the public visibility of Islam in Turkish

[153] Fuller, *The New Turkish Republic: Turkey as a Pivotal State in the Muslim World*.
[154] Ibid.; Soner Cagaptay, *Islam Secularism and Nationalism in Modern Turkey: Who Is a Turk?* (London: Routledge Taylor & Francis Group, 2006).
[155] Kuru, *Secularism and State Policies Towards Religion: The United States, France, and Turkey*.
[156] Dismorr, *Turkey Decoded*.
[157] Feroz Ahmad, "The Historical Background of Turkey's Foreign Policy," in *The Future of Turkish Foreign Policy*, eds. Lenore G. Martin and Dimitris Keridis (Cambridge, MA: MIT Press, 2004).
[158] Pope and Pope, *Turkey Unveiled: A History of Modern Turkey*; Sena Karasipahi, "Comparing Islamic Resurgence Movements in Turkey and Iran," *Middle East Journal* 63, no. 1 (2009).

politics. He opened religious schools throughout the country, had the Arabic call to prayer used in mosques, and started observing Ramadan; his policy changes increased the influence of Islamic groups in Turkish politics.[159] These reforms threatened the military, which overthrew Menderes in 1960, giving way to significant social disruption. The military accused Menderes of violating the constitution and executed him in 1961. Following the coup, a series of weak coalition governments ruled the country in the 1960s and 1970s; widespread clashes occurred among leftists, rightists, and secularists throughout the 1960s and 1970s, and Islamic groups became more active in politics.[160]

Turkey developed closer ties to the United States in the 1950s, although this deteriorated in the 1960s and 1970s. Turkey aligned itself with the United States after World War II in response to concerns about the Soviet Union; Turkey joined NATO, participated in the Korean War, and developed ties with other US allies like Israel. Yet, after the United States refused to support Turkey in its tensions with Greece over Cyprus – beginning in the 1960s – Turkey reached out to Middle Eastern states and the Soviet Union as an alternative to US support.

The 1980 Military Coup and Late 1980s–Early 1990s reforms

Increasing unrest in Turkey in the 1970s led to another military coup in 1980. As was noted, political violence was increasingly intensifying in the 1970s. At the same time, Islamic activism became more pronounced. Islamic groups became more organized and held more frequent protests; a key figure in this was Necmettin Erbakan, who had long been active in politics and would later lead an influential political party and briefly serve as prime minister.[161] The military moved decisively after Erbakan called for Islamic law in the country during a protest against Israel.[162]

The military government attempted to decrease the power of Islamic groups, while at the same time increasing state support for religious

---

[159] Pope and Pope, *Turkey Unveiled: A History of Modern Turkey*; Karasipahi, "Comparing Islamic Resurgence Movements in Turkey and Iran"; Sencer Ayata, "Patronage, Party, and State: The Politicization of Islam in Turkey," ibid., 50 (1996).

[160] Kepel, *Jihad: The Trail of Political Islam*; Pope and Pope, *Turkey Unveiled: A History of Modern Turkey*.

[161] Erbakan led a variety of political parties throughout the next few decades, as they frequently were banned for their religious leanings. These are (in chronological order): the Welfare Party, the Virtue Party, and the Felicity Party.

[162] Pope and Pope, *Turkey Unveiled: A History of Modern Turkey*.

activities.[163] Reforms included the establishment of articles specifically banning Islamic political activity; the military also restricted religious education and set up secular, pro-military parties to compete in elections.[164] At the same time, the military government created the "Turkish-Islamic synthesis," which ideologically fused Turkish nationalism and Islamism to draw both nationalists and Islamists into supporting the regime.[165]

The country transitioned back to civilian leadership under Turgut Ozal, who dramatically changed Turkey's domestic and foreign politics. Ozal liberalized Turkey's economy through a series of reforms that empowered Anatolian middle-class business interests and lower classes in urban areas.[166] He was also close to the United States; Ozal had good relations with both President Bush and Clinton and supported the United States in its military operation against Iraq in the early 1990s.[167] This occurred in the broader context of improving ties with the United States, as the United States began to send aid to Turkey and allow it to buy US arms.[168]

Ozal's reforms also increased the prominence of religion in Turkey. Ozal reformed the state control of religion, increasing the power of the Director of Religious Affairs and facilitating Islamic banking and investment from the Persian Gulf.[169] He also publicly called for the acceptance of religion in Turkish politics and supported religious schools.[170] And Ozal relied heavily on conservative religious voters and Islamic groups for political support.[171]

This created space for an expansion of Islamic contention. Some Islamist parties formed after the end of the military government, and

---

[163] Eric Rouleau, "The Challenges to Turkey," *Foreign Affairs* 72, no. 5 (1993).

[164] Pope and Pope, *Turkey Unveiled: A History of Modern Turkey*; Kuru, *Secularism and State Policies Towards Religion: The United States, France, and Turkey.*

[165] Aybet, *Turkey's Foreign Policy and Its Implications for the West: A Turkish Perspective*; Yavuz, *Secularism and Muslim Democracy in Turkey*; Gordon and Taspinar, *Winning Turkey: How America, Europe, and Turkey Can Revive a Fading Partnership.*

[166] Fuller, *The New Turkish Republic: Turkey as a Pivotal State in the Muslim World.*

[167] Ibid.; Pope and Pope, *Turkey Unveiled: A History of Modern Turkey*; Sabri Sayari, "Turkey and the Middle East in the 1990s," *Journal of Palestine Studies* 26, no. 3 (1997).

[168] Pope and Pope, *Turkey Unveiled: A History of Modern Turkey.*

[169] Ayata, "Patronage, Party, and State: The Politicization of Islam in Turkey"; Pope and Pope, *Turkey Unveiled: A History of Modern Turkey.*

[170] *Turkey Unveiled: A History of Modern Turkey*; Kuru, *Secularism and State Policies Towards Religion: The United States, France, and Turkey.*

[171] Pope and Pope, *Turkey Unveiled: A History of Modern Turkey.*

Islamic publications proliferated.[172] And religiously minded voters became more prominent due to the migration of conservative Anatolians to the cities and the rise of a conservative middle class under Ozal's reforms; at the same time, tensions between secularists and Islamists became more pronounced.[173]

Kurdish unrest began in this period. While this did not directly involve religious contention, the military often saw Kurdish and Islamic activism as linked security threats, necessitating strong measures in response.[174] The Kurds are a non-Turkish ethnic group located in southeast Turkey, Iran, Iraq, and Syria. Kurdish separatism in Turkey emerged in the 1970s and fighting began in the 1980s.[175] The primary combatant on the Kurdish side was the Kurdistan Workers' Party (*Partiya Karkerên Kurdistan*, PKK) a Marxist nationalist. This development greatly concerned both the military and Turkish nationalists, who saw it as a threat to Turkish identity and territorial integrity.[176] The military conducted aggressive campaigns against the PKK, which continued into the 1990s; additionally, fighting broke out between the PKK and Hizballah, an Islamic militant group in the southeast some believed had military ties.[177]

Overview: Persistently Distant Religion–State Ties

Turkey's religion–state relationship is thus nearly the opposite of Pakistan's. Turkey was founded as a secular state, with institutional means to preserve this such as the power of the military. This persisted over several decades, even as Islamic groups increased in prominence and gained electoral office. A political opening of sorts did occur in the late 1980s,

---

[172] Fuller, *The New Turkish Republic: Turkey as a Pivotal State in the Muslim World.*

[173] Nilüfer Gole, "Secularism and Islamism in Turkey: The Making of Elites and Counter-Elites," *Middle East Journal* 51, no. 1 (1997); Michele Penner Angrist, "Party Systems and Regime Formation in the Modern Middle East: Explaining Turkish Exceptionalism," *Comparative Politics* 36, no. 2 (2004); Yavuz, *Secularism and Muslim Democracy in Turkey*; Fuller, *The New Turkish Republic: Turkey as a Pivotal State in the Muslim World*; Yavuz, *Islamic Political Identity in Turkey*; Sayari, "Turkey and the Middle East in the 1990s"; Kuru, *Secularism and State Policies Towards Religion: The United States, France, and Turkey.*

[174] M. Hakan Yavuz, "Turkish-Israeli Relations through the Lens of the Turkish Identity Debate," *Journal of Palestine Studies* 27, no. 1 (1997); Robert Olson, "Turkey-Iran Relations, 1997 to 2000: The Kurdish and Islamist Questions," *Third World Quarterly* 21, no. 5 (2000).

[175] Brown, "The Turkish Imbroglio: Its Kurds."

[176] Ibid.

[177] Hizballah is a Kurdish militant group unconnected to Hezbollah in Lebanon. There is significant debate over its origins and backing; some claim it is backed by the Turkish military to combat the PKK, while some argue it is supported by Iran.

creating space for the Islamic contention and rise of the AKP discussed earlier, but the official separation between religion and state remained.

ANALYSIS

The contrast between Turkey and both Pakistan and the UAE is apparent, particularly how the differing religion–state relationship corresponds to different state response to Islamic contention over counterterrorism. By the time US counterterrorism efforts ramped up, the strict separation between religion and state in Turkey had limited the influence of Islamic groups over Turkish leaders even as these groups became more prominent in the country in the 1990s. As a result, Turkish leaders pursued many policies actively opposed by Islamic groups – such as close ties to the United States and Israel – and stepped in to limit Islamic influence over politics, as when an Islamist prime minister was elected in the mid-1990s. Even when the religiously conservative AKP was elected in 2002, the state persisted in its religiously contentious security policies. This readily translated into close support for US counterterrorism efforts after 9/11.

As with the other chapters, though, I want to further demonstrate this close connection between a *distant religion–state relationship* and *extensive counterterrorism cooperation* with an in-depth analysis of this case. In this section I discuss how the religion–state relationship in Turkey contributed to its extensive counterterrorism cooperation, and provide evidence suggesting my claims on the effects of religion–state relationships are supported by events in Turkey. I am basically analyzing a negative – why Turkey's Islamic politics did not influence its counterterrorism policies – so the evidence is a bit less direct than the positive examples of religious groups influencing Pakistan's counterterrorism. But we can find evidence that Islamic groups were of little concern to leaders, and that counterterrorism policies were not formulated with Islamic opposition in mind. Of course, as always there are other aspects of Turkish politics that could explain its cooperation with the United States. And one may argue that the reason for its cooperation is the relative lack of Islamic contention in Turkey, compared to Pakistan. I draw on the same qualitative methods I used in the other case studies to address these various alternative explanations.

In this section, I will specifically demonstrate that: (1) Turkish leaders formulated its counterterrorism policies in a manner that was divorced from religious considerations, effectively ignoring Islamic opposition when working with the United States, (2) this was possible due to the limits on Islamic political activity the country's religion–state relationship produced, and (3) although Turkey did not cooperate on counterterrorism *because* of its distant religion–state relationship, it would have been unable to do so without it.

The Effect of Turkey's Distant Religion–State Relationship on its Counterterrorism Cooperation

The low religion–state connections in Turkey corresponded to the high level of counterterrorism cooperation between that country and the United States. By the 1990s, religious contention had increased in the country, with Islamic groups and religiously inclined voters becoming more visible. Yet, the state remained officially secular and the military and judiciary intervened to prevent religious groups from influencing state behavior. When Turkey began cooperating with the United States on counterterrorism in the late 1990s, leaders were able to ignore religious opposition to this counterterrorism cooperation due to minimal connections between religion and the state. As a result, counterterrorism cooperation remained high even as opposition increased and tensions emerged between the two countries in other areas.

Like many other majority-Muslim countries, Turkey experienced significant religious contention. Islamist groups were active throughout the time period of this study, pressing for more religiously based policies and attacking the regime when it took steps these groups disagreed with. Many groups also attacked the United States and, by extension, Turkish regimes that were allied with the United States. This continued under the AKP, as it was seen as insufficiently pious and too close to the United States. Turkey also experienced violent contention from domestic religious groups and a few plots by al-Qaeda.

Yet, religion and state remained separate. While Islamic parties were often successful electorally, they rarely made lasting changes to Turkish politics due to interventions from the military and judiciary. The officially secular system in Turkey gave legal justifications for such acts as necessary to uphold the republic. As a result, Islamic groups were unable to translate electoral success into policy impacts. And due to the minimal electoral power of Islamic groups, the state rarely responded to religious contention by changing its behavior. When it did increase ties to religion – as with the 1980s "Turkish-Islamic synthesis" – this was an attempt to maintain control of increasingly active religious groups.[178]

The strongest evidence for the enduring power of Turkey's institutional religion–state separation is the behavior of the AKP once it came to power. Unlike in Pakistan – where religious parties elected to power implemented Islamic law – the AKP for the most part attempted to distance itself from such transformative programs. The AKP's religious policies have focused primarily on expanding the public role of religion in the country.[179] As M. Hakan Yavuz has noted, the AKP is "deeply involved in Islamic social ethics . . . and stresses the religious values and interests of its pious electorate"; it does not, however, "seek the religious transformation of state and society [emphasis removed]."[180] And while it does contain Islamist members, its support base is diverse enough that it is not completely reliant on them to stay in power.[181] Granted, much of this may be strategic; the AKP worried about the military intervening if it made too dramatic a break with existing Turkish foreign policy.[182] Whether the AKP's general adherence to Turkey's secularism was a strategic decision in order to avoid a military coup or due to a sincere acceptance of the distant religion–state relationship, the institutional configuration undoubtedly structured the religious policies of this party once it came to power.

Thus, Turkey's distant religion–state relationship limited the political influence of Islamist groups. And this can be seen in the specific issue of Turkey's counterterrorism policies. In the Pakistan case study, we saw Pakistani leaders attempting to downplay cooperation with the United States, such as Musharraf's use of Islamic history to discuss it as an alliance of convenience. Pakistani leaders also trumpeted their uncooperative behavior in religious terms; as I discussed in that chapter, some Pakistani leaders not only continued supporting Kashmiri militants in contradiction of US preferences, but emphasized the importance of involvement in this conflict as part of solidarity with Muslims around

[178] Turkey: Army's Erratic Policy on Religion Viewed, April 8, 1996.
[179] R. Quinn Mecham, "From the Ashes of Virtue, a Promise of Light: The Transformation of Political Islam in Turkey," *Third World Quarterly* 25, no. 2 (2004); Rabasa and Larrabee, *The Rise of Political Islam in Turkey*; Fuller, *The New Turkish Republic: Turkey as a Pivotal State in the Muslim World*.
[180] Yavuz, *Secularism and Muslim Democracy in Turkey*: 8.
[181] Sultan, "Politics between Market and Islam: The Electoral Puzzles and Changing Prospects of Pro-Islamic Parties"; Carl Vick, "Party Tied to Islam Wins Big in Turkey," *The Washington Post*, November 4, 2002.
[182] Yavuz, *Secularism and Muslim Democracy in Turkey*.

the world. This was because the leaders feared religious backlash for cooperation, and desired to gain religious support for not cooperating. In Turkey, nearly the opposite occurred. Turkey repeatedly emphasized its cooperation with the United States and the two countries' close ties, discussing how important this was for Turkey. And when it broke with the United States, it did not use religious rhetoric to justify this break.

This can be seen in a few examples. In the section on US-Turkish counterterrorism cooperation, I noted the many strong affirmations Turkish leaders made of Turkey's role in the US efforts. It is not unfair to say that many Turkish officials seemed to take pride in the country's prominent place. And Turkish leaders often saw US counterterrorism efforts not as a burden, but as essential to its own domestic priorities. For example, some saw working with the United States on counterterrorism as a way to gain more support for Turkey's efforts against Kurdish separatism.[183] Likewise, Turkish non-cooperation was not framed in religious terms. This is particularly apparent in the US invasion of Iraq. Erdogan framed his opposition to the Iraq War in terms of Turkey's interests, not religion. In a 2003 interview, he pointed to the consequences of the first Gulf War – specifically the lost trade and increasing terrorism in the southeast – and stated that "we do not approach the issue of Iraq from the religious standpoint. We approach it from the standpoint of universal law."[184]

We see this pattern of behavior because Turkish regimes' security policymaking process is insulated from Islamic pressure, due to the distant religion–state relationship. Again, it is difficult to demonstrate a negative – that Turkish regimes *did not* respond to Islamic opposition by limiting cooperation because of the political institutions – but these examples fit with my claims about the effects of religion–state relationships. The distant religion–state relationship in Turkey limited Islamic groups' political power and the salience of religious issues, so the regime could cooperate with the United States with little fear of dramatic repercussions. If this had not been the case – if, as in Pakistan, Islamic groups and issues dominated politics – Turkish leaders would have downplayed their cooperation with the United States and emphasized non-cooperation, not the other way around.

---

[183] Turkey Said Pleased with US Determination to Fight Terrorism, September 22, 2001; Milliyet Column Sees Terrorist Attacks Making US More Sympathetic Toward Turkey, September 12, 2001; Turkey: Column Lauds Government Decision to Send Special Force to Afghanistan, November 2, 2001; Turkey: Erdogan Comments on Kurdish Issue, Presidential System, Regional Issues, November 30, 2012.

[184] Turkey's Erdogan Comments on Role of Army, Iraq, EU, Islam, January 24, 2003.

Historical Legacies of Religion–State Relationship

Even though the distant religion–state relationship seems to be connected with Turkey's counterterrorism cooperation, one could still argue that Turkey's leaders were just responding to short-term political calculations. Islamic groups are not very powerful, and the Turkish state has an interest in working with the United States on counterterrorism. As with the other countries I discussed in this book, however, this political situation was not just leaders responding to immediate political pressure. It arose from the specific manner in which religion–state relationships developed throughout the twentieth century.

The reforms that Ataturk put in place when he formed Turkey established this path-dependent process. By establishing an officially secular state with various policy mechanisms to enforce this secularism, Ataturk created institutions that would structure Turkish politics for decades. This institutional configuration limited Islamic political activity, making it difficult for later religious groups to change the official secularism and leaving only relatively moderate religious groups able to influence political outcomes. And it made it easier for later regimes to further limit Islamic political activity. This took the form of three interlocking path-dependent processes that combined to create the political situation facilitating Turkey's close cooperation with the United States on counterterrorism.

The first was the recurring steps the state took to maintain its distant religion–state relationship. As was noted, Turkey was not only officially secular, it empowered the military to intervene in politics and protect that secularism. It did this primarily through a series of coups against governments the military deemed as too religious. These coups disrupted the ability of Islamic groups to operate and made later governments more hesitant to adopt religious policies. For example, some have argued that the AKP's hesitation to break ties with the United States came partially from its fears of being overthrown.[185] Thus, this institutional system quickly became "locked-in," in part through the military's willingness to step in when politics turned away from the set relationship. This made it very difficult for Islamic groups to change the system in later years.

The second effect was to both make it easier for later regimes to further strengthen the official secularism of Turkey and make it more likely they would do so. The distant religion–state relationship gave regimes political

[185] Yavuz, *Secularism and Muslim Democracy in Turkey*.

and rhetorical tools to increase the distance between religion and state. For example, following the 1960 coup, the military drafted a constitution in 1961 that expanded Ataturk's secularizing policies, establishing official protections for the state's secular system that made it harder for them to be changed in the future.[186] This process continued after the 1980 military coup, as the new constitution put in place further restricted the activities of religious groups; for example, Article 163 banned communism and Islamism. Moreover, these actions increased the power of secularist groups, which challenged Islamic groups for power. In addition to building on earlier legal restrictions on religious politics, the state at times appealed to Turkey's official secularism in justifying these limits. For example, in the 1980s, the military government set up what it called a "Turkish-Islamic synthesis," co-opting religious opposition by tying Islamic beliefs to Turkish nationalism.[187] Thus, in addition to "locking-in" the distant religion–state relationships, Turkey's political institutions also set in place a positive feedback loop in which existing configurations made it more likely that similar policies would be enacted in the future.

Finally, the institutional configuration in Turkey reinforced itself by limiting widespread extremist Islamic contention. As I noted earlier, while violent Islamic militant groups exist, most Islamic parties tend to be nonviolent and relatively moderate. That is, few explicitly call for an Islamic state, and even those that do tend to work within the political system. And the most influential Islamic groups in the country – like the Nur and Gulen movements – advocate pluralism and religious tolerance. Some have argued this was produced by Turkey's religion–state relationship, as the relative openness of the system – compared to the active repression of Islamists in Egypt and pre-Revolution Iran – contributed to the rise of moderate religious politics.[188] This is possible, although it is difficult to demonstrate this, especially in the scope of this book. It is undoubtable, however, that Turkey's religion–state relationship actively discouraged groups from adopting extremist or openly Islamist political platforms. Islamist groups – or even groups suspected of being Islamist – attempting to gain power risked military intervention, as occurred several times in Turkey's history. As Nasr puts it, "Turkey's Islamists learned to adopt

---

[186] Kuru, *Secularism and State Policies Towards Religion: The United States, France, and Turkey.*

[187] M. Hakan Yavuz, "The Politics of Fear: The Rise of the Nationalist Action Party (MHP) in Turkey," *Middle East Journal* 56, no. 2 (2002).

[188] Sena Karasipahi, "Comparing Islamic Resurgence Movements in Turkey and Iran," ibid. 63, no. 1 (2009). Yavuz, *Secularism and Muslim Democracy in Turkey.*

pragmatic policies to avoid the generals' wrath."[189] And those that were elected, such as Erbakan in the 1990s, were limited in their ability to change Turkey's policies due to the strength of the military.[190] Similarly, others argue that the AKP was moderate in its approach to religious issues due to pressure from secularists.[191]

These three aspects of Turkey's historical religion–state relationship contributed to the political situation Turkey's leaders faced when responding to US counterterrorism pressure. The positive feedback loop of the distant religion–state relationship gave leaders rhetorical and legal tools to limit Islamic groups' influence and ignore opposition to working with the United States. And the relative absence of extremist groups or influential Islamist parties due to the limiting effect of the religion–state relationship decreased some of the pressure on the regime to follow these groups' lead. Moreover, the lock-in of the institutions made it difficult for religious groups to change the religion–state relationship, even when the governments were aligned with them. The persistence of Turkey's distant religion–state relationship and the security policies it enabled under the AKP provides evidence for the durable effects of these religion–state relationships on politics.

Alternative Explanations

As the previous explanation shows, the historical development of Turkey's distant religion–state relationship significantly influenced the nature of its religious politics, which in turn enabled its leaders to work closely with the United States on counterterrorism. But the religion–state relationship did not cause Turkey to cooperate with the United States. As I pointed out in Chapter 2, religion influences regimes' calculations but their ultimate counterterrorism policies represent a balance between religious pressure and strategic calculations. As a result, numerous other factors also mattered in US-Turkey counterterrorism cooperation, many of which analysts have pointed to as alternative explanations for the apparent role of religion–state relationships. In this section I address these alternative explanations, demonstrating that, while some of them are valid, we

---

[189] Vali Nasr, "The Rise of 'Muslim Democracy'" *Journal of Democracy* 16, no. 2 (2005): 18.

[190] Bolukbasi, "Behind the Turkish-Israeli Alliance: A Turkish View."

[191] Turkey's Birand Says Anti-AKP Circles Surprised with Outcome of Elections, July 24, 2007; Mecham, " From the Ashes of Virtue, a Promise of Light: The Transformation of Political Islam in Turkey."

cannot understand Turkey's counterterrorism behavior without taking its religion–state relationship into account.

One alternative explanation is that Turkey just faces less Islamic pressure than a state like Pakistan. That is, Islamic groups may not be as opposed to US-Turkish counterterrorism cooperation as they are in other states or there may be fewer active Islamic groups in general. Many have pointed to the "moderate Islam" of Turkey. For example, Murat Somer, a Turkish academic, summed up this argument as the claim that Turkey "[succeeded] because of moderate Islamists."[192] Applied to counterterrorism, this would be the claim that Turkey is a close partner of the United States because of its moderate Islam, which limited the sort of opposition to cooperation seen in a place like Pakistan.

This is a popular argument, but is not very effective in understanding US-Turkish counterterrorism cooperation. As I discussed before, there was significant opposition to counterterrorism cooperation by Islamic groups both before and after 9/11. It is true that many Islamic groups in Turkey are not as extreme as in other majority-Muslim countries, but they still strongly opposed counterterrorism cooperation, so leaders would face pressure against this. And Turkey did face violent threats from militants.

Alternately, some may argue that Turkey's greater cooperation is due to the strength of the Turkish state. Yet, starting in the 1980s, the public increased its influence over the state but counterterrorism cooperation remains high. And while Turkey's military often intervened in politics, the country did experience recurring elections that limited the state's power to act independently of society. Moreover, the nature of the Turkish state's control over society is related to religion–state connections, as the official secularism empowers the military to intervene in politics. Granted, the AKP's reforms may change this, but this would be due to a differing religion–state relationship, which I discuss in the concluding chapter. This explanation is thus partially valid, but not to the detriment of my theory. The Turkish state's strength does not explain all aspects of counterterrorism, and it can actually contextualize the effects of the religion–state relationship as it arose from this institutional configuration.

The inadequacy of this alternative explanation is also apparent from the attending counterfactual. The counterfactual of this alternative explanation is that a strong state with a different religion–state relationship –

---

[192] Murat Somer, "Turkey's Model of 'Moderate' Islamism Can Be Misleading," *The National*, October 1, 2012.

like a strong officially Islamic state – would still cooperate extensively with the United States. The previous chapter on the UAE indicates the weakness of this counterfactual. Yes, the UAE was able to restrict Islamic groups and work with the United States, but this was complicated by its moderately close religion–state relationship. Thus, state strength matters, but it alone does not explain counterterrorism cooperation.

The prominence of Kurdish separatism could also explain the close counterterrorism cooperation. Turkey has long sought international support for its efforts against the Kurds, and fear of Kurdish separatism has affected its foreign policy in the past. Turkey's negative experience with Kurdish unrest after the 1991 US military action against Iraq likely drove its opposition to the 2003 invasion.[193] So Turkey might have worked with the United States on counterterrorism to further this goal.

This is partially valid, but does not undermine my argument. As discussed earlier, Turkey connected its struggle with the PKK to US actions against al-Qaeda. But seeking help with the PKK did not necessarily require the plethora of measures Turkey took on counterterrorism. Turkey launched numerous actions against al-Qaeda elements in the country that had little to do with the PKK, which indicate a commitment to counterterrorism beyond the Kurdish issue. Granted, one could argue this was merely an attempt to gain US support against the PKK in return. But even if true, this would merely contextualize it. Turkey was more amenable to strong counterterrorism policies due to its extant terrorism issue. But Turkey's religion–state relationship minimized the political influence of Islamic groups opposing cooperating with the United States, giving the regime the freedom of movement needed to pursue counterterrorism policies it may have already desired to undertake.

Moreover, there are reasons to question whether Turkish concerns about the PKK are a viable alternative explanation. The first is a counterfactual. This explanation would imply that any country experiencing widespread political violence would cooperate extensively with the United States on counterterrorism. But Pakistan experienced significant terrorism violence – by both the Islamic militants this book focuses on and ethnic separatist ones – that occurred alongside weak counterterrorism cooperation. Indeed, as I discussed in that chapter, some have argued that the violence in Pakistan is the cause of its counterterrorism policies, the

---

[193] Fuller, *The New Turkish Republic: Turkey as a Pivotal State in the Muslim World*; Robins, "Confusion at Home, Confusion Abroad: Turkey between Copenhagen and Iraq."

opposite of the hypothesized effect of domestic terrorism in the case of Turkey. It is difficult to accept that domestic terrorism can both promote counterterrorism cooperation – as some argue in regard to Turkey – and complicate it, as some claim with Pakistan, so this alternative explanation is questionable. Additionally, Turkey was not completely satisfied with US support for its anti-PKK efforts. As I discussed earlier, Turkish officials were rather angered by US criticism of its counterterrorism policies in the 1990s. And while the two became closer after 9/11, Turkey remained frustrated with what it saw as the United States' minimal assistance in countering the PKK. Thus, even if Turkey's counterterrorism cooperation with the United States was driven only by its concerns about the PKK – despite the issues with this claim I have pointed out – Turkish frustrations with US assistance should have led to decreased counterterrorism cooperation.

Additionally, one could argue that Turkey's desire to enter the European Union influenced its decision to cooperate with the United States on counterterrorism. Some have pointed to the EU process influencing several aspects of Erdogan's policies, including his initial positive steps on human rights.[194] Yet, the counterterrorism cooperation was likely not tied to EU accession. US counterterrorism actions were not incredibly popular in Europe, so it is unclear if working closely with the United States would increase support for Turkey's EU accession. Indeed, some in Turkey believed rejecting US requests for help in the 2003 Iraq invasion would endear the country to Europe.[195] And as was noted, Turkey remained frustrated with the lack of European support for its struggle with Kurdish groups. This explanation is thus incidental to the effects of religion–state connections on counterterrorism cooperation.

CONCLUSION

The two things most people seem to think about concerning Turkey's recent politics are the examples I used to open this chapter: the election of the AKP and the break with the United States over the invasion of Iraq. These examples, however, serve only to highlight the broader political dynamics in Turkey. Despite widespread religious contention and increasingly prominent Islamic groups, Turkey's leaders cooperated extensively with the United States on counterterrorism as they could

---

[194] Dismorr, *Turkey Decoded*.
[195] Ibid.

ignore or sidestep Islamic opposition without losing power. This was the result of Turkey's founding institutions, in which an official secularism at the country's founding perpetuated distance between religion groups and the state, minimizing their political power and ability to change Turkey's security policies. Religion can thus explain Turkey's counterterrorism cooperation, although it was the institutional distance between religion and state, not the lack of religious contention or the nature of Turkish Islam.

The case of Turkey provides further support for my argument concerning the role of religion–state relationships in US–Muslim counterterrorism cooperation. Turkey was a case of a distant religion–state relationship facilitating extensive counterterrorism cooperation. As the quantitative analysis suggested, states with more distant religion–state relationships tended to be more cooperative on counterterrorism than those with closer religion–state ties. This case study thus further verifies this finding. Moreover, it validates the mechanisms I suggested lead to this finding. The distant religion–state relationship led to weakened Islamic groups and constrained religiously oriented actors who came to power. Moreover, the insulation of the regime from these groups allowed it to implement policies strongly opposed by Islamic groups in society. But Turkey's cooperation was not overwhelmingly dismissive of religious opposition, and followed the expectations I laid out in Chapter 2. For example, some of the cooperation appears to involve *justification* through appeal to Islam, such as when officials claimed support for US-led actions in Afghanistan was intended to promote true Islam in that country. Combined with the quantitative analysis and the other case studies, this discussion of Turkey thus strongly supports my theorized argument about the role of religion–state relationships in counterterrorism cooperation. In the next and final chapter, I will summarize my argument and findings, discuss how it extends to other cases I have not mentioned here – including other countries' counterterrorism cooperation and Muslim states' reactions to the Arab Spring uprisings – and present its broader implications for the study of international relations.

Conclusion

Religion–State Relationships and Religion Beyond Counterterrorism

We can now answer the questions I posed in this book's introductory chapter. Why did Pakistan refuse to implement US preferences on education but covertly approve many US drone strikes in its territory? Why did Turkey not participate in the 2003 invasion of Iraq but arrest mass numbers of al-Qaeda operatives? Why did the UAE allow terrorist financing in the 1990s, but quickly crack down on these activities after 9/11?

Pakistan's close religion–state relationship made it difficult for elites to cooperate on counterterrorism initiatives that would spark opposition, while it could work with the United States on more covert areas. Turkey's opposition to the Iraq invasion was an outlier in its overwhelmingly cooperative interactions with the United States because its distant religion–state relationship allowed it to cooperate extensively when the regime desired. And the UAE's about-face on counterterrorism was due to the moderate influence Islamic sentiment had over the regime but its ability to ignore push back from Islamic groups when it wanted to work more closely with the United States.

But these are not just country-specific examples. They represent a broader trend in Islamic politics that lets us answer my general question: what explains the varying effects of religion on US–Muslim counterterrorism cooperation? This book's findings demonstrate that the great variation in Muslim states' cooperation with US counterterrorism initiatives was related to religion, specifically to the differing religion–state relationships among Muslim states. The quantitative analysis provided significant evidence that religion–state relationships correspond to lessened counterterrorism cooperation, even when other possible explanations – state strength, ties to the United States, domestic terrorism – are taken into account. It also showed that religion–state relationships' effects are greater than the effects of US aid on cooperation and that they are most significant among domestic aspects of counterterrorism.

The case studies revealed the mechanisms connecting religion–state relationships and counterterrorism. Islamic contention and opposition to counterterrorism was present in all the countries investigated. But the countries with closer religion–state ties faced greater pressure from Islamic groups to oppose US counterterrorism efforts, and were more likely to have regime members sympathetic to religious sentiment on this issue. This led leaders to hedge on counterterrorism in order to maintain support among these groups. These states would be cooperative occasionally, when they could hide their cooperation from the public or when the religion–state relationship made repressing Islamic opposition a better bet than angering the United States. Moreover, the case studies demonstrated that this situation was itself the result of institutional development that occurred over time and structured religious politics.

In the previous chapters, I have demonstrated how the political effects of religion–state relationships and their varying manifestations among Muslim states explain the dynamics of US–Muslim counterterrorism cooperation. In this chapter, I will extend this analysis, demonstrating that my theory holds up in additional cases not covered in the empirical chapters and discussing how the theory expands our understanding of counterterrorism, religion, and politics and broader debates in international relations. I will also apply my theory to new areas of international relations, highlighting how it can provide insights into political changes in Turkey and Middle Eastern states' responses to the Arab Spring and the Islamic State (IS) militant group. I close with concluding thoughts on what this book's findings can tell us about current and future episodes involving religious issues and Muslim states' responses to US international initiatives.

ADDITIONAL CASES

My analysis in this book demonstrates the ability of my institutional approach to religion and international relations to explain the dynamics of US–Muslim counterterrorism cooperation. I did not, however, conduct qualitative analyses of every type of religion–state relationship among Muslim states due to space considerations. I therefore present three short discussions of other types of religion–state relationships within countries not covered by the case studies. These include a country with close religion–state ties but a stronger state than Pakistan (Saudi Arabia), and two authoritarian states that limit Islamic political influence; one that has adopted some trappings of an Islamic state (Egypt) and one that is secular (Azerbaijan). These examples show that the relationship between closer religion–state relationships and lessened counterterrorism cooperation holds for other types of countries than those I analyzed in this book.

Saudi Arabia

The Saudi state has very close ties to Islam. Saudi Arabia has been officially Islamic since its founding, basing its legal code and its very basis for existence on Islam. The state is also closely connected to Islam. Islamic clerics administer the judiciary and oversee state actions and an official morality police enforces conservative Islamic standards. These connections have strengthened in recent decades. The Saudis have financially and rhetorically supported Islamic movements around the world since the 1970s, including the anti-Soviet militants fighting in Afghanistan in the 1980s. Domestically, the Saudi ruler King Fahd adopted the title of "Defender of the Two Holy Sites" in the 1980s in an attempt to gain greater religious legitimacy among Muslims around the world in response to postrevolutionary Iranian criticisms of the Saudis.

Yet, while Saudi Arabia experienced widespread religious contention, the state was usually able to control Islamic groups when needed. Islamic groups in Saudi Arabia have criticized its ties to the United States, beginning with a verbal rebuke of the state's founder for establishing a relationship with the United States after World War II. Islamic opposition also has extended to unrest over modernizing reforms. This contention intensified in the 1990s with calls from both Islamic and liberal groups for the regime to implement political reforms. Due to the extent to which its legitimacy is connected to Islam, these religious critiques at times lead the regime to implement policies in line with Islamic contention. For example, in the 1990s, the Saudi regime initially responded to protests by women over the right to drive with moderation, but took a harsher stance when attacked by Islamic groups.[1] Yet, Islamic opposition to the regime often does little to influence Saudi policy. The Saudi state continues to maintain a closed political system with extensive controls over society through effective repressive capacity and significant oil wealth. As a result, when

[1] Bronson, *Thicker Than Oil: America's Uneasy Partnership with Saudi Arabia*.

Islamic contention seems to threaten the regime it swiftly disrupts the groups involved, as occurred eventually in the 1990s in response to the Islamic critiques of the regime.

This explains the country's counterterrorism cooperation. Saudi Arabia resisted US efforts to push it toward cooperation in the 1990s. The regime was hesitant to move strongly against domestic militants and come out against public support for al-Qaeda and other Islamic militants. This continued even after 9/11, causing some tensions between the United States and Saudi Arabia. After an al-Qaeda affiliated group conducted a series of brutal attacks in Riyadh in 2003, however, Saudi Arabia launched an offensive against militants in the country. Crown Prince Abdullah (who became king in 2005) also initiated reforms of the country's political system intended partially to decrease support for extremism, including changes to educational curricula, a series of official National Dialogues on contentious issues, and local elections. Thus, while Saudi Arabia's close ties to Islam resulted in initial hesitations on counterterrorism, the strength of the state enabled it to move against militants when they threatened the regime.

Egypt

Egypt, in contrast, has maintained a distant religion–state relationship, even while adopting some trappings of an officially Islamic state. Islamic groups became rather influential in Egypt starting in the 1940s, particularly the Muslim Brotherhood. In the 1970s, President Anwar Sadat increased the state's ties to Islam in an attempt to co-opt these Islamic groups.[2] After Islamic militants assassinated Sadat, however, his successor – Hosni Mubarak – actively repressed Islamic groups. For example, Mubarak intensified the crackdown on the influential Gamaah Islamiyah movement. After the group began launching terrorist attacks in the 1990s, the state arrested huge numbers of the group's members. The state also restricted the activities of nonviolent Islamic groups. The Mubarak regime would not allow the Muslim Brotherhood to compete in parliamentary elections, so members of the group ran as independent candidates. Thus, while Egypt has faced often intense Islamic contention, the distance the state kept from religion allowed it to minimize religious influence.

---

[2] Dina Shehata, *Islamists and Secularists in Egypt: Opposition, Conflict and Cooperation* (New York: Routledge, 2010).

Egypt's close counterterrorism cooperation with the United States was connected to the distant nature of its religion–state relationship. The Egyptian state maintained strict control over Islamic political activity by the time period of this report. The state was thus able to easily ignore Islamic opposition to its counterterrorism policies and US ties. Accordingly, Egypt worked closely with the United States on counterterrorism both before and after 9/11 by disrupting both active militant groups and supporters of al-Qaeda in the country.

Azerbaijan

Azerbaijan has a distant religion–state relationship and, unlike Egypt, has adopted few outward signs of a commitment to Islam. There have been reports of the government limiting the ability of unapproved religious groups to operate since the 1990s.[3] And the state actively restricts Islamic groups' activities. The government has refused to register some Islamic groups, such as followers of Said Nursi, which leaves these groups vulnerable to being shut down by the government. The government also closely controls Islamic broadcasting and literature. And there were some reports of actions against Islamic groups. For example, in 2009, a mosque was reportedly closed for failing to receive government approval; the government has also tried to disrupt the activities of Hizb ut-Tahrir members – an extremist but nonviolent Islamic group – in the country.[4]

Azerbaijan's controls over its society, and its limits on Islamic political activity, enabled it to cooperate extensively with the United States on counterterrorism. The distant religion–state relationship limited the rise of influential Islamic groups or militant activity, so the state faced little political risk from working with the United States. Before 9/11, Azerbaijan had cooperated with US counterterrorism efforts, particularly in combating the flow of fighters and resources to Chechnya. The government also took action against groups targeting the United States, such the sentencing of members of Jayshullah – a group that was reportedly planning to attack the US Embassy – to prison in 2000.[5] This cooperation increased after the 9/11 attacks. The state increased its border enforcement to limit the flow of terrorist sympathizers through its territory and shut down several Islamic organizations suspected of ties to terrorism.

---

3 "Azerbaijan: Freedom in the World," (Freedom House 1999).
4 "International Religious Freedom Report," (US Department of State, 2010).
5 "Patterns of Global Terrorism, " ed. US Department of State (2001).

The state also arrested numerous Islamic militants, turning some over to the United States; for example, in 2002 it jailed several individuals who had trained to fight in Chechnya.[6] Its strongest area of cooperation, however, was in support of US military actions in Afghanistan; shortly after the 9/11 attack, Azerbaijan gave the United States extensive overflight rights and the use of its military bases.

WHAT THE EFFECTS OF RELIGION–STATE CONNECTIONS TELL US ABOUT COUNTERTERRORISM, RELIGION, AND INTERNATIONAL RELATIONS

This book provides a compelling and novel explanation for how religion affected US–Muslim counterterrorism cooperation. Its findings present numerous implications, both for this specific topic and broader debates in international relations. My book reveals patterns in the US–Muslim counterterrorism cooperation – specifically how it varied across countries and across time – that would not be explainable using existing approaches to this topic. It also contributes to the study of religion and politics, domestic influences on international relations and international hierarchy.

Implications for US–Muslim Counterterrorism Cooperation

This book's empirical findings provide context for discussions on specific instances of uncooperative behavior and the historical trends behind cooperation. As I discussed in the chapters on Turkey and the United Arab Emirates, popular perceptions of those countries' cooperation have been colored by earlier behavior or single incidents. In the case of Turkey, the defining incident is thought to be its opposition to the 2003 Iraq invasion. For the UAE, the dominant concern has been its history of lax terrorist financing enforcement. Yet, as I showed in those chapters, the overall counterterrorism cooperation of both Turkey and the UAE was greater than these examples indicated. The cross-country and cross-time analysis in this book thus provides greater insight into the aggregate nature of cooperation among countries. Moreover, it suggests trends in counterterrorism cooperation, particularly its sharp increase after 9/11 – as can be expected – but also its more unexpected aggregate decrease as time went on and the significant differences among regions.

---

[6] "Patterns of Global Terrorism," ed. US Department of State (2003).

More importantly, this book's findings highlighted patterns in US–Muslim counterterrorism cooperation that were not apparent before. As I discussed in the introductory chapter, typical explanations for counterterrorism cooperation range from broad-ranging Islamic activism to state-specific security interests. This book shows that a factor not previously considered on a generalizable level – the nature of the religion–state relationship – has much more explanatory power to understand how cooperative a Muslim state was on counterterrorism. That is, the reason Turkey was cooperative on counterterrorism relates to the reason Pakistan was uncooperative (and the reason for the UAE's shifts in cooperation), and all of them had to do with religion. This not only lets us make sense of this crucial episode in US foreign policy, it also points to a political dynamic – the effects of religion–state relationships – that has broader ramifications for the study of religion and politics, as I will discuss further in the next section.

Additionally, it provides an explanation of the nature of US–Muslim counterterrorism cooperation that is superior to alternatives. None of the alternative explanations I presented in the introduction held up under my in-depth analysis. Islam – or more specifically Islamic contention – could not explain the level of cooperation, as differing levels of Islamic activism did not correspond to differing counterterrorism policies. States' strength and capabilities similarly did not correspond to variations in counterterrorism. Ties to the United States mattered – as seen in the effects of US aid in the quantitative analysis – but they cannot explain the effects of religion–state relationships. Additionally, as the case studies showed, three countries with significant ties to the United States can have vastly differing levels of counterterrorism cooperation. And states' security interests either could not explain the specific type of cooperative behavior a state exhibited or actually emerged from the effects of the religion–state relationship. Thus, in this book I am able to provide a comprehensive and nuanced explanation for the differences in Muslim states' counterterrorism policies that other explanations struggle to produce.

The discussion also suggests some next steps in attempts to understand states' responses to the US "Global War on Terror" and other international initiatives. In Chapter 2, I discussed various types of cooperative and uncooperative behavior – such as *hedging, strategic* non-cooperation, and *hiding* cooperation – which I observed in the case studies. I did not explicitly analyze when these behaviors will occur. Follow-on studies examining the particular combinations of political institutions, domestic political dynamics, and US pressure could identify when observers can expect certain types of behavior to occur in response to US international initiatives.

Religion and Politics

This book also provides the field of international relations greater understanding of the role that religion can play in international relations. Specifically, the book can broaden and clarify what religious contention is. It also helps scholars to focus on the conditions under which religion matters in international relations, not merely whether or not it does matter.

My findings highlight the importance of both religion and political conditions. Scholars do not need to – and should not – decide between whether a situation was driven by "religion" or "politics." Religious activism alone does not influence state behavior, and studies focused only on religious movements or rhetoric are incomplete. At the same time, religion is not epiphenomenal to political conditions, because religion determines the nature of the pressure states face – and thus the policies they may implement in response – and often catalyzes activism that drives states to action. Those studies that focus on the interaction between religious contention and political institutions have the greatest promise to explain how religion affects international relations.[7] My investigation also makes clear that examples of religious influence over international relations – like US–Muslim counterterrorism cooperation – can be studied alongside and inform similar non-religious issues.[8]

Second, the book clarifies what we mean by religious politics. Studies that attempt to identify instances of states or social groups acting based on religious beliefs, or religion having a direct effect on conflicts or other aspects of world politics, are important and should be continued. But scholarly argument about the relationship between religion

---

[7] For similar points, see Fox and Sandler, *Bringing Religion into International Relations*; Anthony Gill, "Religion and Comparative Politics," *Annual Review of Political Science* 4 (2001); Daniel Philpott, "Has the Study of Global Politics Found Religion?," ibid. 12 (2009); Grim and Finke, *The Price of Freedom Denied: Religious Persecution and Conflict in the Twenty-First Century*.

[8] For similar points, see Daniel H. Nexon, "Religion and International Relations: No Leap of Faith Required," in *Religion and International Relations Theory*, ed. Jack Snyder (New York: Columbia University Press, 2011); Kenneth D. Wald and Clyde Wilcox, "Getting Religion: Has Political Science Rediscovered the Faith Factor?," *American Political Science Review* 100, no. 4 (2006); Bellin, "Faith in Politics: New Trends in the Study of Religion and Politics."

and politics may be more effective if we focus on religion's nuanced effects, such as altering the incentives of regimes or combining with political institutions to produce unexpected outcomes. This requires stepping back from some of the more dramatic claims about religion, but could still be a fruitful source of well-grounded empirical analysis. For example, research into religion and American politics has produced numerous valuable works demonstrating the nature of religious belief and religious influence over politics that could be useful for scholars of international relations.[9]

Additionally, the variety of states' responses to religious contention – even within the broader categories of "cooperative" or "uncooperative" – highlight the powerful but subtle nature of religious contention. Even cooperation was not complete; as I discussed, the UAE had to justify its cooperative behaviors to their publics while Pakistan often had to hide its cooperation. This suggests the power of religious contention: even regimes at minimal risk of losing power from upsetting religious groups would still avoid upsetting them unnecessarily. At the same time, uncooperative behavior was complicated, with states still attempting to cooperate as much as they could while avoiding upsetting Islamic groups. These dynamics second the measured approach to religion and politics I call for in the earlier chapters.

Finally, I would make some tentative meta-theoretical or methodological points. Namely, that religion need not be approached as a unique phenomenon or one that requires an abandonment of conventional forms of analysis. Some have made this argument, claiming religion's nature precludes positivist analyses or confounds all existing models.[10] This book, and the research on religion and politics on which it builds, suggests a more cautious perspective. Religious contention, in my study, functioned much like non-religious contention in its interaction with political structures and pressure on regimes. It differs in its content, and also arguably in the extent of pressure it places on states, but in form it resembles

[9] Clyde Wilcox, Kenneth D. Wald, and Ted G. Jelen, "Religious Preferences and Social Science: A Second Look," *The Journal of Politics* 70, no. 3 (2008); James L. Guth *et al.*, "Faith and Foreign Policy: A View from the Pews," *The Review of Faith and International Affairs* 3, no. 2 (2005); David C. Leege and Lyman A. Kellstedt, eds., *Rediscovering the Religious Factor in American Politics* (M. E. Sharpe, Inc, 1993).

[10] Thomas, *The Global Resurgence of Religion*; Elizabeth Shakman Hurd, "The Political Authority of Secularism in International Relations," *European Journal of International Relations* 10, no. 2 (2004); Joshua Mitchell, "Religion Is Not a Preference," *The Journal of Politics* 69, no. 2 (2007).

other transnational belief systems.[11] Scholars of religion and politics make their jobs much harder by rejecting all theories and concepts that were not designed specifically for the study of religion. Moreover, even though I used a rather strictly neopositivist research design with quantitative methods, I was still able to detect the influence of religion.[12] I may have identified deeper or more dramatic aspects of religious contention through an interpretive study, but such an approach is not necessary to effectively analyze religious politics. I had some incentives to adopt this meta-theoretical stance, of course. Several scholars have called for a closer connection between the study of religion and other aspects of world politics.[13] One of the most effective ways to do this is to demonstrate that studies of religion and politics can be conventional exercises in political science (or sociology, anthropology, etc.) and do not need to be cordoned off as an experimental or disruptive trend in a discipline.

There are a few ways this book's analysis could be extended. Studies could apply the institutional approach to religion and international relations to other issues in international and domestic politics, including interstate conflict and diplomatic interactions. The scope of the analysis could also be expanded to look further at the rise of different religion-state relationships or dynamics outside of Muslim countries. A deeper look at the transnational aspects of religious contention – which I touch on in this book but did not examine in-depth – could also highlight how religion differs from other belief systems. Moreover, looking into what issues become religiously contentious over time, and how this occurs, would be very valuable.

Domestic Politics and International Relations

The theoretical implications of this book extend beyond the study of religion, however. If we take a step back from my theoretical arguments involving religion–state connections and counterterrorism cooperation,

---

[11] For similar points, see Nexon, "Religion and International Relations: No Leap of Faith Required"; Wald and Wilcox, "Getting Religion: Has Political Science Rediscovered the Faith Factor?"; Bellin, "Faith in Politics: New Trends in the Study of Religion and Politics."

[12] For discussion on neopositivism and other approaches to social science, see Patrick Thaddeus Jackson, *The Conduct of Inquiry in International Relations* (New York: Routledge, 2011).

[13] Bellin, "Faith in Politics: New Trends in the Study of Religion and Politics"; Wald and Wilcox, "Getting Religion: Has Political Science Rediscovered the Faith Factor?"

what I am really talking about is the conditions under which domestic politics – specifically domestic ideational politics – affect international hierarchical relations. The findings from this book could thus engage with other research areas in the field. I will discuss each of these in turn.

International relations experts have expended significant effort understanding whether – and how – domestic politics affect states' international behavior. A few influential works have discussed how the study of religion could fit into existing paradigms of international relations, and domestic politics is an additional avenue for exploration.[14] This research program deals with high-level questions about the nature of international relations – such as the perennial debate between systemic and state-level explanations for phenomena such as war – and analyses of specific issues like economic growth or diplomatic negotiations.[15] As I discussed in Chapter 1, the general theoretical work I base my explanation on involves domestic politics and international relations, specifically the effects of political institutions on state behavior. As a result, the findings of this book can speak to this general research program, and by extension to broad issues in international relations.

First, it provides support for studies based on Bueno de Mesquita *et al.*'s selectorate theory, which I discussed in Chapter 1. This book aligns well with other studies that have demonstrated how differing winning coalition sizes have varied effects on state behavior both domestically and internationally. But it also extends selectorate theory with its emphasis on the content of the pressure states face from society – in this case religious contention – and the manner in which the winning coalition is connected to groups in society, specifically religion–state connections. This book points to an aspect of Bueno de Mesquita *et al.*'s initial work, affinity, which has been developed to a lesser extent in follow-on studies than their insights into winning coalitions. Affinity refers to personal or ideational attachments between a regime and segments of society that can

---

[14] Fox and Sandler, *Bringing Religion into International Relations.*; Jack Snyder, "Introduction," in *Religion and International Relations Theory*, ed. Jack Snyder (New York: Columbia University Press, 2011); Nukhet Sandal and Jonathan Fox, *Religion in International Relations Theory: Concepts, Tools, and Debates* (London: Routledge, 2013).

[15] James Fearon, "Domestic Politics, Foreign Policy, and Theories of International Relations," *Annual Review of Political Science* 1 (1998); Helen Milner, *Interests, Institutions, and Information: Domestic Politics and International Relations* (Princeton: Princeton University Press, 1997); Robert D. Putnam, "Diplomacy and Domestic Politics: The Logic of Two-Level Games," *International Organization* 42, no. 3 (1988); Alastair Smith, "International Crises and Domestic Politics," *American Political Science Review* 92, no. 3 (1998); Bueno de Mesquita *et al.*, *The Logic of Political Survival.*

interact with the effects of the winning coalition size. The religion–state connections I point to could be reframed as a particular type of affinity.

Beyond domestic politics and international relations, the book's findings can also speak to a specific growing research program: the study of international hierarchy. I should note that my argument is not focused directly on international hierarchy. Yet, it does deal with hierarchy in terms of understanding how Islamic contention led Muslim states to refuse to comply with US power, which constituted a form of hierarchical influence. This field of study is quickly developing out of pioneering early work by scholars like David Lake, Hendrik Spruyt, and John Ruggie, who conceptualized international hierarchy and pointed to some areas in which it seems to hold.[16] Recent studies have extended these works to various examples of international hierarchy as well as how hierarchical ties affect relations among states.[17]

While I focused on the conditions under which religion undermined cooperation in this book – rather than the hierarchical ties between the United States and Muslim states that promoted this cooperation – my findings can point to hierarchy's presence in the international system. Scholars have emphasized various examples of hierarchy, including Nexon and Wright's analysis of US power and Cooley's study of hierarchical relations in the Soviet Union.[18] This book's findings point to an additional area of international hierarchy. The network of diplomatic ties, aid and trade flows, and security assurances that developed between the United States and Muslim states gave the United States significant control over both the international and domestic policies of Muslim states. Muslim states' counterterrorism policies thus did not occur in a pure state of anarchy, but instead were disciplined by US power. Even uncooperative states like Pakistan could not blatantly disregard US pressure and had to

---

[16] Hendrik Spruyt, *The Sovereign State and Its Competitors: An Analysis of Systems Change* (Princeton: Princeton University Press, 1994); John G. Ruggie, "Territoriality and Beyond," *International Organization* 47, no. 1 (1993); David A. Lake, "Anarchy, Hierarchy and the Variety of International Relations," ibid. 50 (1996).

[17] "Escape from the State of Nature: Authority and Hierarchy in World Politics"; Cooley, *Logics of Hierarchy: The Organization of Empires, States and Military Occupations*; Jack Donnelly, "Sovereign Inequalities and Hierarchy in Anarchy: American Power and International Security," *European Journal of International Relations* 12, no. 2 (2006); Ann E. Towns, "Norms and Social Hierarchies: Understanding International Policy Diffusion 'from Below'," *International Organization* 66, no. 2 (2012); Daniel H. Nexon, "What's This, Then? 'Romanes Eunt Domus'?," *International Studies Perspectives* 9, no. 3 (2008); Nexon and Wright, "What's at Stake in the American Empire Debate?"

[18] "What's at Stake in the American Empire Debate?"; Cooley, *Logics of Hierarchy: The Organization of Empires, States and Military Occupations*.

either secretly cooperate or tentatively balance uncooperative behavior with cooperative moves. This moves beyond weak states merely acquiescing to strong states, and extends to the United States determining the domestic and foreign conduct of nations.

This book validates a particular approach to international hierarchy. One could conceive of US–Muslim state relations as a hierarchical structure maintained through constant interactions between the states, rather than a fixed authority system of norms or institutions. This has two implications for the study of international hierarchy. First, this supports conceptions of hierarchy focused on the relational nature of hierarchical and suggests the importance of the broader relational approach to contentious politics.[19] That is, rather than attempting to investigate broad normative agreements or insidious hegemonic discourses to understand hierarchy, we should focus on the interactions among states of different power that produce hierarchical arrangements. Second, it indicates that domestic and transnational contention – in this case religious opposition to US counterterrorism efforts – can undermine these hierarchical ties, especially when combined with unstable political institutions. Similar dynamics have been noted by Nexon in his study of religious contention and the early modern state system and Cooley in his work on US military bases.[20]

This book's implications for the study of hierarchy present a few suggestions for future research. Systematic analyses of issue-areas – such as my measurement of counterterrorism cooperation – may be particularly useful to identify varying levels of hierarchy in international relations. My approach to US–Muslim counterterrorism cooperation presents a model for other hierarchical situations to be analyzed quantitatively, which could potentially expand the research program on this issue. As I noted earlier, my focus in this book was on why and how Muslim states broke from hierarchical ties, not how the United States established and enforced those ties in the first place. Follow-up studies on this aspect of US counterterrorism efforts or other areas of its interaction with weak states may be very valuable.

---

[19] Nexon and Wright, "What's at Stake in the American Empire Debate?"; McAdam, Tarrow, and Tilly, *Dynamics of Contention*; Charles Tilly, *The Politics of Collective Violence* (New York: Columbia University Press, 2003); *Identities, Boundaries and Social Ties* (Boulder, CO: Paradigm Publishers, 2005).

[20] Nexon, *The Struggle for Power in Early Modern Europe: Religious Conflict, Dynastic Empires and International Change*; Alexander Cooley, *Base Politics: Democratic Change and the US Military Overseas* (Ithaca, NY: Cornell University Press, 2008).

EXPANDED DISCUSSION

This book's findings provide significant insight into the nature of US–Muslim counterterrorism cooperation and can also elucidate broader aspects of international relations, such as religion and politics, US international influence, and international hierarchy. But can my theoretical framework – focused on the effects of religion–state connections – provide insight into other empirical areas of international relations? Indeed, this is one of the best tests of a theory's power, if it can provide similar findings through application to a new set of data. For theories involving treatment for disease or psychological issues, this could involve repeating an experiment with a new set of individuals. For theories of international relations, it involves determining whether the dynamics posited by a theory can explain new empirical areas. I have conducted some of this in my other scholarly works, which have applied this institutional theory of religion and international relations to interstate conflict, United Nations voting, and forced migration.[21] In this section I will broaden this theory's applicability by looking at how it can explain two areas of crucial importance to contemporary policy debates that fell outside this book's scope: political changes in Turkey and Middle East states' response to the Arab Spring and the Islamic State.

Institutional Change in Turkey

It is very possible that the institutional configurations we see in Muslim states will change over time, with corresponding shifts in their foreign policies. I discuss how institutional religion–state relationships develop, but focus primarily on how they lock-in certain types of political conditions for later actors. I thus do not deal with the question of how these institutions change. Could my theory take into account changing religion–state relationships in Muslim states, and provide some expectations for how these changes would affect international relations?

Turkey is the best test of this extension of my theory. As I noted in the chapter on this country, the idea of Turkey having a distant religion–state relationship may be puzzling to many observers. While this configuration persisted through the time period of this study, changes that began after the AKP came to power and gradually intensified over time

---

[21] Henne, "The Two Swords: Religion–State Connections and Interstate Conflict"; "The Domestic Politics of International Religious Defamation"; Melanie Kolbe and Peter S. Henne, "The Effect of Religious Restrictions on Forced Migration," ibid. 7, no. 4 (2014).

may alter this arrangement. Prime Minister and later President Erdogan has weakened the military's power, removing one of the policy tools that maintained the state's secularism. He has also loosened restrictions on public religiosity and increased state support to Islamic schools. Erdogan may also have increased the chance of elites – particularly military elites – being sympathetic to religious sentiment. For example, he has pushed reforms of military education including adding classes on Islam to military academies.[22] At the same time, we have seen the ties between the AKP and the influential Gulen movement unravel.[23] This suggests increasing ties between religion and state, but not the more direct "Islamization" some claim occurred in Pakistan, in which we would see Islamic groups gaining influence over the regime.

While it is risky to assume a political trajectory will continue, it is possible Erdogan's reforms will eventually change the nature of Turkey's religion–state relationship. The reduction in the military's influence and the weakening of the secularist opposition parties limit the self-perpetuating nature of Turkey's official secularism. Likewise, the religious nature of the AKP intensifies the political connections between religious groups and the Turkish government. Finally, the opening of space for religious expression decreases restrictions on religious activity. Assuming Turkey's political system remains open, Turkey could come to resemble Pakistan in many ways, at least in terms of its religion–state ties. But the tensions with the Gulen movement indicate there is still some distance between the regime and Islamic groups. As a result, Turkey may end up occupying an unstable space between the two categories for the near future, which will be resolved eventually in favor of a more official Islamic state or secular retrenchment.

These changes have already started to alter its policies toward religious issues. Remember that its counterterrorism policies under the AKP primarily maintained the country's historically tough stance on terrorism even as it increased its outreach on religious issues. This is because the religious nature of the AKP was not intense enough to undermine the institutional distance between religion and state. As this institutional distance fades, we may see more instances of Turkey acting in line with religious sentiment even if it upsets the United States. This is not because Turkey's regime is becoming more radical or erratic: it is because the

---

[22] "Turkish Army 'Bans' Game of Thrones, Prepares for Islam Classes," *Hurriyet Daily News*, November 7, 2014.
[23] "Turkey's Political Imams: The Gulenists Fight Back," *The Economist*, May 18, 2013.

institutional arrangement that gave Turkish elites an incentive to cooperate with the United States on contentious security issues is disappearing. That explains some of the tensions that emerged between Turkey and the United States on Middle East issues in the case study, as well as its behavior in response to the Arab Spring and Islamic State, which I will discuss later.

In addition to explaining some of the changes in Turkey's foreign policy, its shifting religion–state relationship can also validate work on institutional change. Exogenous change is the most visible and dramatic sign of institutional change; some external event, such as a revolution or invasion, creates new institutions. But, as Mahoney and Thelen argue, gradual change can often have dramatic effects. They present a framework for analyzing different types of gradual institutional change, depending on how strong veto players are – those able to limit change – and how much discretion there is in the manner in which institutional guidelines are enforced. When veto players are strong and there is limited discretion, we will see *subversive* actors effecting *layering*, in which new institutional patterns are added to existing ones. When strong vetoes combine with broad discretion, we will instead see *drift*, in which actors change the purposes of existing institutions. If veto players are weak, in contrast, and there is broad discretion, *opportunist* actors will actively *convert* institutions into new ones. And when weak veto players combine with limited discretion, we will see *insurrectionaries displace* institutions with new ones.[24]

Applying this work to the previous discussion of changes in Turkey provides some insight into the way religion–state relationships may change. Following Mahoney and Thelen's formulation, Turkey's changing religion–state relationship takes the form of *layering* giving way to *displacement*.[25] At first, actors layer new institutional patterns to existing ones that push the state toward a new religion–state relationship; in this case of Turkey, this is the AKP's outreach to religious groups. As the institutional change picks up and the veto possibilities decrease, the change accelerates into *displacement*. In the case of Turkey, this occurred as the military's ability to block the AKP's reforms is undermined. At the same time, more aggressive elements in the AKP – such as Erdogan – have been able to accelerate their reforms.

---

[24] James Mahoney and Kathleen Thelen, A Theory of Gradual Institutional Change, in *Explaining Institutional Change: Ambiguity, Agency, and Power*, eds. James Mahoney and Kathleen Thelen (New York: Cambridge University Press, 2010).
[25] Ibid.

Religion–State Connections, the Arab Spring, and the Islamic State

As I stated in the introductory chapter, this book covers a time period from the 1990s up through the height of the US struggle against al-Qaeda. As a result, my investigation did not focus directly on the series of political struggles that began in 2011 and came to be known as the "Arab Spring," or the rise of the vicious Islamic State (IS) movement in Syria and elsewhere. This was intended to maintain a tight scope for this book, but the theoretical insights I advanced – relating to the political effects of religion–state connections – can inform our understanding of these issues.

In this section I will provide some background on the Arab Spring and the Islamic State movement and briefly discuss how one could extend my study to understand states' responses to these phenomena. This is intended not to advance a comprehensive explanation for all aspects of this issue, but rather to highlight how my theory could be used in such a study. Granted, this situation is much more complicated than that of Muslim state responses to US counterterrorism operations. In that case, states faced clear external pressure – to work with the United States – and countervailing domestic religious pressure against the cooperation. US pressure following the Arab Spring was more muddled, so there was less of a clear scale of cooperation/non-cooperation. But as I will discuss next, we did see the emergence of a religious issue in the Arab Spring uprisings and the emergence of IS. religion–state connections affected regional states' reactions to these events in a generally similar manner to their effects on US counterterrorism cooperation.

The Arab Spring began in 2011, when a vendor in Tunisia set himself on fire in protest against government regulation and corruption.[26] This set off a series of anti-government protests in that country that soon spread throughout the region. The president of Tunisia fled and relatively democratic elections were soon held, while mass protests in Egypt resulted in the resignation and arrest of long-time authoritarian leader Hosni Mubarak. Yemen soon followed suit. More violent uprisings occurred in Libya and Syria. Saudi Arabia remained relatively stable, although it experienced some unrest and sent troops into Bahrain to quell anti-government activism in that country. The sudden and broad-ranging

---

[26] For useful overviews of the Arab Spring, see Marc Lynch, *The Arab Uprising: The Unfinished Revolutions of the New Middle East* (New York: Public Affairs, 2013); Ken Pollack and Daniel Byman, *The Arab Awakening: America and the Transformation of the Middle East* (Washington, DC: Brookings Institution Press, 2011).

nature of these uprisings led some to compare them to earlier widespread cross-national episodes of political change, calling this period the "Arab Spring."

While many countries settled back into authoritarian patterns or simmered in persistent civil conflict, Syria took a more brutal turn. Broad protests against the rule of Bashar al-Assad turned violent after strong state repression, and a loose collection of groups – many from the country's Sunni Arab majority – began waging open conflict against the state. Some of the combatants were relatively secular movements, but the conflict attracted the interest of regional Islamic movements. An al-Qaeda affiliate – al-Nusra front – emerged and a small breakaway faction of that group adopted the name Islamic State in Iraq and Syria (later known as just the Islamic State, or IS). IS soon overshadowed all other combatants, launching brutal attacks against both Syrian government forces and civilians in a bid to establish an Islamic state in the region. The group's activities spilled over into Iraq and it began enslaving and massacring non-Muslim groups – like Christians and Yazidis – as it gained territory in northern Iraq. The group also inspired followers around the world to travel to Syria and join it, commit attacks in the group's name, and even organize IS-affiliated militant chapters in countries like Libya.

The causes and dynamics of the Arab Spring uprisings and the savage tactics of IS are important to understand, but a crucial aspect of this entire episode is the differing manner in which regional states responded to this turmoil. The Arab Spring uprisings represented a political challenge to existing regimes. While the protests initially started out secular in nature, just like contention over counterterrorism they took on a religious salience. Many of the early protests were not Islamic ones, but they often were directed against secular regimes that severely limited religious groups' activity. As a result, religious belief and practice came to be part of the protests, as seen in the numerous protests occurring after Friday prayers and the iconic photograph from Egypt of protesters bowing in Muslim prayer before regime water cannons.[27] Moreover, Islamic groups were often the most powerful opposition movements in many countries, so they eventually came to lead anti-government actions. This is apparent in Tunisia, where the previously banned al-Nahda group returned to prominence as the government fell.

[27] Mairi MacKay, "Prayer and Politics: How Friday Became the Middle East's Day of Protest," *CNN*, June 20, 2011.

I would argue that the Arab Spring and IS came to be a religious issue, similar in nature to US counterterrorism efforts. Because US counterterrorism efforts were seen as targeting Muslims and Islam, Muslim states faced pressure (from both Islamic groups and broader religious sentiment) to not work with the United States. With the Arab Spring becoming seen as a religious struggle against repressive secular regimes, Middle Eastern regimes would face calls from Islamic groups to take action in support of this struggle. Likewise, there may be more diffuse, religiously based sympathy with the protesters among their publics. And while few in the region actively supported IS, just like with al-Qaeda, states may fear that harsh actions against the group could be seen as targeting Islamic movements. Because of this pressure arising from the religious nature of the Arab Spring and IS, regional states' responses would be filtered through their religion–state relationships.

One group of responses was from the Persian Gulf countries, notably Saudi Arabia, Qatar, and the UAE. These countries initially had a muddled response, supporting some aspects of the political uprisings but also trying to channel activism. For example, Qatar reportedly supported Islamic movements throughout the region and provided economic assistance to Egypt's post-Mubarak Muslim Brotherhood government.[28] And Saudi Arabia allowed its citizens to support people in Syria affected by the conflict but restricted their ability to do so outside of state control.[29] Once the focus turned to IS' militant activities, many of these countries were at the vanguard of attempts to disrupt the group. For example, the UAE was a significant contributor to the airstrikes against IS that began in 2014 under US direction.[30]

A second group of countries were those that tried to weather the Arab Spring uprisings and stay out of much of the anti-IS campaigns. As protests spread outward from Tunisia, Morocco and Jordan implemented some political reforms but also drew closer to the Saudi-dominated Gulf Cooperation Council in an attempt to gain support against opposition forces. Algeria, in turn, primarily held fast against political turmoil. And once IS emerged as a powerful force, many of these countries – including

---

[28] Kristian Coates Ulrichsen, "Qatar and the Arab Spring: Policy Drivers and Regional Implications," (Carnegie Endowment for International Peace, 2014).

[29] Ben Gilbert, "Saudi Arabia Walks a Fine Line in Backing Syrian Rebellion," *Al-Jazeera America*, January 10, 2014; Robert F. Worth, "Saudis Back Syrian Rebels Despite Risks," *New York Times*, January 7, 2014.

[30] Helen Cooper, "United Arab Emirates, Key US Ally in Isis Effort, Disengaged in December," ibid., February 3, 2015.

Egypt, which by then had reverted to a Mubarak-esque military government – stayed out of the fight. There are some reports Egypt actually opposed the actions against IS. In May 2015, reports emerged that Egypt's ties with Saudi Arabia had become tense due to the latter's actions in Syria, although both countries denied this.[31] Egypt did launch airstrikes into Libya against IS forces there.[32]

Finally, there is Turkey, which is a complicated case. Turkey initially called for restraint from Egypt and Syria's regimes in the face of protests. When the government response became violent in Syria, Turkey pushed more strongly for political reforms. Its support for anti-Assad forces in Syria intensified as the conflict did, with one of the leading umbrella groups for the opposition setting up its headquarters in Turkey.[33] The situation became murkier as IS rose. Some have accused Turkey of supporting IS, although this is mostly uncorroborated.[34] But Turkey has undoubtedly proven more resistant to moving against IS than other states. It did launch airstrikes against IS after the group killed a Turkish solder in a border clash in July 2015.[35] Beyond that, however, Turkey has been less willing to commit to strong actions against IS than have states like the UAE, and some have suggested the 2015 moves by Turkey were driven by internal political dynamics.[36]

There are numerous explanations for these countries' differing responses to the Arab Spring and IS. Many are the conventional drivers of international relations like geopolitical tensions or domestic instability. For example, Sunni states in the region are concerned about Iran's influence due to long-standing rivalries with that country. As a result, states like Saudi Arabia were eager to see the Iran-aligned Basher al-Assad fall. Likewise, states were wary of the Arab Spring protests spreading to their countries and compelling political reforms. They were even more concerned about IS' violent campaigns infecting their territory and causing an outbreak of civil conflict. And Turkey's fears of Syrian Kurds gaining

---

[31] "Egypt and Saudi Arabia Deny Split over Syria," *Al-Jazeera*, May 31, 2015.
[32] David D. Kirkpatrick, "Egypt Launches Airstrike in Libya against Isis Branch," *New York Times*, February 16, 2015.
[33] "Syria's Opposition Opens Office in Turkey," *Al-Jazeera*, December 14, 2011.
[34] Alexander Christie-Miller, "Kurds Accuse Turkish Government of Supporting Isis," *Newsweek*, October 22, 2014.
[35] Gul Tuysuz, "Turkish Warplanes Bomb Isis Positions in Syria for the First Time," *CNN*, July 25, 2015.
[36] Tim Arango and Ceylan Yeginsu, "Turkey's Push into War Is Seen as Erdogan's Political Strategy," *New York Times*, August 5, 2015.

power there and promoting secessionism in Turkey's Kurdish population likely drove some of its policies toward Syria and IS.

But the political effects of religion–state connections, which played such a major part in states' responses to the US Global War on Terror, also affected state behavior in this episode. religion–state connections affected states' responses by influencing the extent to which they were threatened by these uprisings, and the opportunity the uprisings presented. Two potential opportunities presented themselves for Middle Eastern states during the Arab Spring. As the uprisings came to be seen as a religious struggle, countries that backed opposition groups could claim to support a religious cause and hopefully gain the support of domestic and international Islamic groups. For example, if replacing Egypt's Mubarak with an Islamic-oriented leader is viewed as a success for Islamic groups, then states that helped bring that about may gain greater religious prestige. Similarly, these protests give states an opportunity to replace secular regimes with sympathetic religious regimes. At the same time, the initial Arab Spring uprisings and the more violent outburst that occurred later presented a potential threat to regional states. IS presents an obvious security threat, while the nonviolent protests proved capable of destabilizing regimes. But their religious element could intensify the threat. For regimes that rely on Islamic symbols and argument to justify their rule, a religious opposition movement not only threatens regime stability but also the reason for the regime's existence.

The seesawing pattern of states like Saudi Arabia, Qatar, and the UAE reflects their religion–state relationships. The officially Islamic nature of these countries gives them an incentive to appear to take a stance in support of the religious cause behind some of the Arab Spring uprisings, particularly the fight against Assad and Mubarak. The increased political salience of religious issues as a result of this situation, however, makes them wary of powerful religious actors that could threaten their regimes' stability. Moreover, their small winning coalition and distance from Islamic groups in society gave them a window to move against groups like IS. Thus, these states followed the pattern of their earlier counterterrorism behavior; they initially followed religious sentiment as the Arab Spring took off by supporting protest movements, but did so warily and led the charge against IS once these regimes saw its activities as threatening.

Egypt similarly followed the pattern seen in the Global War on Terror. Even though Hosni Mubarak resigned from power and was succeeded by the Muslim Brotherhood's President Morsi, Egypt's religion–state

connections have persisted as the post-Morsi military government continues to restrict Islamic political activity and keep its distance from Islam.
As a result, the government had little to gain from supporting the religious
opposition movements in other countries and also little to fear in terms of
backlash from the rise of groups like IS. It is only when the militants pose
a direct threat to the country – as when they killed Egyptian citizens –
that the regime was threatened enough to take action.

Finally, Turkey's more mixed record on its involvement with the Arab
Spring uprisings is in line with its changing religion–state relationship that
I mentioned earlier. Turkey's activist approach to the initial Arab Spring
uprisings is in line with Turkey's increasing international assertiveness
under Erdogan's AKP generally, but also the increasing salience of religious issues in Turkish politics under the party. This made Turkish leaders
more amenable to supporting religious causes and gave them more of an
incentive to do so. But Turkey's religion–state ties were not yet as close as
those in the UAE or Saudi Arabia, so the violent uprising of IS presented
less of an ideological threat to Turkey's regime. As a result, Turkey felt
less compelled to move against IS until it presented a direct security threat.

Beyond IS, the Saudi-led response to the rise of Houthi forces in
Yemen also illustrates the effects of religion–state connections. Arab
Spring protests spread quickly to Yemen, threatening the stability of the
regime under Ali Abdullah Saleh. In June of 2011 Saleh was injured in
an explosion at his palace and left for medical treatment in Saudi Arabia;
he resigned as president in November. Yemen's turmoil continued, however, as al-Qaeda affiliated forces and Houthi rebels fought against the
government. The Houthis proved the more effective force; the movement
is composed of Zaydi Yemenis, an Islamic sect related to Shia Islam, who
began to oppose the Yemeni government in 2004. The group reportedly
developed close ties with and received supplies from Iran. The Houthis
succeeded in overthrowing the government in 2014. This prompted a
swift response from Saudi Arabia. The country organized a bombing campaign against the group with other countries in the region and launched
devastating attacks that have reportedly resulted in numerous civilian
casualties.

The effects of religion–state connections on the conflict in Yemen can
be seen in Saudi Arabia's motivations behind it. The religious salience
of the conflict in Yemen went beyond much of the other Arab Spring
uprisings due to the prominence of Iran, with which Saudi Arabia had
tense relations since the Iranian Revolution of 1979. Much of this was
geopolitical, as the two are powerful countries that lie on opposite sides

of the Persian Gulf, both of which attempt to influence the behavior of weaker Middle Eastern states. They also lie on opposite sides of the Sunni-Shia divide. Moreover, both states are officially Islamic and justify much of their existence and behavior through their dedication to global Islamic causes. Due to these close religion–state ties, Iranian actions in the region represent not just a geopolitical threat, but also an ideological one; a loss to a competing state with a differing religious ideology could undermine support for the Saudi regime due to their own dependence on religion. This aspect of the Saudi-Iranian rivalry heightened the threat the Houthi uprising posed to Saudi Arabia, which in turn led to Saudi Arabia responding in as strong a manner as it did.

Just as differing religion–state relationships among Muslim countries influenced the extent to which they cooperated with the United States on counterterrorism, so too did these religion–state ties affect how states responded to the Arab Spring and the emergence of IS. What we saw was a religious issue prompting pressure on states from their publics to respond and worries about the implications for regime stability. Those states with close religion–state relationships supported many of the protest movements but later took strong action when opposition forces posed a threat to these regimes. States with more distant relationships, in contrast, generally stayed out of the fray. And Turkey, experiencing transitions in its religion–state relationship, adopted an accordingly complex stance on the Arab Spring and IS.

As always, numerous other conditions affected how states responded to this issue, and one could easily construct detailed "just-so" stories for each country's behavior since the beginning of the Arab Spring that had nothing to do with differing religion–state relationships. But it is striking how Middle Eastern states' behavior generally lined up with the theorized effects of religion–state relationships I laid out in this book. My institutional theory of religion and international relations to explain US–Muslim counterterrorism cooperation can thus also explain states' responses to the Arab Spring and IS, providing greater insight into this crucial aspect of contemporary international relations.

CONCLUDING THOUGHTS

The explanation I laid out in this book for US–Muslim counterterrorism cooperation can therefore clarify the nature of religious tensions in Muslim countries and the prospects for US international efforts on contentious international issues. It provides greater insight into how much influence the United States can actually exert in the international system. It also suggests what is likely to occur as Muslim states respond to international religious issues.

This book can speak to perennial debates among policymakers and scholars over the nature of US influence over the international system. Is the United States in decline? Is it able to drive international cooperation or organize alliances to advance its interests? In the case of counter-terrorism cooperation, the United States was neither able to wield complete dominance over the international system nor face a broad-ranging rejection of US power. Instead, US counterterrorism efforts involved constant outreach and adjustment in its relations with Muslim states, and the necessity of balancing its expectations with the domestic political realities of these states. This likely extends to other aspects of the United States' international standing, especially involving Muslim states or contentious religious issues.

Second, it can speak to the nature of international tensions between the United States and Muslim states. Religious issues in Muslim countries are not the inevitable result of infusing Islam or religion in general into politics. But neither are they irrelevant to religious beliefs, arising from economic angst or ethnic tensions. Instead, they relate to these states' political institutions, particularly the ties between Islam and the state and the manner in which the state restricts religious practices of Muslims and non-Muslims. Some have noted this, and this book extends this argument, by pointing out that this dynamic explains not just social religious tensions but also tensions between the United States and Muslim states.[37]

When the United States encounters resistance or hostility from Muslim states over its future international actions relating to contentious religious issues, these reactions arise from such domestic dynamics. Erratic or frustrating behavior (from the US perspective) is rarely a sign of a regime's religious zeal or self-defeating apocalypticism. Muslim regimes are driven primarily by the desire to survive in the face of external pressures and often-intense domestic Islamic contention over an issue. When religion and state are close, a regime will have an incentive to implement policies advocated for by religious groups. Given the unpopularity of the United States in the region, states often accomplish this by breaking with

---

[37] Toft, Philpott, and Shah, *God's Century: Resurgent Religion and Global Politics*; Grim and Finke, *The Price of Freedom Denied: Religious Persecution and Conflict in the Twenty-First Century.*

the United States and advancing policies that are a careful balance of cooperation when possible and hesitation when needed. Attempts to understand Muslim states' responses to international religious issues or US difficulty in advancing an international agenda should focus less on whether the United States is being legitimate or forceful enough, and more on these domestic institutional dynamics.

This book also highlights the role of an emerging topic in tensions between the United States and Muslim states: religious freedom. Some point to political repression in Muslim countries – particularly repression of religious groups, Muslim or otherwise – as a cause of the terrorist activities of groups like al-Qaeda.[38] And a few observers, such as Thomas Farr, argue that greater religious freedom will have positive benefits for international relations, limiting extremism and instability.[39] Others worry that a strong push for political reforms – which may include religious freedom – could increase instability and extremism.[40] Similarly, commentators have pointed to countries like the UAE as good examples of limits on religious expression coupled with economic development.[41] Still others suggest the terminology of "religious freedom" and its mobilization through policy initiatives are problematic.[42] These attitudes may suggest a negative effect from religious freedom.

My findings present mixed results for what effect religious freedom has on episodes like US–Muslim tensions over counterterrorism. The countries with the least amount of counterterrorism cooperation had limited religious freedom, like Pakistan. But some of the more cooperative countries, like Egypt, also had little religious freedom; even though they did not actively advance or support Islamic groups, like Pakistan, they still restricted the ability of Muslim and non-Muslim religious groups to operate freely. The close ties to religious groups and an officially Islamic state that resulted in Pakistan's minimal religious freedom also produced greater tensions with the United States over counterterrorism. But the limited religious freedom produced by strict repression of Islamic groups in

---

38 Toft, Philpott, and Shah, *God's Century: Resurgent Religion and Global Politics.*
39 Thomas Farr, *World of Faith and Freedom: Why International Religious Liberty Is Vital to American National Security* (New York: Oxford University Press, 2008).
40 Eva Bellin, "Democratization and Its Discontents: Should America Push Political Reform in the Middle East?," *Foreign Affairs* 87, no. 4 (2008).
41 Thomas L. Friedman, "Dubai and Dunces," *New York Times*, March 15, 2006.
42 Elizabeth Shakman Hurd, *Beyond Religious Freedom: The New Global Politics of Religion* (Princeton, NJ: Princeton University Press, 2015).

countries like Egypt allowed for greater cooperation on counterterrorism. That being said, Muslim states with relatively high religious freedom levels – like Senegal or Bosnia – also had good counterterrorism records.

In conclusion, the US Global War on Terrorism may have slowed down with the withdrawal of US troops from Iraq and Afghanistan and the death of Osama bin Ladin. But this will undoubtedly not be the last time the United States – or other prominent states in the international community – will attempt to advance a set of policies on a contentious international religious issue that provokes widespread opposition in Muslim countries. When this occurs, the political dynamics we saw in the context of US counterterrorism efforts will likely re-emerge, with Islamic contention being filtered through the differing institutions in Muslim states. This book's insights, and the lessons it provides from the US experience with international counterterrorism, will thus continue to be relevant to policymakers, scholars, and the general public for the foreseeable future.

Methodological Appendix

In this appendix, I provide more details on the calculation of the Counterterrorism Cooperation Scale and the Religion–State variable, the statistical methods I used and robustness checks for the quantitative analyses in Chapter 3.

THE COUNTERTERRORISM COOPERATION SCALE

The dependent variable is an original measure of counterterrorism cooperation, the Counterterrorism Cooperation Scale (CTCS). It measures the balance of cooperative to uncooperative behaviors among Muslim states in response to US counterterrorism efforts, running from -10 to 10.

This scale measures a latent variable with two dimensions – cooperation and non-cooperation. I developed a series of questions for whether or not a state took a specific counterterrorism-related action, either cooperative or non-cooperative, and used these as dichotomous variables that I coded for each country by year. These cover: actions against domestic terrorist targets, institutional reforms, compliance with US preferences on domestic counterterrorism policies, and support for US-led military actions. I exclude two commonly discussed areas of counterterrorism cooperation: official designation as a terrorist sponsor by the United States, and cooperation in the United Nations and other international forums. Official designation of terrorist sponsorship often includes historical behaviors and tends not to change due to the bureaucratic and political procedures involved; as a result, this does not closely correspond to other aspects of counterterrorism. Likewise, behavior in the United Nations – such as voting on resolutions – often involves different motivations and behaviors than active counterterrorism policies, and thus may not measure the same phenomenon as the other measures. Indeed, the distinctness of these measures is apparent methodologically, as they decrease the reliability of the full set of measures when included. For most questions, there are both cooperative and uncooperative behaviors; that is, there is a variable for cooperating on arresting terrorist suspects and a variable for not cooperating on terrorist suspects.

Each country is given a 1 for a question if the action occurred. I base the coding on US State Department Counterterrorism Country Reports.[1] These reports, released annually since 1996, provide official US assessments of the level of terrorist activity in countries, state counterterrorism actions, the extent to which states are complying with US and international counterterrorism standards, and the list of states that the United States designates as terrorist sponsors.

I calculate the CTCS by averaging states' cooperative and uncooperative behaviors separately, and then taking the balance of them. This captures both the level and full range of counterterrorism cooperation. Countries with no information for a year – that is, in which no counterterrorism activity occurred – received zeros. I use the average of the behaviors, rather than the raw count, because using the count as the basis for the calculation would result in countries more active in counterterrorism receiving larger scores. Taking the average score, however, equalizes countries allowing for greater comparison. I also created sub-scales for international and domestic counterterrorism. I weight all components of the CTCS equally.

The CTCS is a valid measure of counterterrorism cooperation on both mathematical and intuitive grounds. The scale reliability coefficient for the full set of variables is 0.68; the standard for such scores is 0.7 or above, although with difficulties involved in gaining information on counterterrorism cooperation a score that is almost at the optimal level indicates it is a useful measure. When exploratory factor analysis is used, two clear factors resulted from the factor analysis. These factors generally line up with the domestic and international aspects of counterterrorism.

There are some potential biases with the CTCS, but these are unlikely to undermine the analysis. First, as a high-stakes security issue, much information on counterterrorism is classified. But if a certain type of cooperation is not reported – such as the details of intelligence-sharing agreements – then it would not be reported for every country; while this

---

[1] Reports are available at www.state.gov/j/ct/rls/crt/index.htm.

decreases the amount of information available, it most likely does not bias the results. A related issue has to do with changing reporting over time, as US attention to counterterrorism increased after 2001. Any change in information as a result would affect all countries, however. Also, I addressed time period differences in a robustness check. Finally, because the CTCS is the average of cooperative and uncooperative behaviors, it is not as sensitive to change in the overall amount of counterterrorism activity as it would if it used a count of counterterrorism-related behaviors. Another potential issue is the biasing of the reporting by US interests. This likely occurs, although this issue does not bias the CTCS. Based on CTCS scores, Pakistan has been rather non-cooperative with the United States; the extent of its non-cooperation might be even greater, but even with this conservative bias the results still are intuitively plausible. I also ran numerous robustness checks using alternate versions of the CTCS, as discussed in Table A.1; the results of the statistical tests were consistent across all these alternate tests.

Extended Discussion: Religion–State

The independent variable is an ordinal measure that is an index measuring the religion–state relationships in Muslim states. There are two components of the index, following the previous discussion of the modified selectorate theory. The first is the size of the winning coalition. I follow Bueno de Mesquita's calculation, which makes use of the Polity dataset's measures of the competitiveness of executive recruitment, openness of executive recruitment, competitiveness of participation, and regulation of executive recruitment.[2] The result is a four-level ordinal variable, from which I take the yearly winning coalition size, the median winning coalition size for the entire length of the study, and the five-year maximum winning coalition size. I then created a set of variables that are dichotomous measures, using these three specifications; states receive a 1 – for having a small winning coalition – if the winning coalition size is less than 3.

The second is the extent of religion–state connections, which comprises three variables. The first, *Official Religion* measures whether or not the state has established Islam as the official religion, or extensively draws on Islam in its legal codes. The second, *Political Ties*, measures whether there are extensive political ties between the regime and religious groups,

---

[2] For discussion of the winning coalition size, see Bueno de Mesquita *et al.*, 2005. Data are available at www.nyu.edu/gsas/dept/politics/data/bdm2s2/Logic.htm.

either through political parties or membership in non-democratic regime coalitions. Finally, *Restricts Religion*, measures whether the state extensively restricts religious practice and belief, of either Muslims or non-Muslims. I base the coding for the three variables on a variety of sources: the Pew Research Center's "Global Restrictions on Religion" project, Jonathan Fox's "Religion and State Database," and the US State Department's annual International Religious Freedom reports.[3]

I combine the three religion–state connection variables with the five-year value for *Small Winning Coalition* to develop the religion–state relationship index. Because year-to-year changes in the winning coalition size may not have an immediate effect on the overall relationship between religion and state, the five-year value for *Small Winning Coalition* is more appropriate. I create a five-level ordinal variable, *Religion–State*: 0 represents the most distant religion–state relationship, and 4 is the closest. I also use alternate measures of religion–state relationship in robustness checks – presented in Table A.2 – which did not affect the results significantly.

METHODS

The dataset covers 47 countries with 14-year observations per country, and the CTCS is a bounded continuous variable, running from −10 to 10.[4] I use a generalized estimating equation (GEE) with autoregressive within-cluster correlation, a flexible and robust estimator that accounts for the longitudinal data and correlation among observations.[5] I use three main models. Model 1 includes CTCS and *Religion–State*, Model 2 includes the domestic control variables, and Model 3 adds the international control variables. Two additional models separate the domestic and international aspects of counterterrorism. The results are presented in Table A.3 and A.4, and information on robustness checks is available in Table A.5. I ran numerous alternate models as robustness checks, presented in Table A.6; the results were consistent across these checks.

---

[3] Pew data is available at www.pewforum.org/2012/09/20/rising-tide-of-restrictions-on-religion-findings/, Fox's data are available at www.religionandstate.org, and the US State Department reports are available at www.state.gov/j/drl/irf/rpt/index.htm.

[4] Robustness checks using the dichotomous version of the CTCS can deal with issues with the bounded dependent variable.

[5] See Zorn, "Generalized Estimating Equation Models for Correlated Data: A Review with Applications."

APPENDIX LISTS AND TABLES

Alternate Versions of the Counterterrorism Cooperation Scale

Separate cooperative and non-cooperative variables
Count of counterterrorism behaviors
Including only components that have cooperative and non-cooperative
    versions
Replace 0 values with missing
Dichotomous version with 1 as cooperative
Predicted scores from factor analysis results as variables
Weighted version using principal component analysis

TABLE A.1. *Results from Models 1–3 in Chapter 3*

	Model		
	(1)	(2)	(3)
Religion–State	−0.44*	−0.46*	−0.62**
	(0.20)	(0.23)	(0.21)
Alliance			3.09***
			(0.62)
US MID			0.33
			(0.85)
Diplomatic Representation			0.03
			(0.28)
Terrorism		0.03	−0.12
		(0.11)	(0.10)
Affinity			−1.30
			(0.65)
Small Winning Coalition		−0.50	−0.32
		(0.40)	(0.40)
GDP		0.18	0.12
		(0.18)	(0.20)
US Aid			0.00***
			(0.00)
Trade			0.00
			(0.00)
Islamist Activity		0.16	0.42
		(0.35)	(0.35)
Constant	1.25***	0.14	−0.23
	(0.33)	(1.36)	(2.00)
Observations	658	604	564

Robust standard errors in parentheses
*** $p < 0.001$, ** $p < 0.01$, * $p < 0.05$

Alternate Versions of Religion–State

Collapsed levels 2 and 3
religion–state and winning coalition components as separate variables
All levels of religion–state as separate variables
Yearly varying calculation of winning coalition as component
Median level of winning coalition across entire time period

TABLE A.2. *Results from Models 4 and 5 in Chapter 3*

	Model	
	(4) International	(5) Domestic
Religion–State	−0.14	−0.74**
	(0.12)	(0.24)
Alliance	2.35***	1.99***
	(0.44)	(0.66)
US MID	0.03	−0.06
	(0.33)	(1.12)
Diplomatic Representation	0.31	−0.00
	(0.31)	(0.31)
Terrorism	−0.00	−0.14
	(0.07)	(0.12)
Affinity	0.41	−1.59
	(0.45)	(0.83)
Small Winning Coalition	−0.49*	−0.09
	(0.29)	(0.48)
GDP	−0.05	0.24
	(0.17)	(0.25)
US Aid	0.00***	0.00***
	(0.00)	(0.00)
Trade	0.00	0.00
	(0.00)	(0.00)
Constant	0.49	−0.94
	(1.83)	(2.33)
Observations	564	564

Robust standard errors in parentheses
*** p < 0.001, ** p < 0.01, * p < 0.05

TABLE A.3. *Information on Control Variables from Chapter 3*

Control Variable	Calculation
GDP[6]	log of GDP using PPP and current US dollars
Terrorism[7]	two-year rolling averages of deaths from attacks
Islamist Activity[8]	active Islamic groups, Islamic political parties, Islamist parties in government
US aid[9]	US military and economic aid as percentage of target country GDP
Trade[10]	Log of country's US trade
Alliance[11]	presence of official alliance with the United States
Diplomatic Representation[12]	maximum level of diplomatic ties between the United States and country
Affinity[13]	similarity of country votes with the US in the UN
MID[14]	had a MID with the United States since 1990

[6] World Bank data available at http://data.worldbank.org/.

[7] Data from the Global Terrorism Database, available at http://start.umd.edu/gtd/.

[8] Data from CIA World Factbook, available at www.cia.gov/library/publications/the-world-factbook/; Charles Kurzman's data on Islamist parties, available at http://kurzman.unc.edu/islamic-parties/; the US State Department's Country Reports on Terrorism, available at www.state.gov/r/pa/prs/ps/2013/05/210.htm; and the American Foreign Policy Council's "World Almanac of Islamism," available at http://almanac.afpc.org/.

[9] Data available at http://usoda.eads.usaidallnet.gov/.

[10] Data from Katherine Barbieri, Omar M. G. Keshk, and Brian Pollins, "Trading Data: Evaluating Our Assumptions and Coding Rules," *Conflict Management and Peace Science* 26, no. 5 (2009).

[11] Data from Douglas M. Gibler and Meredith Sarkees, "Measuring Alliances: The Correlates of War Formal Interstate Alliance Data Set, 1816–2000," *Journal of Peace Research* 41, no. 2 (2004).

[12] Data from Reşat Bayer, "Diplomatic Exchange Data Set, V2006.1," (2006).

[13] Data from Erik Gartzke, "Kant We All Just Get Along? Opportunity, Willingness, and the Origins of the Democratic Peace," *American Journal of Political Science* 42, no. 1 (1998).

[14] Data from Faten Ghosn, Glenn Palmer Palmer, and Stuart Bremer, "The Mid3 Data Set, 1993–2001: Procedures, Coding Rules, and Description," *Conflict Management and Peace Science* 21, no. 133–154 (2004).

TABLE A.4. *Robustness Checks for Chapter 3*

Robustness Check	Affect results?
Control for regions	No
Remove Iraq, Afghanistan	No
Control for time periods	No
CTCS count version	No
CTCS proportion version	No
CTCS principle components version	No
CTCS missing values removed	No
CTCS sum version	No
CTCS paired indicators	No
CTCS only cooperative	Yes, not significant
CTCS only non-coopeative	No
Separate levels of religion–state	No
Religion–state w/o five-year	No
Religion–state constant	No
Religion–state w/o winning coalition	No
Religion–state three levels	No
OLS	No
Fixed Effects	No
Random Effects	No
GEE, exchangeable correlation	No
Random Coefficients	No
Logit with dichotomous CTCS	No
Sum of Islamist activity	No
Dichotomous Islamist activity	No
Polity control	No
Democracy and Dictatorship control	No
Economic and Military aid separate	No
Conflict intensity control	No
Terrorism categorical severity control	No
Terrorism each year control	No
State power control	No
Ally of Russia or China control	No
Public approval of US as control	No
Average value of all variables across entire time period	No

References

Databases Referenced

Foreign Broadcast Information Service/World News Connection
ProQuest

Periodicals

al-Akhbar
Al-Arabiya
The Arab American News
Asian News International
Asian Wall Street Journal
BBC Monitoring
BBC News
Christian Science Monitor
CNN Online
Daily News Egypt
The Daily Star
The Daily Telegraph
Financial Times
The Gazette
The Guardian
The Hindustan Times
The Irish Examiner
IPS-InterPress Service
Irish Times
Jerusalem Post
Khaleej Times
Los Angeles Times
International Herald Tribune
Mideast Mirror

The National
National Post
New York Times
The New Zealand Herald
Newsweek
The Ottawa Citizen
Reuters
al-Shorfa
Sunday Times
The Times
Toronto Star
Wall Street Journal
The Washington Post

Books and Journal Articles

The 9/11 Commission. *The 9/11 Commission Report: Final Report of the National Commission on Terrorist Attacks Upon the United States*. New York: W. W. Norton and Company, 2004.

Acemoglu, Daron, and James A. Robinson. *Why Nations Fail: The Origins of Power, Prosperity and Poverty*. New York: Crown Business, 2012.

Adams, T. W. "The American Concern in Cyprus." *Annals of the American Academy of Political and Social Science*, 401 (May 1972): 95–105.

Ahmad, Feroz. "The Historical Background of Turkey's Foreign Policy" in *The Future of Turkish Foreign Policy*, edited by Lenore G. Martin and Dimitris Keridis, 9–36. Cambridge, MA: MIT Press, 2004.

Ahmed, Ishtiaq. "The Spectre of Islamic Fundamentalism over Pakistan" in *Pakistan in Regional and Global Politics*, edited by Rajshree Jetly, 150–80. London: Routledge Taylor & Francis Group, 2009.

Ahmed, Samina. "The United States and Terrorism in Southwest Asia: September 11 and Beyond." *International Security* 26, no. 3 (2002).

Aktay, Yasin. "Politics at Home, Politics in the World the Return of the Political in Turkish Foreign Policy." *Mediterranean Quarterly* 21, no. 1 (Winter 2010): 61–75.

al-Qasimi, Noor "Immodest Modesty: Accommodating Dissent and the 'Abaya-as-Fashion in the Arab Gulf States." *Journal of Middle East Women's Studies* 6, no. 1 (2010).

Angrist, Michele Penner. "Party Systems and Regime Formation in the Modern Middle East: Explaining Turkish Exceptionalism," *Comparative Politics* 36, no. 2 (January 2004): 229–49.

Appiah, Kwame Anthony. "Causes of Quarrel: What's Special about Religious Disputes?" in *Religious Pluralism, Globalization, and World Politics*, edited by Thomas Banchoff, 41–65. New York: Oxford University Press, 2008.

Arango, Tim, and Ceylan Yeginsu. "Turkey's Push into War Is Seen as Erdogan's Political Strategy." *New York Times*, August 5, 2015.

Aras, Bulent. *Palestinian Israeli Peace Process and Turkey*. Commack, NY: Nova Science Publishers, Inc., 1998.

Ayata, Sencer. "Patronage, Party and State: The Politicization of Islam in Turkey." *Middle East Journal* 50, no. 1 (Winter 1996): 40–56.

Aybet, Gulnur. *Turkey's Foreign Policy and Its Implications for the West: A Turkish Perspective*. Rusi Whitehall Paper Series. Dorset: Roal United Services Institute for Defence Studies, 1994.

"Azerbaijan: Freedom in the World." Freedom House, 1999.

Aziz, Mazhar. *Military Control in Pakistan: The Parallel State*. New York: Routledge, 2008.

Bajpai, Kanti. "Managing Ambivalence: Pakistan's Relations with the United States and China since 2001" in *Pakistan in Regional and Global Politics*, edited by Rajshree Jetly, 63–97. London: Routledge Taylor & Francis Group, 2009.

Banchoff, Thomas. "Introduction: Religious Pluralism in World Affairs" in *Religious Pluralism, Globalization, and World Politics*, edited by Thomas Banchoff, 3–41. New York: Oxford University Press, 2008.

   ed. *Religious Pluralism, Globalization and World Politics*. New York: Oxford University Press, 2008.

Bandyopadhyay, Subhayu, Todd Sandler, and Javed Younas. "Foreign Aid as Counterterrorism Policy." *Oxford Economic Papers* 63, no. 3 (2011): 423–47.

Barbieri, Katherine, Omar M. G. Keshk, and Brian Pollins. "Trading Data: Evaluating Our Assumptions and Coding Rules." *Conflict Management and Peace Science* 26, no. 5 (November 2009): 471–91.

Bayer, Reşat. "Diplomatic Exchange Data Set, V2006.1." 2006.

Bellin, Eva. "Democratization and Its Discontents: Should America Push Political Reform in the Middle East?" *Foreign Affairs* 87, no. 4 (July 1, 2008).

   "Faith in Politics: New Trends in the Study of Religion and Politics." *World Politics* 60, no. 2 (January 2008): 315–47.

Bennett, Andrew. "Process Tracing and Causal Inference" in *Rethinking Social Inquiry: Diverse Tools, Shared Standards*, edited by Henry Brady and David Collier, 207–21. Lanham, MD: Rowman & Littlefield Publishers, 2010.

Bennett, Andrew, and Jeffrey Checkel. "Process Tracing: From Philosophical Roots to Best Practices" in *Process Tracing: From Metaphor to Analytic Tool*, edited by Andrew Bennett and Jeffrey Checkel. New York: Cambridge University Press, 2014.

Bennett, Andrew, and Colin Elman. "Qualitative Research: Recent Developments in Case Study Methods." *Annual Review of Political Science* 9 (2006): 455–76.

Bergen, Peter. *The Longest War: The Enduring Conflict between Al-Qaeda and America*. New York: Free Press, 2011.

Beyer, Peter. *Religions in Global Society*. New York: Routledge, 2006.

Blum, Douglas W. "Beyond Blood and Belief: Culture and Foreign Policy Conduct" in *The Limits of Culture: Islam and Foreign Policy*, edited by Brenda Shaffer, 65–83. Cambridge, MA: MIT Press, 2006.

Bolukbasi, Suha. "Behind the Turkish-Israeli Alliance: A Turkish View." *Journal of Palestine Studies* 29, no. 1 (Autumn 1999): 21–35.

Bronson, Rachel. *Thicker Than Oil: America's Uneasy Partnership with Saudi Arabia*. New York: Oxford University Press, 2006.

Brooks, Stephen G., and William C. Wohlforth. *World Out of Balance: International Relations and the Challenge of American Primacy*. Princeton: Princeton University Press, 2008.

Brown, James. "The Turkish Imbroglio: Its Kurds." *Annals of the American Academy of Political and Social Science*, 541 (September 1995): 116–29.

Brown, Sophie. "Malaysian Court to Christians: You Can't Say 'Allah'." *CNN Online*, June 24, 2014.

Brumberg, Daniel. "Authoritarian Legacies and Reform Strategies in the Muslim World" in *Political Liberalization and Democratization in the Arab World*, edited by Rex Brynen, Bahgat Korany, and Paul Noble, 229–60. Boulder, CO: Lynne Reiner Publishers, 1995.

"Survival Strategies versus Democratic Bargaining: The Politics of Economic Reform in Contemporary Egypt" in *The Politics of Economic Reform in the Middle East*, edited by Henri Barkey, 73–105. New York: Palgrave MacMillan, 1992.

Bueno de Mesquita, Bruce, and Alastair Smith. "Leader Survival, Revolutions, and the Nature of Government Finance." *American Journal of Political Science* 54, no. 4 (2010): 936–50.

Bueno de Mesquita, Bruce, Alastair Smith, Randolph M. Siverson, and James D. Morrow. *The Logic of Political Survival*. Cambridge, MA: The MIT Press, 2003.

Bushku, Michael B. "Albania and the Middle East." *Mediterranean Quarterly* 24, no. 2 (2013).

Butt, Gerald. "Oil and Gas in the UAE" in *United Arab Emirates: A New Perspective*, edited by Ibrahim al-Abed and Peter Hellyer, 231–49. London: Trident Press, 1997.

Byman, Daniel. *Al Qaeda, the Islamic State, and the Global Jihadist Movement: What Everyone Needs to Know*. New York: Oxford University Press, 2015.

Deadly Connections: States That Sponsor Terrorism. New York: Cambridge University Press, 2007.

"Friends Like These: Counterinsurgency and the War on Terrorism." *International Security* 31, no. 2 (2006): 79–115.

Cagaptay, Soner. *Islam Secularism and Nationalism in Modern Turkey: Who Is a Turk?*. London: Routledge Taylor & Francis Group, 2006.

Cagaptay, Soner, and Mark Parris. "Turkey after the Iraq War: Still a US Ally?" in *Policy Analysis*: Washington Institute for Near East Policy, 2003.

Carlson, John D., and Erik C. Owens. "Introduction: Reconsidering Westphalia's Legacy for Religion and International Politics" in *The Sacred and the Sovereign: Religion and International Politics*, edited by John D. Carlson and Erik C. Owens, 1–41. Washington, DC: Georgetown University Press, 2003.

Carpenter, Ted Galen. "Estrangement: The United States and Turkey in a Multipolar Era." *Mediterranean Quarterly* 21, no. 4 (Fall 2010): 27–37.

Casanova, Jose. "Globalizing Catholicism and the Return to a 'Universal' Church" in *Transnational Religion and Fading States*, edited by Susanna

Hoeber and James Piscatori Rudoplh, 121–43. Boulder, CO: Westview Press, 1996.

Public Religions in the Modern World. Chicago: University of Chicago Press, 1994.

Chellany, Brahma. "Fighting Terrorism in Southern Asia: The Lessons of History." *International Security* 26, no. 3 (2002).

Chengappa, Bidanda M. *Pakistan: Islamisation, Army and Foreign Policy.* New Delhi: A.P.H. Publishing Corporation, 2004.

Christie-Miller, Alexander. "Kurds Accuse Turkish Government of Supporting Isis." *Newsweek*, October 22, 2014.

Cloud, David S. "Pakistan Shuts Down US 'Intelligence Fusion' Cells." *The Los Angeles Times*, May 27, 2011.

Cohen, Stephen Philip. *The Idea of Pakistan.* Washington, DC: Brookings Institution Press, 2004.

Coll, Steve. *Ghost Wars: The Secret History of the CIA, Afghanistan and bin Ladin, from the Soviet Invasion to September 10, 2011.* New York: Penguin Press, 2004.

Collier, David, and Henry Brady, eds. *Rethinking Social Inquiry: Diverse Tools, Shared Standards.* Lanham, MD: Rowman & Littlefield Publishers, 2010.

Cooley, Alexander. *Base Politics: Democratic Change and the US Military Overseas* Ithaca, NY: Cornell University Press, 2008.

Logics of Hierarchy: The Organization of Empires, States and Military Occupations. Ithaca, NY: Cornell University Press, 2005.

Cooper, Helen. "United Arab Emirates, Key US Ally in Isis Effort, Disengaged in December." *New York Times*, February 3, 2015.

"Country Reports on Terrorism 2003," edited by US Department of State, 2004.

"Country Reports on Terrorism 2008: Chapter 2. Country Reports: Africa Overview." US Department of State, 2009.

"Country Reports on Terrorism 2009: Chapter 2. Country Reports: Africa Overview." US Department of State, 2010.

Dagi, Ihsan. "Turkey's AKP in Power." *Journal of Democracy* 19, no. 3 (July 2008): 25–30.

Dark, K. R. "Large-Scale Religious Change and World Politics" in *Religion in International Relations*, edited by K. R. Dark, 50–82. New York: St. Martin's Press, 2000.

Davidson, Christoper M. *Dubai: The Vulnerability of Success.* New York: Columbia University Press, 2008.

The United Arab Emirates: A Study in Survival. Boulder, CO: Lynne Reiner Publishers, 2005.

Dawisha, Adeed. "Islam in Foreign Policy: Some Methodological Issues" in *Islam in Foreign Policy*, edited by Adeed Dawisha. New York: Cambridge University Press, 1985.

Dismorr, Anne. *Turkey Decoded.* London: Saqi, 2008.

Donnelly, Jack. "Sovereign Inequalities and Hierarchy in Anarchy: American Power and International Security." *European Journal of International Relations* 12, no. 2 (2006): 139–70.

"Egypt and Saudi Arabia Deny Split over Syria." *Al-Jazeera*, May 31, 2015.

Ehteshami, Anoushiravan, and Steven Wright. "Political Change in the Arab Oil Monarchies: From Liberalization to Enfranchisement." *Royal Institute of International Affairs* 83, no. 5 (2007).

Esposito, John. *The Islamic Threat: Myth or Reality?* New York: Oxford University Press, 1992.

"Fact Sheet on the Global Counterterrorism Forum." www.cfr.org/counter terrorism/fact-sheet-global-counterterrorism-forum/p28460.

Fair, C. Christine Fair. "Pakistan's Relations with Central Asia" in *Pakistan in Regional and Global Politics*, edited by Rajshree Jetly, 125–49. London: Routledge Taylor and Francis Group, 2009.

Fair, C. Christine Fair, Keith Crane, Christopher C. Chivvis, Samir Puri, and Michael Spirtas. *Pakistan: Can the United States Secure an Insecure State?* RAND Corporation, 2010.

Farr, Thomas. *World of Faith and Freedom: Why International Religious Liberty Is Vital to American National Security.* New York: Oxford University Press, 2008.

Fearon, James. "Domestic Politics, Foreign Policy, and Theories of International Relations." *Annual Review of Political Science* 1 (1998): 289–313.

Fearon, James D. "Counterfactuals and Hypothesis Testing in Political Science." *World Politics* 43, no. 2 (January 1991): 169–95.

"Domestic Political Audiences and the Escalation of International Disputes." *American Political Science Review* 88, no. 3 (September 1994): 577–92.

Finnemore, Martha. "Legitimacy, Hypocrisy, and the Social Structure of Unipolarity: Why Being a Unipole Isn't All It's Cracked up to Be." *World Politics* 61, no. 1 (January 2009): 58–85.

Fox, Jonathan. "Ethnoreligious Conflict in the Third World: The Role of Religion as a Cause of Conflict." *Nationalism and Ethnic Politics* 9, no. 1 (Spring 2003): 101–25.

A World Survey of Religion and the State. New York: Cambridge University Press, 2008.

Fox, Jonathan, and Nukhet Sandal. "State Religious Exclusivity and International Crises between 1990 and 2002" in *Religion, Identity and Global Governance: Theory, Evidence, and Practice*, edited by Patrick James. Toronto: University of Toronto Press, 2010.

Fox, Jonathan, and Shmuel Sandler. *Bringing Religion into International Relations.* New York: Palgrave MacMillan, 2004.

Friedman, Thomas L. "Dubai and Dunces." *New York Times*, March 15, 2006.

Fuller, Graham E. *The New Turkish Republic: Turkey as a Pivotal State in the Muslim World.* Washington, DC: United States Institute of Peace Press, 2008.

Gartzke, Erik. "Kant We All Just Get Along? Opportunity, Willingness, and the Origins of the Democratic Peace." *American Journal of Political Science* 42, no. 1 (1998): 1–27.

Gartzke, Erik, and Kristian Skrede Gleditsch. "Identity and Conflict: Ties That Bind and Differences That Divide." *European Journal of International Relations* 12, no. 1 (2006): 53–87.

George, Alexander, and Andrew Bennett. *Case Studies and Theory Development in the Social Sciences.* Cambridge, MA: MIT Press, 2005.

Ghosn, Faten, Glenn Palmer Palmer, and Stuart Bremer. "The Mid3 Data Set, 1993–2001: Procedures, Coding Rules, and Description." *Conflict Management and Peace Science* 21, no. 133–54 (2004).

Gibler, Douglas M., and Meredith Sarkees. "Measuring Alliances: The Correlates of War Formal Interstate Alliance Data Set, 1816–2000." *Journal of Peace Research* 41, no. 2 (2004): 211–22.

Gilbert, Ben. "Saudi Arabia Walks a Fine Line in Backing Syrian Rebellion." *Al-Jazeera America*, January 10, 2014.

Gill, Anthony. *The Political Origins of Religious Liberty*. New York: Cambridge University Press, 2008.

"Religion and Comparative Politics." *Annual Review of Political Science* 4 (2001): 117–38.

Rendering Unto Caesar: The Catholic Church and the State in Latin America. Chicago: University of Chicago Press, 1998.

"Global Restrictions on Religion." Washington, DC: Pew Research Center, 2009.

Gole, Nilüfer. "Secularism and Islamism in Turkey: The Making of Elites and Counter-Elites." *Middle East Journal* 51, no. 1 (Winter 1997): 46–58.

Gordon, Philip H., and Omer Taspinar. *Winning Turkey: How America, Europe and Turkey Can Revive a Fading Partnership.* Washington, DC: Brookings Institution Press, 2008.

Griesa, Thomas, Daniel Meierrieksb, and Margarete Redlinc. "Oppressive Governments, Dependence on the USA, and Anti-American Terrorism." *Oxford Economic Papers* 67, no. 1 (2015): 83–103.

Grigoriadis, Ioannis N. "Friends No More? The Rise of Anti-American Nationalism in Turkey." *Middle East Journal* 64, no. 1 (Winter 2010): 51–66.

Grim, Brian J., and Roger Finke. *The Price of Freedom Denied: Religious Persecution and Conflict in the Twenty-First Century.* New York: Cambridge University Press, 2010.

Gul, Imtiaz. *The Most Dangerous Place: Pakistan's Lawless Frontier.* New York: Penguin Books, 2011.

Gunaratna, Rohan. *Inside Al Qaeda.* New York: Berkley Books, 2003.

Guth, James L., John C. Green, Lyman A. Kellstedt, and Corwin E. Smidt. "Faith and Foreign Policy: A View from the Pews." *The Review of Faith and International Affairs* 3, no. 2 (2005): 3–10.

Hafez, Mohammed M. *Why Muslims Rebel: Repression and Resistance in the Muslim World.* Boulder, CO: Lynne Reiner Publishers, 2003.

Haider, Ziad. *The Ideological Struggle for Pakistan.* Stanford: Hoover Institute Press, 2010.

Haleem, Irm. "Ethnic and Sectarian Violence and the Propensity Towards Praetorianism in Pakistan." *Third World Quarterly* 24, no. 3 (June 2003): 463–77.

Haqqani, Husain. *Pakistan: Between Mosque and Military.* Washington, DC: Carnegie Endowment for International Peace, 2005.

Harrison, Selig. "Global Terrorism: US Policy after 9/11 and Its Impact on the Domestic Politics and Foreign Relations of Terrorism" in *Pakistan in Regional and Global Politics*, edited by Rajshree Jetly, 20–45. London: Routledge Taylor and Francis Group, 2009.

Hassner, Ron E. "Blasphemy and Violence." *International Studies Quarterly* 55, no. 1 (March 2011): 23–47.

"To Halve and to Hold: Conflicts over Sacred Space and the Problem of Indivisibility." *Security Studies* 12, no. 4 (Summer 2003): 1–33.

Haydar, Afak. "The Sipah-E-Sahaba Pakistan" in *Pakistan: Founders' Aspirations and Today's Realities*, edited by Hafeez Malik, 263–86. New York: Oxford University Press, 2001.

Heard-Bey, Frauke. "The United Arab Emirates: Statehood and Nation-Building in a Traditional Society." *Middle East Journal* 59, no. 3 (2005).

Hellyer, Peter. "Evolution of UAE Foreign Policy" in *United Arab Emirates: A New Perspective*, edited by Ibrahim al-Abed and Peter Hellyer, 161–79. London: Trident Press, 1997.

Henne, Peter S. "The Domestic Politics of International Religious Defamation." *Politics and Religion* 6, no. 3 (2013).

"The Two Swords: Religion-State Connections and Interstate Conflict." *Journal of Peace Research* 49, no. 6 (2012): 753–68.

Hoffman, Bruce. *Inside Terrorism*. New York: Columbia University Press, 2006.

Horowitz, Michael. "Long Time Going: Religion and the Duration of Crusading." *International Security* 34, no. 2 (Fall 2009).

Hunter, Shireen T. "Religion, Politics and Security in Central Asia." *SAIS Review* 2, no. 1 (2001).

Huntington, Samuel P. *The Clash of Civilizations and the Remaking of World Order*. New York: Simon & Schuster, 1996.

Hurd, Elizabeth Shakman. *Beyond Religious Freedom: The New Global Politics of Religion*. Princeton, NJ: Princeton University Press, 2015.

"The Political Authority of Secularism in International Relations." *European Journal of International Relations* 10, no. 2 (June 2004): 235–62.

Iannaccone, Lawrence, Roger Finke, and Rodney Stark. "Deregulating Religion: The Economics of Church and State." *Economic Inquiry* 35, no. 2 (1997): 350–64.

"International Religious Freedom Report." US Department of State, 2010.

Jackson, Patrick Thaddeus. *The Conduct of Inquiry in International Relations*. New York: Routledge, 2011.

Jalal, Ayesha. *The Sole Spokesman: Jinnah, the Muslim League and the Demand for Pakistan*. London: Cambridge University Press, 1985.

Jenkins, Gareth. "Muslim Democrats in Turkey?" *Survival* 45, no. 1 (Spring 2003): 45–66.

Jones, Seth. "The Rise of Afghanistan's Insurgency: State Failure and Jihad." *International Security* 32, no. 4 (2008).

Juergensmeyer, Mark. *The New Cold War?: Religious Nationalism Confronts the Secular State*. Berkeley: University of California Press, 1993.

Jung, Dietrich, and Wolfango Piccoli. *Turkey at the Crossroads: Ottoman Legacies and a Greater Middle East*. London: Zed Books, 2001.

Karasipahi, Sena. "Comparing Islamic Resurgence Movements in Turkey and Iran." *Middle East Journal* 63, no. 1 (Winter 2009).

"Kazakhstan Promotes Central Asian Interests within OIC." In *Eurasia Daily Monitor*, Jamestown Foundation, 2013.

Keohane, Robert O., and Peter J. Katzenstein. *Anti-Americanisms in World Politics*. Ithaca, NY: Cornell University Press, 2007.

Kepel, Gilles. *Jihad: The Trail of Political Islam*. Cambridge, MA: The Belknap Press of Harvard University, 2002.

Kirchgaesser, Stephanie. "US Coast Guard Warned on Dubai Ports Deal." February 28, 2006.

Kirkpatrick, David D. "Egypt Launches Airstrike in Libya against ISIS Branch." *New York Times*, February 16, 2015.

Kizilbash, Hamid H. "Anti-Americanism in Pakistan." *Annals of the American Academy of Political and Social Science*, 497 (May 1988): 58–67.

Kolbe, Melanie, and Peter S. Henne. "The Effect of Religious Restrictions on Forced Migration." *Politics and Religion* 7, no. 4 (2014): 665–83.

Krause, Wanda. *Women in Civil Society: The State, Islamism and Networks in the UAE*. New York: Palgrave MacMillan, 2008.

Krebs, Ronald R., and Patrick Thaddeus Jackson. "Twisting Tongues and Twisting Arms: The Power of Political Rhetoric." *European Journal of International Relations* 13, no. 1 (2007): 35–66.

Kull, Steven. *Feeling Betrayed: The Roots of Muslim Anger at America*. Washington, DC: Brookings Institution Press, 2011.

Kupchan, Charles A. *The End of the American Era: US Foreign Policy and the Geopolitics of the Twentieth Century*. New York: Random House, 2002.

Kuru, Ahmet T. *Secularism and State Policies Towards Religion: The United States, France, and Turkey*. New York: Cambridge University Press, 2009.

Lake, David A. "Anarchy, Hierarchy and the Variety of International Relations." *International Organization* 50, no. 1 (1996): 1–33.

"Escape from the State of Nature: Authority and Hierarchy in World Politics." *International Security* 32, no. 1 (Summer 2007): 47–79.

"Legitimating Power: The Domestic Politics of US International Hierarchy." *International Security* 38, no. 2 (Fall 2013).

Lalami, Laila. "Islamophobia and Its Discontents," *The Nation*, July 2, 2012.

Larrabee, F. Stephen. *Troubled Partnership: US-Turkish Relations in an Era of Global Geopolitical Change*. Washington, DC: The RAND Corporation, 2010.

Larrabee, F. Stephen, and Ian O. Lesser. *Turkish Foreign Policy in an Age of Uncertainty*. Santa Monica, CA: The RAND Corporation, 2003.

Leege, David C., and Lyman A. Kellstedt, eds. *Rediscovering the Religious Factor in American Politics*. New York: M. E. Sharpe, Inc, 1993.

Lewis, Bernard. *The Crisis of Islam*. New York: Random House Trade Paperbacks, 2003.

"The Roots of Muslim Rage." *The Atlantic Monthly* (September 1990): 47–60.

Lieber, Kier A., and Gerard Alexander. "Waiting for Balancing: Why the World Is Not Pushing Back." *International Security* 30 no. 1 (Summer 2005): 109–39.

Lieber, Robert J. *The American Era: Power and Strategy for the 21st Century*. New York: Cambridge University Press, 2007.

Lieberman, Evan S. "Nested Analysis as a Mixed-Method Strategy for Comparative Research." *American Political Science Review* 99, no. 3 (August 2005): 435–52.

Lynch, Marc. *The Arab Uprising: The Unfinished Revolutions of the New Middle East*. New York: Public Affairs, 2013.

MacKay, Mairi. "Prayer and Politics: How Friday Became the Middle East's Day of Protest." *CNN*, June 20, 2011.

Mahoney, James. "Path Dependence in Historical Sociology." *Theory and Society* 29, no. 4 (2000): 507–48.

"Strategies of Causal Assessment in Comparative Historical Analysis" in *Comparative Historical Analysis in the Social Sciences*, edited by James Mahoney and Dietrich Rueschemeyer, 337–73. New York: Cambridge University Press, 2003.

Mahoney, James, and Gary Goertz. "A Tale of Two Cultures: Contrasting Quantitative and Qualitative Research." *Political Analysis* 14, no. 3 (Summer 2006): 227–48.

Mahoney, James, Erin Kimball, and Kenra L. Koivu. "The Logic of Historical Explanation in the Social Sciences." *Comparative Political Studies* 42, no. 1 (November 2008): 114–46.

Mahoney, James, and Kathleen Thelen, eds. *Explaining Institutional Change: Ambiguity, Agency, and Power*. New York: Cambridge University Press, 2010.

"A Theory of Gradual Institutional Change" in *Explaining Institutional Change: Ambiguity, Agency, and Power*, edited by James Mahoney and Kathleen Thelen, 1–38. New York: Cambridge University Press, 2010.

Malik, Anas. *Political Survival in Pakistan: Beyond Ideology*. New York: Routledge, 2011.

Malik, Hafeez. *Pakistan: Founders' Aspirations and Today's Realities*. New York: Oxford University Press, 2001.

Martin, Lenore G. "Turkey's Middle East Foreign Policy" in *The Future of Turkish Foreign Policy*, edited by Lenore G. and Dimitris Keridis Martin, 157–90. Cambridge, MA: MIT Press, 2004.

Masood, Salman. "In Protest over Nato Strike, Pakistan Will Skip Afghan Conference." *The New York Times*, November 29, 2011, 6.

Mazaheri, Nimah. "Iraq and the Domestic Political Effects of Economic Sanctions." *The Middle East Journal* 64, no. 2 (2010).

McAdam, Douglas, Sidney Tarrow, and Charles Tilly. *Dynamics of Contention*. New York: Cambridge University Press, 2001.

McGillivray, Fiona, and Alastair Smith. *Punishing the Prince: A Theory of Interstate Relations, Political Institutions, and Regime Change*. Princeton, NJ: Princeton University Press, 2008.

Mecham, R. Quinn. "From the Ashes of Virtue, a Promise of Light: The Transformation of Political Islam In Turkey." *Third World Quarterly* 25, no. 2 (2004): 339–58.

Mehta, Pratap Bhanu. "On the Possibility of Religious Pluralism" in *Religious Pluralism, Globalization, and World Politics*, edited by Thomas Banchoff, 65–89. New York: Oxford University Press, 2008.

Milner, Helen. *Interests, Institutions, and Information: Domestic Politics and International Relations*. Princeton: Princeton University Press, 1997.

Mitchell, Joshua. "Religion Is Not a Preference." *The Journal of Politics* 69, no. 2 (May 2007): 351–62.

Morrow, James D., Bruce Bueno de Mesquita, Randolph M. Siversion, and Alastair Smith. "Retesting Selectorate Theory: Separating the Effects of W from Other Elements of Democracy." *American Political Science Review* 102, no. 3 (2008): 393–400.

Mousseau, Michael. "Market Civilization and Its Clash with Terror." *International Security* 27, no. 3 (Winter 2002): 5–29.

Mufti, Malik. "Daring and Caution in Turkish Foreign Policy." *Middle East Journal* 52, no. 1 (Winter 1998): 32–50.

Munir, Metin. "Principles Come at a Price." *Euromoney*, April 2003.

Myers, Steven Lee. "Tumult of Arab Spring Prompts Worries in Washington." *The New York Times*, September 17, 2011.

Nasr, S. V. R. *Islamic Leviathan: Islam and the Making of State Power*. New York: Oxford University Press, 2001.

Nasr, Vali. "International Politics, Domestic Imperatives, and Identity Mobilization: Sectarianism in Pakistan." *Comparative Politics* 32, no. 2 (January 2000): 171–90.

"Regional Implications of Shi'a Revival in Iraq." *The Washington Monthly* 27, no. 3 (2004).

"The Rise of 'Muslim Democracy'." *Journal of Democracy* 16, no. 2 (April 2005): 13–27.

Nexon, Daniel H. "Religion and International Relations: No Leap of Faith Required" in *Religion and International Relations Theory*, edited by Jack Snyder. New York: Columbia University Press, 2011.

The Struggle for Power in Early Modern Europe: Religious Conflict, Dynastic Empires and International Change. Princeton: Princeton University Press, 2009.

"What's This, Then? 'Romanes Eunt Domus'?' *International Studies Perspectives* 9, no. 3 (August 2008): 300–8.

Nexon, Daniel H., and Thomas Wright. "What's at Stake in the American Empire Debate?" *American Political Science Review* 101, no. 2 (May 2007): 253–71.

Niaz, Ilhan. *The Culture of Governance and Power in Pakistan, 1947–2008*. New York: Oxford University Press, 2010.

The Culture of Power and Governance of Pakistan, 1947–2008. Karachi: Oxford University Press, 2010.

Olson, Robert. "Turkey-Iran Relations, 1997 to 2000: The Kurdish and Islamist Questions." *Third World Quarterly* 21, no. 5 (October 2000): 871–90.

Owen, John M. IV. *The Clash of Ideas in World Politics: Transnational Networks, States, and Regime Change, 1510–2010*. Princeton: Princeton University Press, 2010.

"Pakistani Public Opinion." Pew Research Center, 2009.

"Patterns of Global Terrorism." edited by US Department of State, 2001.

"Patterns of Global Terrorism." edited by US Department of State, 2003.

"Patterns of Global Terrorism 2002: Eurasia Overview." US Department of State, 2003.

"Patterns of Global Terrorism 2002: Europe Overview." US Department of State, 2003.

"Peter King: Dubai Ports Company in 'Al Qaeda Heartland'." *NewsMax Online*, February 20, 2006.

Philpott, Daniel. "Explaining the Political Ambivalence of Religion." *American Political Science Review* 101, no. 3 (August 2007): 505–25.

"Has the Study of Global Politics Found Religion?" *Annual Review of Political Science* 12 (2009): 183–202.

"The Religious Roots of Modern International Relations." *World Politics* 52, no. 2 (January 2000): 206–45.

Pierson, Paul. *Politics in Time: History, Institutions, and Social Analysis*. Princeton, NJ: Princeton University Press, 2004.

Pinto, Vania Carvalho. *Nation-Building, State, and the Genderframing of Women's Rights in the United Arab Emirates (1971–2009)*. Reading, UK: Ithaca Press, 2012.

Piscatori, James P. "Islamic Values and National Interest: The Foreign Policy of Saudi Arabia" in *Islam in Foreign Policy*, edited by Adeed Dawisha, 1–8. New York: Cambridge University Press, 1983.

"Religion and Realpolitik: Islamic Responses to the Gulf War" in *Islamic Fundamentalisms and the Gulf Crisis*, edited by James P. Piscatori, 1–27. Chicago: University of Chicago Press, 1991.

Pollack, Ken, and Daniel Byman. *The Arab Awakening: America and the Transformation of the Middle East*. Washington, DC: Brookings Institution Press, 2011.

Pope, Nicole, and Hugh Pope. *Turkey Unveiled: A History of Modern Turkey*. Woodstock, NY and New York, NY: The Overlook Press, 1997.

Putnam, Robert D. "Diplomacy and Domestic Politics: The Logic of Two-Level Games." *International Organization* 42, no. 3 (Summer 1988).

Rabasa, Angel, and F. Stephen Larrabee. *The Rise of Political Islam in Turkey*. Washington, DC: The RAND Corporation, 2008.

Rapoport, David C. "Fear and Trembling: Terrorism in Three Religious Traditions." *American Political Science Review* 78, no. 3 (December 1983): 658–77.

"The Fourth Wave: September 11 in the History of Terrorism." *Current History* 100, no. 650 (December 2001): 419–24.

Reetz, Dietrich Reetz. "The Deoband Universe: What Makes a Transcultural and Transnational Educational Movement of Islam?" *Comparative Studies of South Asia, Africa, and the Middle East* 27, no. 1 (2007).

Robins, Philip. "Confusion at Home, Confusion Abroad: Turkey between Copenhagen and Iraq." *International Affairs* 79, no. 3 (May 2003): 547–66.

Ross, Michael L. "Does Oil Hinder Democracy?" *World Politics* 53, no. 3 (2001): 325–61.

Rouleau, Eric. "The Challenges to Turkey." *Foreign Affairs* 72, no. 5 (November–December 1993): 110–26.

Roy, Olivier. *Globalized Islam: The Search for a New Umma*. New York: Columbia University Press, 2004.

Rudolph, Susanna Hoeber. "Introduction: Religion, States and Transnational Civil Society" in *Transnational Religions and Fading States*, edited by Susanna Hoeber and James Piscatori Rudoplh, 1–26. Boulder, CO: Westview Press, 1997.

Ruggie, John G. "Territoriality and Beyond." *International Organization* 47, no. 1 (1993).

Rugh, William A. *Diplomacy and Defense Policy of the United Arab Emirates.* London: Emirates Center for Strategic Studies and Research, 2002.

Saif, Lubna. *Authoritarianism and Underdevelopment in Pakistan 1947–1958: The Role of the Punjab.* New York: Oxford University Press, 2011.

Saikal, Amin. "Musharraf and Pakistan's Crisis" in *Pakistan in Regional and Global Politics*, edited by Rajshree Jetly, 1–19. London: Routledge Taylor & Francis Group, 2009.

Sandal, Nukhet. "Religious Actors as Epistemic Communities in Conflict Transformation: The Cases of South Africa and Northern Ireland." *Review of International Studies* 37, no. 3 (July 2011): 929–49.

Sandal, Nukhet, and Jonathan Fox. *Religion in International Relations Theory: Concepts, Tools, and Debates.* London: Routledge, 2013.

Sarkissian, Ani. *The Varieties of Religious Repression: Why Governments Restrict Religion.* New York: Oxford University Press, 2015.

Sayari, Sabri. "Turkey and the Middle East in the 1990s." *Journal of Palestine Studies* 26, no. 3 (Spring 1997): 44–55.

Schanzer, Jonathan. *Al-Qaeda's Armies: Middle East Affiliate Groups and the Next Generation of Terror.* Washington, DC: Washington Institute for Near East Policy, 2005.

Schmidt, John R. *The Unravelling: Pakistan in the Age of Jihad.* New York: Farrar, Strauss & Giroux, 2011.

Seawright, Jason, and John Gerring. "Case Selection Techniques in Case Study Research: A Menu of Qualitative and Quantitative Options." *Political Research Quarterly* 61, no. 2 (June 2008): 294–308.

Sever, Ayegul. "Turkey's Constraining Position on Western Reform Initiatives in the Middle East." *Mediterranean Quarterly* 18, no. 4 (Fall 2007): 131–48.

Shaffer, Brenda, ed. *The Limits of Culture: Islam and Foreign Policy.* Cambridge, MA: MIT Press, 2006.

Shaffer, Brenda. "Introduction: The Limits of Culture" in *The Limits of Culture: Islam and Foreign Policy*, edited by Brenda Shaffer, 1–26. Cambridge: MIT Press, 2006.

Shehata, Dina. *Islamists and Secularists in Egypt: Opposition, Conflict and Cooperation.* New York: Routledge, 2010.

Smith, Alastair. "International Crises and Domestic Politics." *American Political Science Review* 92, no. 3 (September 1998): 623–38.

"Political Groups, Leader Change, and the Pattern of International Cooperation." *Journal of Conflict Resolution* 53, no. 6 (2009): 853–77.

Smith, Alastair, and Bruce Bueno de Mesquita. "Contingent Prize Allocation and Pivotal Voting," *British Journal of Middle Eastern Studies* 42, no. 2 (2011): 371–92.

Smith, Alastair, Bruce Bueno de Mesquita, and Tom LaGatta. "Group Incentives and Rational Voting." *Journal of Theoretical Politics* (forthcoming).

Smith, Christian. "Correcting a Curious Neglect, or Bringing Religion Back In" in *Disruptive Religion: The Force of Faith in Social-Movement Activism*, edited by Christian Smith, 1–28. New York: Routledge, 1996.

Snyder, Jack. "Introduction" in *Religion and International Relations Theory*, edited by Jack Snyder. New York: Columbia University Press, 2011.

Somer, Murat. "Turkey's Model of 'Moderate' Islamism Can Be Misleading." *The National*, October 1, 2012.

Soysal, Mumtaz. "The Future of Turkish Foreign Policy" in *The Future of Turkish Foreign Policy*, edited by Lenore G. and Dimitris Keridis Martin, 37–46. Cambridge, MA: 2004.

Spruyt, Hendrik. *The Sovereign State and Its Competitors: An Analysis of Systems Change*. Princeton: Princeton University Press, 1994.

Steinmo, Sven, Kathleen Thelen, and Frank Longstreth, eds. *Structuring Politics: Historical Institutionalism in Comparative Politics*. New York: Cambridge University Press, 1992.

Stern, Jessica. *Terror in the Name of God: Why Religious Militants Kill*. New York: Harper Collins, 2003.

Streeck, Wolfgang, and Kathleen Thelen. "Introduction: Institutional Change in Advanced Political Economies" in *Beyond Continuity: Institutional Change in Advanced Political Economies*, edited by Wolfgang Streeck and Kathleen Thelen. New York: Oxford University Press, 2005.

Sultan, Tepe. "Politics between Market and Islam: The Electoral Puzzles and Changing Prospects of Pro-Islamic Parties." *Mediterranean Quarterly* 18, no. 2 (Spring 2007): 107–35.

Syed, Anwar H. "The Sunni-Shia Conflict in Pakistan" in *Pakistan: Founders' Aspirations and Todays' Realities*, edited by Hafeez Malik Malik, 244–62. New York: Oxford University Press, 2001.

"Syria's Opposition Opens Office in Turkey." *Al-Jazeera*, December 14, 2011.

Tahir-Khelli, Shirin. "In Search of an Identity: Islam and Pakistan's Foreign Policy." In *Islam in Foreign Policy*, edited by Adeed Dawisha, 68–83. New York: Cambridge University Press, 1985.

Talbot, Ian. *Pakistan: A Modern History*. New York: Palgrave MacMillan, 2005.

Thelen, Kathleen. "How Institutions Evolve: Insights from Comparative Historical Analysis" in *Comparative Historical Analysis in the Social Sciences*, edited by James Mahoney and Dietrich Rueschemeyer, 208–41. New York: Cambridge University Press, 2003.

Thomas, Scott. *The Global Resurgence of Religion and the Transformation of International Relations: The Struggle for the Soul of the Twenty-First Century*. New York: Palgrave Macmillan, 2005.

"Religion and International Conflict" in *Religion and International Relations*, edited by K. R. Dark, 1–23. New York: St. Martin's Press, 2000.

Tilly, Charles. *Identities, Boundaries, and Social Ties*. Boulder, CO: Paradigm Publishers, 2005.

The Politics of Collective Violence. New York: Columbia University Press, 2003.

"Terror, Terrorism, Terrorists." *Sociological Theory* 22, no. 1 (March 2004): 5–20.

Toft, Monica Duffy, Daniel Philpott, and Timothy Samuel Shah. *God's Century: Resurgent Religion and Global Politics.* New York: W. W. Norton and Company, 2011.

Towns, Ann E. "Norms and Social Hierarchies: Understanding International Policy Diffusion 'from Below'." *International Organization* 66, no. 2 (2012): 179–209.

Tschirgi, Dan. "Turkey and the Arab World in the New Millenium" in *Turkey's Foreign Policy in the 21st Century,* edited by Tareq Y. and Mustafa Aydin Ismael, 103–20. Burlington, VT: Ashgate, 2003.

"Turkey's Political Imams: The Gulenists Fight Back." *The Economist,* May 18, 2013.

"Turkish Army 'Bans' Game of Thrones, Prepares for Islam Classes." *Hurriyet Daily News,* November 7, 2014.

"Turkish Parliament Approves Anti-Terrorism Financing Law." *Reuters,* February 7, 2013.

Tuysuz, Gul. "Turkish Warplanes Bomb Isis Positions in Syria for the First Time." *CNN,* July 25, 2015.

Ulrichsen, Kristian Coates. "The Persian Gulf States and Afghanistan: Regional Geopolitics and Competing Interests." *Asia Policy* 17 (2014).

"Qatar and the Arab Spring: Policy Drivers and Regional Implications." Carnegie Endowment for International Peace, 2014.

"US 'Threatened to Bomb' Pakistan." *BBC News Online,* September 22, 2006.

Vick, Carl. "Party Tied to Islam Wins Big in Turkey." *The Washington Post,* November 4, 2002.

Voeten, Erik. "Resisting the Lonely Superpower: Responses of States in the United Nations to US Dominance." *The Journal of Politics* 66, no. 3 (2004): 729–54.

Wald, Kenneth D., and Clyde Wilcox. "Getting Religion: Has Political Science Rediscovered the 'Faith Factor'?" *American Political Science Review* 100, no. 4 (November 2006): 523–29.

Walker, Joshua. "Turkey and Israel's Relationship in the Middle East." *Mediterranean Quarterly* 17, no. 4 (Fall 2006): 60–90.

Walker, Joshua. "Reexamining the US-Turkish Alliance." *The Washington Quarterly* 31, no. 1 (Winter 2007/2008): 93–109.

Walsh, Declan. "Pakistani Media 'Name' Cia Station Chief in Islamabad." *The Guardian,* May 9, 2011.

Watsi, Tahir. *The Application of Islamic Criminal Law in Pakistan: Shariah in Practice.* Leiden: Brill, 2009.

Watson, Katy. "Dubai Dress Code: 'Cover up', UAE Women Tell Foreigners." *BBC News Online,* July 5, 2012.

White, Joshua T. "Pakistan's Islamist Frontier: Islamic Politics and US Policy in Pakistan's North-West Frontier." *CFIA Religion and Security Monograph Series,* 2008.

Wickham, Carrie Rosefsky. "Interests, Ideas and Islamist Outreach in Egypt" in *Islamic Activism: A Social Movement Approach*, edited by Quintan Wiktorowicz, 231–50. Bloomington, IN: Indiana University Press, 2004.

   Mobilizing Islam: Religion, Activism, and Political Change in Egypt. New York: Columbia University Press, 2002.

Wilcox, Clyde, Kenneth D. Wald, and Ted G. Jelen. "Religious Preferences and Social Science: A Second Look." *The Journal of Politics* 70, no. 3 (July 2008): 874–79.

Willoughby, John. "Segmented Feminization and the Decline of Neopatriarchy in GCC Countries of the Persian Gulf." *Comparative Studies of South Asia, Africa, and the Middle East* 28, no. 1 (2008).

Worth, Robert F. "Saudis Back Syrian Rebels Despite Risks." *New York Times*, January 7, 2014.

Wright, Lawrence. *The Looming Tower: Al-Qaeda and the Road to 9/11*. New York: Vintage Books, 2006.

Yacoubian, Mona. "Bridging the Divide: US Efforts to Engage the Muslim World." *The Middle East Journal* 63, no. 3 (2009).

Yavuz, M. Hakan, ed. *The Emergence of a New Turkey: Democracy and the Ak Parti*. Salt Lake City: University of Utah Press, 2006.

   Islamic Political Identity in Turkey. New York: Oxford University Press, 2003.

   "The Politics of Fear: The Rise of the Nationalist Action Party (MHP) in Turkey." *Middle East Journal* 56, no. 2 (Spring 2002): 200–21.

   Secularism and Muslim Democracy in Turkey. New York: Cambridge University Press, 2008.

   "Turkish-Israeli Relations through the Lens of the Turkish Identity Debate." *Journal of Palestine Studies* 27, no. 1 (Autumn 1997): 22–37.

Zahlan, Rosemarie Said. *The Origins of the United Arab Emirates*. New York: St. Martin's Press, 1978.

Zayani, Mohamed. "Civil Society and Democratic Change in the Arab World: Promises and Impediments." *Comparative Studies of South Asia, Africa, and the Middle East* 32, no. 3 (2012).

Ziring, Lawrence. *Pakistan in the Twentieth Century: A Political History*. Karachi: Oxford University Press, 1997.

   "Weak State, Failed State, Garrison State: The Pakistan Saga" in *South Asia's Weak States: Understanding the Regional Insecurity Predicament*, edited by T. V. Paul, 170–95. Stanford, CA: Stanford University Press, 2010.

Zorn, Christopher J. W. "Generalized Estimating Equation Models for Correlated Data: A Review with Applications." *American Journal of Political Science* 45, no. 2 (2001).

Index

For EU product safety concerns, contact us at Calle de José Abascal, 56–1°,
28003 Madrid, Spain or eugpsr@cambridge.org.